II

Secrets of the Wine Whisperer Or, How I Learned to Drink Wine
and Found Ecstasy, Joy, Peace, Happiness, Life, and Salvation

For information contact:

Creative Projects International, Ltd.
1440 Plumas Street, Reno, NV 89509.
www.bookpubintl.com

ISBN-978-0-9818222-5-9

Library of Congress: 2012955550

Design & Typography: Marion Redmond www.kirks-graphics.com
Cover Design: Dave Drotleff / Merlin Creative

Secrets of the Wine Whisperer
Or, How I Learned to Drink Wine
and Found Ecstasy,
Joy, Peace, Happiness,
Life, and Salvation

Life's too short
to drink bad
wine!
Cheers!

Jerry Greenfield
The Wine Whisperer

Dedication

*T*his work is dedicated to the friends who have helped us build, and then deplete, our collection through the years. To the warm and gracious winemakers who have welcomed us into their cellars, homes, and lives, and have been such an important part of our wine education. Many of them are part of this story. The others know who they are.

But mostly, this is dedicated to my wife Debi, with whom I share many passions other than this.

Also by Jerold A. Greenfield
Maverick—The Personal War of a Vietnam Cobra Pilot
With Dennis J. Marvicsin

Table of Contents

Prologue

What the Hell Happened to Us?
> How a normal middle-class couple's developing addiction
> to wine changed their lives (for the better), their friends
> (for the better), and their financial situation (for the worse).

Falling Down the Rabbit Hole
> Everyone who's passionate about wine has had some kind
> of epiphany. Here's how it happened to us.

Buying Fever
> Once we knew we liked it, we started buying it. We
> graduated from buying a few bottles at a time to buying a
> case. Then two. Then three.

Getting Into the Tasting Game
> Wine clubs. Another so-called nail in the coffin, to mix
> a metaphor.

extremely controversial screw cap instead of the time-
honored cork.

Wine and the Sports Hero

The wine world is a magnet for celebrities. At one point, we became haunted by the appearance of Hall of Fame baseball player Rusty Staub. He's everywhere, and we can't get rid of him.

Wine Friends, and Friends of Friends

Thanks to our love of wine, and our willingness to spend silly amounts of money buying it, we've developed relationships that we truly treasure. We have also eliminated from our lives anyone who doesn't drink. Shame on us.

Big Time Tastings

As we developed a taste for wine, we graduated from the monthly tastings at the local wine store and start traveling to larger-scale wine events that cost a lot more money. A lot more.

Wine Festing in Naples

There ain't no bigger wine life event than the Naples Winter Wine Festival, held in Southwest Florida at the end of January. It's attended by the superstars of the wine, sports, and entertainment world, including Judge Judy, Regis Philbin, Kyle McLachlan, and, of course, Rusty Staub.

Prologue

"If you ever have the desire to write a prologue, break all your fingers." Anonymous

There are times I've felt the only thing my wife and I had in common was the ability to breathe air, walk upright and (actively or vestigially) give milk.

Life offers us many transformational experiences, and most of them involve pain. So it was encouraging (not to mention powerfully reaffirming) when we were simultaneously altered in the same happy manner, discovering a mutual interest that quickly turned into a mutual passion. There are those passions that ignite a relationship, but if we're lucky they ultimately settle down to a warm quotidian glow. Then there are passions that maintain the relationship, and discovering them is one of the things that helps us keep the promise about until death do us part.

Fortunately, wife Debi is blessed with an olfactory acuity that borders on the supernatural. Several local law enforcement agencies persist in asking her to help track

escaped convicts through the swamps, but she'd rather
drink wine, where her uncanny sense of smell does us both
the most good. From a palate point of view, she's the kind
of cook who can taste something one time and come home
and make it. That's how we wound up with the recipe for
charcoal grilled sea scallops in white chocolate sauce with
capers and dill.

Like life itself, this wine enthusiasm, thirst, passion, avidity,
zeal, craze, infatuation, addiction, contains within it, we have
discovered, aspects of both the triumphant and the tragic.
Floating within each bottle we have come to know and love
is the seed of its own extinction. Unlike wheat, which is
harvested three or four times a year, grapes ripen only once
a year, and there is just a single make-or-break vintage for
each lovely ripening. No matter how good the wine is, no
matter how legendary the vintage, there is an exactly finite
amount of that particular liquid on the planet. When Debi
and I drink a bottle, we, in our own small way, diminish the
supply, even if that supply is tens of thousand of cases. At
first the wines we love may be plentiful, then they become
an endangered species, and finally they are loved to the
point of extinction. Sometimes we find more on auction
web sites, or through diligent search, but we know the cost
will be far beyond what we originally paid. Point is, when
it's gone, it's gone, and we mourn. But the triumphant part
is we know we'll find something else new and different and
interesting at the next tasting. Or the one after that. We
are driven by the tingling tension between the known and
the yet-to-be-known.

Then there's the whole money thing. Wine prices, we
find, are a favorite topic among wine lovers, a fact we
discovered as soon as we got serious about haunting the

wine stores. We've met people who could spend whatever they want on whatever they want, but they don't live at our house, where the resources are far more modest. I remember reading about five executives from Barclay's Bank in London who celebrated the completion of a big deal by going on some kind of celebrity wine toot at one of the city's priciest restaurants. They ordered, among other rarities, three bottles of insanely expensive Bordeaux from the 1945, 1946, and 1947 vintages and rounded out the evening with a bottle of France's most expensive dessert wine that was 100 years old. The evening cost them about $80,000, which upset their Barclay bosses more than somewhat, and got them fired, or sacked, as they say over there. Even more distressing is that they paid about three times what the bottles were actually worth. Restaurants are certainly entitled to a markup on wine, but those financial geniuses got bent over and driven home.

To this day, the lamentable lack of a sizable personal fortune or trust fund prevents us (and the large majority of our similarly-addicted friends) from fulfilling our wine urges as completely as we'd like. The expansion of our meager wine collection figures prominently in my "when we win the lottery" fantasies.

Some couples spend a portion of their discretionary income fixing up a part of the basement as a gynecological gymnasium, while others devote the spare space and money to a home theater complete with a popcorn machine and candy counter. Point is, we don't know how we got here. Or can't remember, which is a lot worse.

CHAPTER 1

What the Hell
Happened to Me?

The beginning of the end. How a normal middle-class couple's developing passion for wine changed their lives (for the better), their friends (for the better), and their financial situation (for the worse).

October, 2000

"Robert Mondavi just kissed me on both cheeks."

Debi had been on her way up to the dais at the banquet, because she wanted to ask Eric de Rothschild to sign the bottle of 1988 Lafite she'd bought that afternoon. Now she was back, all a-flutter, with flushed face and rapid breath.

"Really. He did." I wasn't jealous. Sure, Robert Mondavi was a bit older than I at the time, a lot richer, and a lot more famous, but okay. Deb has long ago gotten tired of everybody telling her how much she looks like Shelley Long, so I can't blame Bob for feeling the urge to plant one on her – two, actually – and besides, it's not every day that one of the world's most famous winemakers introduces himself with such Old World charm. Later, we found out that the double-cheek kiss was a Mondavian behavioral trademark.

That's when it hit me. What were we even doing in the same banquet room with Robert Mondavi, or with all those other legendary winemakers sitting up at the table of honor? Before us were the owners of the world's oldest, most famous chateaux, internationally glamorous highly polished people, duchesses and marcheses, whose families had been making wine for six hundred years. How the hell did we get here?

We were seated, that evening in late October, at a $300-a-head New York black tie wine gala with all these... *people* in the room. Rock stars of the wine world who live on inherited estates, fly Super First Class on Air France, and spend a week or two whenever they feel like it on the Costa Smerelda in Sardinia. Francis Ford Coppola was there, smoking a Cohiba the size of the Hindenburg.

Question was, what were *we* doing there? Little old us. We weren't anybody. Sure, we knew a bit about wine, having spent the previous five or six years gloriously gliding down the slope into the obsession, but still. To be at this three-day wine event, we'd spent over five grand, which represented a significant percentage of our annual discretionary income, including registration fees, air fare, hotel, cab rides and such, not counting the accumulated capital we'd invested at some of the city's most difficult restaurants.

What *were* we doing there? And where did all that wine in our house come from? What were we doing *there*? In our previous life, we went to the beach on vacation, watched the water all day, did a little snorkeling, maybe, strolled at night, ate at family restaurants. But over the past five years we had lurched (perhaps stumbled is the more appropriate term) into the wine life. We lost friends who didn't enjoy wine, and made new friends who did. And all our vacations, all our dinner reservations, most of our recreational activities, and a truly frightening amount of our mutual income, revolved around vineyard visits, treks to Tuscany, wine tastings, wine auctions, wine shopping, and other insane quests that will be dealt with more extensively later on.

So as we sat in that banquet room, we gazed at each other, at the expensive bottles on the table before us, at the fabled personages in the front of the room, and asked ourselves again: what the hell happened to us?

CHAPTER 2

Falling Down the Rabbit Hole

The revelation. Everyone who's ever become really excited about wine has had some kind of epiphany. It's a common experience to taste a glass of something and think, "Holy moley...I never knew anything could taste like this," after which you're hopelessly hooked. Here's how it happened to us.

July, 1997

We didn't come to the wine life on our own. People just don't discover twisted addictions all by themselves: somebody has to offer that first free sample. In our case, the slide began when a new friend handed us a glass of something that changed our lives. The bottle said "Drink Me," and so we did. And just like Alice, we tumbled down the rabbit hole. Difference is, Alice came back, but we never did.

In one of the most memorable scenes in the surprise hit movie *Sideways*, the characters played by Paul Giamatti and Virginia Madsen are talking about how they got interested in wine. Giamatti asks, "What was the bottle that did it

for you?" And that's the Big Question for every wine lover,
because each of us has a story about the Bottle That Did
It For Us. In our experience, everyone who's been lifted
up and carried off by a passion for wine tells us they went
through some kind of revelation or epiphany. Ours was not
as extreme as Saul of Tarsus getting knocked off his horse,
but we were nevertheless blinded by the light.

Debi and I had never planned to be obsessive about
anything, or addicted to anything, except maybe each other.
But it happened, and it was because somebody lit the lamp,
opened the door, set our feet upon the path. His name was
Larry Burns. Still is. I believe that everyone has some kind
of natural talent. There are people who can play the piano
by ear, others pick up languages quickly. Larry has the gift
of personality. He is thoroughly engaging, overwhelmingly
genial and unfailingly good natured. Warmth and fellowship
flow from him in a Falstaffian torrent the second he appears.
If he ran for office, everyone would vote for him early and
often. Larry and his equally priceless wife Charlene came
into our lives in late July of 1997, right after my birthday. We
were introduced by mutual friends shortly after Debi and I
had moved into our first real house. It was a casual meeting
at a happy hour near a poolside bar on the river. Hi, how
are ya, gladtaseeya. But then, in the weeks afterward, we
started running into them in restaurants, at malls, at the
movies, everywhere. After more chance encounters than
any two married couples should decently have, and not
realizing the consequences of our action, we invited them
over to our new place for dinner. That's when they did
it to us.

It happens that Larry is a sales representative for a major
wine and spirits company, which we sort of knew in

advance, but really didn't think much of until he showed up for canapés hauling this huge square space-age thermally insulated bag over his shoulder.

"These people look serious," I whispered to Debi.

"What's in the bag?"

In the bag was no simple dinner gift, like flowers or a plant or a pie. Not even a single moderately-priced token bottle like normal people bring to the home of someone they hardly know. Larry had brought half a case of assorted bottles. He apparently felt strongly that dinner would require at least a bottle for appetizers, two for the main course, and one for dessert. Plus a few in reserve, just in case the evening went long…which it did. What did we know? Getting into the wine life requires a guide. There he was—bag and all.

Before the transformative invasion of Larry and Charlene, Deb had been mostly happy with vodka martinis or top shelf margaritas, and I'd always been pretty much of a beer man. I had, in fact, written and actually been paid for a series of magazine articles on the subject.

Up until Larry showed up, one of my proudest accomplishments, and the veritable high point of my early beverage appreciation career, had been a trip to the National Beer Wholesaler's Association trade show in New Orleans. The editor of *Tampa Bay Monthly* finally caved in to my strenuous and pathetic importunings, bought me a ticket and sent me there to write an article on the event.

I spent two fuzzy days working my way through an expo hall full of brews from all over the world (including Nigeria, even) and taking frequent bathroom breaks. I loved it, but somehow never got really fanatical about the stuff. Was never driven to visit any breweries, even though I lived in Tampa where Busch has a garden, a brewery, and a huge tasting room. Never had the impulse or desire to go on a tour of the rolling hills of central Germany to see the hops grow, or even fight my way through Oktoberfest in Munich. The closest I came was an afternoon in a microbrewery beer garden somewhere in northern California, where the outdoor patio was strung with cascades of hops dangling from overhead wires. The patrons were mostly farmers from way back up in the hills who grew certain highly desirable but decidedly illegal crops in commercial quantities, and looked it. From a beer standpoint, my fondest wish had been to someday make a pilgrimage to Dublin, and drink real Guinness at the Real Place, which, I understand, occupies half the town, and is a larger tourist attraction than the Blarney Stone. As far as wine experience went, we'd been limited to those embarrassing carafes of anonymous Chianti at the neighborhood red checkered tablecloth place, and the occasional marginally better bottle at somewhat more expensive dining establishments. Call it lack of concern, indifference, ignorance. But when Larry and Charlene appeared with their goody bag, everything changed. It took them no more than ten minutes to derail our lives completely and corrupt us thoroughly. I can't thank them enough.

After greetings and air kisses, the four of us grouped around the island in the middle of the kitchen, and Larry unzipped the bag. It wasn't as though he showed up with some $200 bottle of St. Emilion, or any rare treasure that wine collectors would strangle each other for, but again, what the hell did we know? His first offering was just a bottle of 1993 Cloudy Bay Sauvignon Blanc from New Zealand, maybe $30 retail, though Larry never pays for wine because he's always up to his ass in professional samples. We'd never even heard of Sauvignon Blanc, barely knew what a grape was, and could find New Zealand on a map only under extreme duress. But here was Larry with that first free sample.

Somehow sensing that he was among the uninitiated, Larry even had the acumen to bring his own stemware. We watched as he took four thin crystal glasses from the padded bag and arranged them in a line. He poured, then he and Charlene got serious. The Wine Demeanor overtook them, they swirled the straw-colored liquid around, they actually stuck their noses *down inside the glass*, made small sniffing noises like a couple of puppies, and offered arcane comments about the herbaceousness, the grapefruit and citrus aromas on the nose, the floral echoes on the finish, the crisp acidity…

"What the hell are these people talking about?" Debi wanted to know.

I admit it. We were intimidated. Confused. Intrigued. It all seemed so…*sophisticated*, somehow, and esoteric and elitist. But then we tasted the stuff, and an immediate warm glow suffused the two of us, an expansion of consciousness that I hadn't experienced since my college days. Our interest was piqued. Great word, piqued. A combination of getting pinched, sitting up, taking notice, opening your eyes a little wider.

This was most assuredly not beer. Grass and grapefruit aromas wisped up from the glass, beckoning tendrils, strange perfumes of flowers, flavors that tasted like colors.

There were smells and sensations that were most un-grapelike, which was a further revelation. We actually paid attention to what we were tasting and smelling, deconstructing the sensations, the flavors unfolding, blossoming on our tongues. We smiled a lot, and the four of us became very good friends. Wine will do that.

By the time Larry and Charlene were finished with us, it was well past two in the morning, we'd executed the last two extra bottles, and he'd taken us through a crash course about complexity, body, tannins, mouth feel, legs, and probably some other insider wine stuff that we just plain don't remember, and he'd kept pouring until our focus had wandered off into the wilderness of the night and I was face down in my shortcake, with no idea of what was going to happen next.

CHAPTER 3

Buying Fever

*nce we knew we liked it, we started buying
it. This, quite naturally, led to the acquisition (by
several means) of a variety of racking equipment: the
kind we built ourselves from a kit, a few scavenged
from wine stores, and they multiplied like rabbits
on Viagra. As the collection grew, so did our other
obsessions. Traveling to wine country, going to wine
dinners, attending every tasting night at every wine
store within 50 miles. Then it got really serious.*

August, 1997

Wine became an obsession practically the very next day.
We had no idea where to start, so we went to dinner. At a
neighborhood restaurant, we ordered a real bottle of wine
off a real wine list. Never done that before, except maybe
on anniversaries.

We liked the wine we ordered, and decided at some
point before dessert to buy it in quantity. Also a first. We
were so dumb and stupid that it never remotely occurred
to us to go to a wine store. We ordered a case from the
manager of the restaurant, who was a friend, but to this day

I don't know how friendly she was on the price. Maybe she gave us a break and passed it through at wholesale, maybe she marked it up, but it's too late now to worry about it.

One case led to another. We happened on a few wine stores, which, it turned out, had been there all the time, and by the time the holidays hit us at the end of 1997 we had about 50-60 bottles in the house. Debi went to some kind of Crate and Barrel place and bought one of those "easy to assemble in five minutes" wine racks, and I was naive enough to believe the "easy to assemble" part. It came as a bunch of dowels and sockets, like nothing more than a Tinker Toy set made out of fragrant wood. During a fun-filled five hours, we put it together in the kitchen pantry, loaded it up, and afterwards just opened the cabinet door and stood there together, staring at it.

Meanwhile, we'd become very good friends with Larry and Charlene, who continued to ply us with bottles of stuff we didn't know from places we'd barely heard of, either at one of our respective houses, or at restaurants that didn't mind Larry bringing his own bottles. I came to discover that he, in his wine salesman capacity, was on golfing terms with just about every restaurant owner, bartender, and food and beverage club manager within a hundred miles. Everyone at every restaurant knew him, and greeted him with hale fellowship. The education continued.

We began to discuss what we were drinking, picking out flavors and textures in the liquid, concentrating on what's going on down there in the glass, gaining the habit of focus, of really paying attention, and it gradually lapped over into everything else we ate or drank. As soon as we started focusing on the wine, our food became a lot more interesting, not only because we generally killed at least half a bottle while preparing the meal, but because we started getting *involved* in it for a change. We got crazy about matching dishes up with wine, buying food and wine cookbooks, knocking off two glasses (instead of one) while we were prepping the meal, because dishes of really great food that match with wine take longer to prepare than a plate of spaghetti, and that meant we were munching, which got us to wine and cheese, which drove us to find out about bridge flavors and the food chemistry of why Valtellina Sfursat tastes better with *this* than with *that*.

I'm starting to understand how crazy all this was, then I remember how it got worse.

Predictably, we outgrew the wood wine rack that we'd laboriously constructed in the pantry. As all the cooking and swilling was going on, we were shopping at neighborhood wine stores like most moderately normal people, though our purchases were larger than most, and that's when Deb heard about this thing they do called a "tasting." More about that later, but the point is we'd been buying wine. Lots of it. When we hit a hundred bottles, Debi said, "It's time to call Larry."

Larry's company maintains a whole separate warehouse where they store all the wine and spirits crap that distributors give retail stores to push product. Shelf talkers, window banners, hats, t-shirts…and really decent wire wine racks, capacity 36 to 48 bottles each, with signs on top promoting a certain wine brand. The warehouse was full of them, and I came home with three sticking out of my car windows.

Well, that took care of the stock on hand, and allowed a little room for some additional purchases, which we were certain would occur. Not to worry.

Meanwhile, we were cooking. My parents were in the restaurant business, and I like playing in the kitchen. This is a personal quality that Debi treasures about me, because my culinary efforts always include an obsessive-compulsive cleanup at the end of the process, during which Debi relaxes and opens another bottle.

Even those who don't drink wine understand that there's a thing called wine and food pairing. We were later to discover that in some countries, most notably Italy, wine is a food, and not even considered a separate beverage. We never grasped the implications of that until we staggered into the wine life. The pursuit of wine and food pairing impelled us to try dishes we had never dreamed of making at home, because we don't cook like Emeril Lagasse or Alice Waters or Mario Batali. We started cooking more elaborate meals, eating out more often, going to different restaurants. More expensive ones. We should have known better.

There are people who order dinner and then decide what kind of wine might go with it. We turned into the people who order the wine and then figure out what to eat. By the end of the year we owned about 140 bottles and things had become very unwell.

The wine rack nuttiness is only part of the story. This is also the time when we started traveling with wine in mind, or at least being introduced to the (quite lovely) places where grapes are grown, harvested, and crushed.

A few years earlier, in the summer of 1994, about six months before Debi and I got married, I had the opportunity to do a book project with a woman named Julia Densmore. If the last name sounds even a bit familiar, it's because her ex-husband John was the drummer for The Doors. She had—to put it quite mildly—some interesting stories to tell about the heyday of rock and roll (at least the days she could remember), and her various relationships with some of the most famous bands of the time, and I wanted to write it.

Julia had rented a house in a place called Geyserville which was, though I didn't know it at the time, smack in the middle of Sonoma Valley. After meeting her twice in Miami and Los Angeles, I flew to San Francisco, rented a car, and made my way up to her place to get started on the project. Motoring up through the valley, I admired the rolling rows of grapevines, heavy with purple bunches, that stretched off into the hazy distance on both sides of the road, but I'm ashamed to say they meant nothing to me. Just peaceful scenery on the long ride up from the city. I had not yet been awakened.

My second trip to even-more-spectacular wine country, this time with Debi along, took place shortly afterward. It was another lamentably missed opportunity, and another consequence of our as-yet unaltered consciousness.

We were hired to go to Florence, Italy to shoot a television program for a national client. The day before the project began, one of the partners in the production company we were working with out of Paris took us on a little excursion down through Tuscany to visit a friend. More spectacular than the pleasant vistas of Sonoma, the ancient hillsides unrolled on all sides, carpeted with grapevines and dotted with utterly charming brown stone farmhouses surrounded by ranks and files of deep green cypress trees. Pretty, and certainly affecting from the scenic standpoint, but utterly lacking the obsessive wine component we would come to suffer (and appreciate) later on.

Might as well tell the rest of the story. After we returned from our nice ride down the Chianti Highway, the production company found us a little hotel west of downtown (our room smelled like *pipi du chat*, and Debi refused to stay there). Right around the corner was a neighborhood restaurant called Baldini. As far as I know, it's still there.

It was convenient, the food was beyond our wildest, and well worth twice what it cost, the place being parsecs beyond the "neighborhood Italian" some of us may have grown up with. No checkered tablecloths, no bottles of Chianti in straw baskets. Just the most authentic Italian home cooking we had ever eaten.

Anyway. There were about eight of us on the video crew and we were in Florence for two weeks, so we ate there almost every night, eschewing the Michelin-starred restaurants of the city (which we had foolishly failed to include in the production cost estimate we had submitted to the client) in favor of the geniality and authenticity of Signore Baldini and his merry men. After our third visit in as many nights, we and the management had established an everlasting personal bond. A few evenings later, as the check was being presented, Franco, our waiter and new best friend, clunked a bottle of grappa down on the middle of the table.

"We didn't order this," said Ed, the owner of the video production company.

"*E della casa*," said Franco, and we didn't have to know a whole lot of Italian to realize we were staring at a complimentary bottle of intoxicating spirits. Ed, never one to ignore warm Italian hospitality or a free bottle of anything, appointed himself our server, pouring with the characteristic generosity I love him for, and we didn't give a damn about the shape of the glass. The inevitable ensued, we all missed our call time the next morning, I tasted distilled grape stems for two days afterward, and that's why we don't keep it in the house.

CHAPTER 4

Getting Into the Tasting Game

irst, we discovered the monthly tastings at local wine shops, then we discovered that if we signed up for the mailing list, we'd get notified of special sales, closeouts, and other bargains. And what about sniffers, sippers, and swillers?

November, 1998

After Larry and Charlene epiphanized us with that bottle of Cloudy Bay and the three or four bottles that followed, we slowly came to understand the need to have a dependable wine source. No longer did we naively order cases from the restaurant. We had found the wine aisle of the supermarket (but were still a long way from paying more than about $12 a bottle), and had inkled the idea that there were retail outlets in our area making a living from selling it. As I noted in the previous chapter, they had shelves full of the stuff.

Our area is a major tourist and seasonal resident destination, and the population more than doubles between October and April. So toward the end of 1998 "the season" and the concomitant nightly high life were in full swing at exactly the right time. The symphony was up and running, new restaurants were opening and getting mobbed, there were charity balls, auctions, and events at every major intersection. Best of all, an encouraging number of wine stores were holding tastings at least once a month.

Debi did the research, I did the driving.

"The first step at these places," she said, "is to get into the wine club."

"What does it cost?"

"It doesn't." It didn't. In fact, it was no more complex or demanding than writing down our name and address, which is not too far beyond our capabilities. And an email address, of course. Club members get discounts (very important), and mailings that reveal when the next tasting will take place. It was at these tastings that a significant number of our burgeoning wine impulses kicked in.

Life confronts us with one sad fact after the other, and some of them make me want to just curl up, suck my thumb, turn the electric blanket up to 12 and twirl my hair. Like the idea that every marriage ends in either divorce or death. Or, more tragic still, the fact that there is on this planet a precise quantity of every wine that's produced, and when it's gone, it's gone. Which is one reason the more seriously afflicted wine lifers go to tastings.

It's the end of 1998, we've laid in our first hundred or hundred fifty bottles practically without even knowing it, and it suddenly hit us that all the bottles in those wire wine racks, including the ones we'd splurged on over Christmas the previous year ($28 a bottle) will definitely get sucked up sooner or later. Probably sooner. The wines we're discovering and loving today we will inevitably love to death, transforming then into mere wisps of fond memory. The winemakers, sad to say, have played us like the slavering junkies we are, cynically and without mercy. The sobering (perhaps that's not exactly the right word) fact is that there's a very finite amount of Domaine la Whatever in existence. It may be 400 cases, 4,000, or, in the case of wineries like Gallo, 4,000,000. Doesn't matter. When it's gone, it's gone. Even at that early stage we understood that if it isn't consumed, it disappears into cellars and private collections. We hadn't yet discovered that we would be able to buy it later on, at auction, at five times the original price.

Almost overnight, the new obsession toppled our misbegotten souls into a constant search for the next Big Thing. As the Eagles had sung so many years before, we were hot for the action, blinded by thirst. And we certainly didn't see the stop sign.

Looking back, it's now more than apparent that this impulse, drive, whatever, was (and is) an inevitable and maybe even necessary step on the stairway down to happy ruination. Fortunately, running after wine is a mite more comfortable (and reputable) than scuffling around dark alleys and even damper basements looking for that dime bag (which I actually did once, in Copenhagen, much to my eternal regret), but even so, as novice wine junkies we did rush out, jonesing, lusting to sample the world, wanting to do it as close to for free as we could manage. Some tastings were agreeably gratis, but most of them charged at least something, a token of $10 or $20 or so to keep the freeloaders out. In our area, the customary hit is ten dollars, but at tastings where they're pouring the real biggies, it could run as high as thirty-five. That *really* keeps the freeloaders out.

So after participating in a few Thursday night events of this type, and after coming home with three or six or twelve bottles of this or that, we were considered Good Customers.

("You have to buy at least three," Debi would tell me. "If we buy one and we like it, we'll go back for more and it'll be gone." Quite often, her characteristic yet charming pessimism has real practical value).

So by the end of the tourist season we'd been to two or three tastings at one particular store, plus a few events at other stores, spending a couple hundred a month, taking home cases at a time. It got to the point where they just handed us a glass before we were even through the door. Charge us ten dollars? Don't be silly.

Whatever it cost to get in, it didn't matter. We knew there was always the chance of discovering something really extraordinary that's priced way below market. Like Louis Bernard Cotes du Rhône Villages, which came out in 1998. Ten bucks a bottle, delicious, and we were all over it. Must've bought two cases, and drank them with unbecoming eagerness. (Flash forward: A few years later, in 2001, *Wine Spectator* magazine selected it as one of the top 100 wines of the year. While the magazine's annual Top 100 list is viciously excoriated by a certain portion of the wine life community, which is a phenomenon that deserves more discussion and will certainly receive it, they do sometimes come up with a winner. It was number 41 on the list, and we felt like people who had bought Apple at eight dollars a share).

We were all signed up at several shops, inveterate Wine

Clubbers, and every day we looked for that postcard or email announcing the next tasting. These tended to be cheery notices which said something like, "Come to our store on Thursday between five and eight PM, bring your credit card, and we'll put it to death for you." Some racket. Invite a bunch of people to your store, pour them 30 or 40 one-ounce samples, and they stumble out with cases and cases. There's an old saying that it's always happy hour somewhere, so we were on the list at six or seven stores. Not a week went by without an eager, smiling merchant pouring something at one location or another. That's the good news.

The bad news is that every time we went to one, there was some new kind of Clos du Something or Fattoria Nessuno that we liked. Three to six bottles of each. Every time.

"I have an idea," I said to Debi one day when we were stowing cases of our new purchases in the bottom of the closet. Larry's wine racks had long been suffering under the burden of their full capacity. "Let's start buying more expensive wine. That way, we can spend the same amount of money and have fewer bottles. Problem solved." She gave me one of her looks.

The tasting whirl turned into a routine. As I mentioned, it's always happy hour (or tasting time) somewhere, so we found ourselves scheduling our social calendar around the second-Wednesday-of-the-month tasting, the last-Thursday-of-the-month tasting, and the third-Friday-of-the-month tasting. We didn't tell anybody we were doing it.

There are, of course, other reasons to go to tastings. As the wine sickness tightened its grip, we gradually began to buy wine according to the recommendations of our more knowledgeable friends and wine store owners, and that was when my first issue of *Wine Spectator* arrived. Debi had bought me a surprise subscription.

I started reading the ratings that critics give to wine, on a hundred-point scale, copying them down, compelled to discover new wineries, new tastes, and new varietals. I even worked out an Excel spreadsheet (this is kind of embarrassing) that figured out the "value ratio" of a wine by dividing the price by the number of points the critics gave it, arriving at a cost per point, which can also be expressed as a percentage, if the inclination strikes. Meanwhile, this whole idea of "rating" wines bubbled on the back burner. It was something I'd have to come back to, sooner or later.

It took a while for the varietals thing to kick in for us, but oh, when it did. At first, we stayed with the stuff that Larry and Charlene had hooked us on…New Zealand Sauvignon Blanc, California Cabernets, and Zinfandel. We eat a lot of pasta, and Italy is never very far from our hearts, so we'd already discovered a few acceptable (we believed at the time) Chiantis and Tuscan blends. But looking back, it's clear that our condition was laughably primitive, and our tastes severely circumscribed, almost parochial. We hadn't nearly begun to discover all the different kinds of wine we would ultimately like, and hadn't nearly begun to discover how much money they could cost.

It's like the person who, one day, is struggling to choke down his first oyster, and two years later he's discussing the merits of raspberry points from Prince Edward Island over the Chesapeake varieties. Same with caviar and other luxury foods.

Wine is the worst. The burgeoning obsession forced us (*forced* us, I say) into an intensive, arduous schedule of samplings. First, there were the covetous glances at bottles of Pinot Noir. Then I, who had been repulsed at the outset by the peppery taste of Syrah, performed, at some unknown point, a complete about face and started sucking up information on Australia and the Rhône Valley. Things went downhill like one of those funny little sleds at the winter Olympics, except we were riding headfirst instead of the other way around. One year, for Christmas, Deb's mother gave me a copy of *Wines of the Rhone* by Robert Parker, and not only did it change my life, it caused nearly fatal damage to my FICO score. I don't know what happens after we die, but if there's an office or a place where I can stand in front of a desk staffed by some ethereal being who's charged with sending me to spend eternity in this place or that, I'm going to tell him I want to go to Hermitage.

Back to the tastings. It seemed that each wine store attracted a different kind of crowd, and no matter how hard we looked at them, we could honestly never tell about those people. There's an extremely spiffy shop in the next town, which sits in the middle of ridiculously expensive homes occupied by hilariously wealthy people. The store owner always gave us a liberal discount, because every once in a while we would find a bargain and buy a case or two. Besides, the glassfuls he poured at his tastings were more than generous.

Frankly, we didn't buy *that* much wine from him, because his prices were close to stratospheric. We'd been to enough wine shops to know what the most common brands cost, so I asked him once why he charged so much. He said,

"Because I can. These people will pay it." And they did. We were at a tasting one afternoon in late summer of 1998 (samplings at this particular store were more like happy hours…we just all sat around and opened a bottle of this, and a bottle of that) and this twentysomething guy walked in who looked like Ted Nugent on a bad day, accompanied by a barefooted girlfriend in a tank top and cutoffs who reminded us of Patti Smith on any kind of a day. They had that wasted, on the road again, took the brown acid at Woodstock aura that tells you they're either a couple of insanely famous people from a grunge band and we didn't recognize them, or they're two degenerates who just spend most of their lives amicably divorced from reality as most of us experience it.

Except they strolled the store for half an hour, put together a case of exquisite bottles, none of which cost under $120, slapped down a Platinum American Express card, hit it for around a grand and a half, and lugged their newfound treasures to their Jaguar. As Scott Joplin said, "One never knows, do one?" One never do.

By the end of that summer, after dozens of tastings and many hours of elbow-bent observation, we found ourselves classifying the wine tasting crowd into three fairly broad classes: the sippers, the swillers, and the sniffers. The sippers enjoy wine, but not to the point where they'll buy books or go to classes about it. They stand with arm crooked, holding their glass out for the next pour, listening to the distributor's rep talk about malolactic fermentation and carbonic maceration, taking it in, treating themselves to tiny little sips before dumping it in the bucket and going on to the next. They like it, they drink it, but they'd never actually collect it.

The sniffers make up the large middle class. When we first came down with the disease, we never expected to have 100 bottles in the house, but they somehow started to pile up. These people have at least that, they know their stuff, they look for bargains, but don't mind paying the higher two figures or lower three for something that awes them. These are the fun people, who, when they sip, seek that fine balance between inevitability and surprise. Typically, they drink a bottle a night. They enjoy, and they appreciate. We recognized ourselves in them, in an incipient way.

You can tell by the way they swirl, putting the glass down on the table and moving it in small circles as they hold it flat against the surface. They learned long ago that if they swirl a glass in midair the liquid explodes out of it, and their Dolce & Gabbana silk blouse becomes a dishrag. They put their noses way down deep in the glass (even though the wine store uses this little birdfart stemware they rent from the party supply company), close their eyes to focus all their sensibility on the wafting aromas, breathe deeply, and then they sip, sucking the wine into their mouths with little slurping sounds and chewing it around a bit.

Swillers come in two types. The first doesn't know a lot about wine, but he knows when the tastings are, and he knows he can drink all night for ten bucks. There aren't many of these people, because sooner or later they run out of wine stores. The second kind is what we came to know as the cork dork, our discovery that if any pursuit, hobby, or interest can lead to pretentiousness and elitism, wine is at the top of the list.

We used to have one cork dork at our last-Thursday-of-the-month tastings, a chest-out-chin-down amply-stomached gray lump of a man, about seventy years old and well over 260 pounds, who wore a *tastevin* around his neck. It's one of those little silver faceted cups that fancy wine stewards sometimes wear when the restaurant wants patrons to think the place is a real Wine Destination. I'd never seen anyone actually do that before, and he didn't bring it off.

(When I was in college I had a roommate who came from a wealthy Spanish family. He owned an honest-to-God opera cape, black with red silk lining, which he would wear to plays and concerts on campus. He looked great in it. One night my other roommate, Ron, borrowed it to wear to some event at the student center. Poor guy just couldn't make it work. He was hoping to look like the Count of Monte Cristo, but he just looked like some schmuck in an opera cape).

There were regular tastings, the ones we planned our weeks around, and then there were the accidental ones, the blessed events, like when we strolled into Morrell's insanely upscale wine store in Rockefeller Center and found ourselves in front of tables laden with bottles, wine reps pouring, and strangers standing around sipping, sniffing, smiling, and getting to know each other. The surprise ones are the best.

CHAPTER 5

MMMM! These Pencil Shavings are Delicious!

ine tastes like almost everything but grape juice. Decoding "descriptors," the words wine writers and critics use to describe the flavors and aromas of wine, is something of a skill. I've never seen this subject explained anywhere else. This could be a first.

September, 1999

It was sometime after the summer of 1999 when I realized that almost exactly two years earlier I couldn't even spell Trockenbeerenauslese Neusiedlersee, and now I had six bottles of it in an official wine rack in the back bedroom. Not only that, I could find its place of origin in eastern Austria on a map, and wanted to go there. It was turning into an interesting year.

By becoming regulars at the tastings around town, we'd met more than a few people who were much more hopelessly consumed by the wine life than we were. Inevitably, our conversation worked its way around to the question, "What do you like most about wine?" We asked a lot of people, and kept getting a lot of the same answer. Wine is some kind of miraculous liquid, it seems, where living microbiological things happen within it from the time the grapes are crushed until we swirl, sniff, and sip. There are seeds, there are spores, even. Yeast comes alive. Through a natural process powerful enough to inspire reverence and awe in even the most godless of us, there occurs the miraculous conversion of sugar into alcohol. In some cases there's even a process of putrefaction called noble rot that attacks grapes on the vine, turning them into disgusting gray and black lumps, wrinkled, oozy, and drippy, with whiskers and fuzzy growth all over, and it all actually makes the juice taste even better, which is astonishing because that makes no sense at all. I've seen pictures of grape bunches all slimy with noble rot, and can't imagine the mentality of the first guy who looked at them and thought, "Hey…I bet those rotten disgusting grapes would make terrific wine." Kind of like that first brave soul who ever ate an oyster.

I started wishing I could take courses on what happens to grapes when you squeeze them, like running off to the University of California at Davis or Fresno State, but it really wasn't an option. Point is, there really are better things for better living through chemistry, which is how plain old grape juice winds up tasting like…almost anything else. To me, that's the real wonder of it. I've read the description of how it happens, the way the fruit sugar molecules get rearranged during fermentation, read about the polysaccharides and all the rest of the multisyllabic science, but I'd rather just enjoy the phenomenon. Apple juice tastes like apples, more or less, and orange juice tastes like oranges. Let either of them ferment, and the result is lousy-tasting juice that will probably kill anyone who drinks it. But when grape juice becomes wine the final product is far from the original liquid. Why wine doesn't taste like the grape juice it's made of is a primary puzzlement upon entry into the wine life. It's one of the wonderments that first sucked me in.

I had been reading about wine obsessively ever since the Larry and Charlene revelation, and all the books told me scads about what wine is, how it's made, where it comes from, in as much detail as I cared to absorb. But not one of them (until the middle of 1999) told me squat about what wine *isn't*. I was taken aback just a bit when I found out that, through the ages, the problem was not getting grape juice to ferment, but getting it *not* to. Enter Dr. Thomas Welch (this was one of those aha moments) who lived, appropriately enough, in Vineland, New Jersey in the mid 1800s. The county was dry, and since local lawmakers had little respect for the requirements of religious observance, it posed a big problem for churches that needed wine for communion (and synagogues, if there were any in the neighborhood, that needed it for Passover). Being a pious man, the good doctor rose to the challenge and became the first person in history to figure out how to make "non-fermented wine," which was his naïve name for it. Assisted by his son, he crushed the grapes, put the liquid in bottles, and boiled them. Today we call it grape juice, and Dr. Welch's descendants, when they go shopping, never have to ask how much things cost.

Compared to other fruit extracts, grape juice is a horse of a different wheelbase. Wine can be made out of just about any fruit juice, or dandelions, even, or whatever rots and goes bad, and people actually do that. I don't know why they bother, because, out of all the grape species in the world, only the species *vitis vinifera* ferments with style, with feeling, with imagination and inspiration. Kind of like some apples are good for sauce, others for pies, and still others for eating. As the mysterious chemical rearrangements of fermentation occur, the juice gives up flavors that have no resemblance to what Dr. Welch was boiling in the bottle. The white grapes yield up often-stunning sensations of citrus, white fruit, flowers, herbs and minerals, and some of the whites from Burgundy would set me back upwards of $400 a bottle, were I silly enough to buy them. The best reds, we discovered in our nightly swirlings, hit us with cherries, berries, plum, spice, and deeper, darker flavors.

For us, back in the early stages of the addiction, it started with the super-fruity styles of wine that come out of California and onto the wine aisle at the local supermarket. Big, juicy, obvious, and cheap. As soon as we began to read the wine critics, and graduated from the $10 bottles to the just-under $20 bottles, those deeper, darker flavors made themselves known, along with others, considerably more strange.

A lot can be learned about wine just by talking to people. At the many, many tastings we attended, we chatted with like-minded aficionados, and inevitably compared the sensations we were experiencing. Few subjects are more, well, subjective than wine, and everybody who sniffs and sips tastes something different. One person says, "Well, I get a little hint of mushroom on the finish," and I'm standing there with the taste of mushrooms the farthest thing from my mind. Sometimes, a fellow sipper will mention a flavor or aroma, and the other people in the group will detect it just by power of suggestion. Fortunately, there are no wrong answers. You taste wet leaves and forest floor? Go right ahead.

The ability to really pay attention to what taste buds are saying takes a lot of practice, and probably a bit of inborn talent, as well. People go into the perfume business (they're called "Noses") because they have naturally acute olfactory talent. I once asked a professional hockey player what made Wayne Gretzy so good, and he told me, "He sees the puck better than anyone." So the Great One was gifted with visual acuity and uncommon depth perception, as well as the ability to wear ice skates and remain upright.

We'd been applying ourselves assiduously to the tasting task for at least two years, and we realized that most of it could be consciously learned. But we had help. *Wine Spectator* magazine had been arriving regularly, thanks to Debi's nice surprise, and I customarily opened it to the wine ratings page even as I walked from the mailbox to the house. Reading the tasting notes, I marveled at the twisted tastes the magazine's critics discovered as they swirled, sniffed, sipped, and spat. I never tasted the flavors they claimed to detect, so I had to conclude that they were either completely full of crap or, alternatively, that their palates were more educated than mine, more sensitive, like some people who see the puck better than I ever will. Because these writers have been thusly blessed, they've found a way to drink wine for a living, damn them. Their worldliness and sophistication surpass mine as well, hard as that is to admit. But these people seem to pinpoint flavors in wine that I didn't even want to think about, let alone put past my lips. And the vocabulary they use to describe them is a psycholinguistic study in itself, requiring readers to come at the English language from a perspective that's more than a little out of plumb.

Let's take the second situation first. Since I majored in the

subject in college, and words are the substance of my trade,
I'm aware that English happens to be among the richer of
languages, endowed with tons of words that provide subtle
nuances of distinction. Other languages have different
virtues. Italian, for example, has thousands of words that all
end in the same sound, so Dante had no problem rhyming
canto after canto, piling them up one upon another, from
the first circle of Hell to the ninth. English, alas, is rhyme-
poor, but more than compensates by being adjective-rich.
People who make a living studying this kind of thing have
tabulated all the adverbs, conjunctions, pronouns, and
other parts of speech in our language alongside others and
they assure us that when it comes to adjectives, English
speakers are (ahem) exceptionally well endowed. Wine
writers exploit that richness with Dickensian fervor, flinging
adjectives about with joyful abandon.

They talk about wine having "backbone," and "stuffing."
There are wines that are "muscular," and others that are
"shy" or "supple." Some words, especially those that
try to describe the way wine feels in the mouth, are
fairly expected. Wine can taste silky, harsh, rough, all
those things. But then there is "opulence" in wine, there
is "vibrance." Tannins can be "velvety." Wine can be
"chunky," and "chewy," or even "jammy." It can "resonate,"
it can be "round," and certainly "seductive." Clearly, wine
writers are especially adept at putting a little… well, English
on the language.

But the words that express feeling are nothing compared
to the words that attempt to convey flavors. These words,
we learned, are called "descriptors." Here, the language
soars skyward like an exultation of larks, but the flavors go
in exactly the opposite direction. The well-read and well-

traveled critics who write for the major wine magazines and web sites are drinking $500 bottles, and seem to love it when they experience flavors like saddle sweat or wet animal fur. For them, the fouler the flavor, the better the beverage.

Just to show that I'm not making any of this up, here's a sample of actual reviews of some top end wines that often sell at auction for outer-spatial prices.

"...exotic nose of barbeque spices, burning wood, and sweet cherry fruit..."

"...scents of underbrush, smoke, saddle leather, soy, and other assorted Asian spices begin to emerge along with kirsch liqueur and black fruit notes."

"...cooked apple, lemon, and petrol." I think that means gasoline.

"...perfumed, nuanced aromas of cherry, faded rose, wood smoke and bacon fat." Wood smoke again. And breakfast flavors, too.

"Reticent but lively aromas of black raspberry and blackberry syrup...Very expressive, super-ripe flavors of plum, nuts, game and animal fur." Animal fur? Do we even want to know what kind of animal?

What's creepy about all this is that when these flavors show up in a wine glass, they *work*. It's a marvel to me that wine can taste like just about anything, and the more we progressed (or degenerated) in our enthusiasm during the course of the year, the more we understood the appeal of those "barnyard overtones" and "hints of forest floor."

Deb once bought me what I guess would be called a wine appreciation course in a box. It's a largish container, designed with sophisticated graphics in rich gold and purple brown, and inside there are about 50 little plastic vials, each one containing a smell, aroma, or odor. The idea is to snort these things one at a time, thereby developing sense memory and training the olfactory facilities to identify the scents and savors when they are encountered in the glass. Professional wine people and perfumers use kits like this in their training, but I never did find a vial that smelled like animal fur, and I looked. Most of the scents are pretty benign, and even lovely. Honeysuckle, strawberry, apricot, black cherry, lemon drop. Those aren't the problem. It's the others.

The best winemakers manage to make their grapes give up aromas not only of bacon fat and animal fur, but of slate, peach pits, and gun flint, which are only the more normal sensations. Since grapes soak up the characteristics of the ground in which they're grown (the *terroir*, as the French, who have a word for everything, like to say), stone-type flavors aren't too much of a surprise. There are, in fact, wines called "Stony Hill" and "Gravelly Meadow." But if the wine tastes like animal fur, it's hard not to think of what else might be going on in the vineyard.

But it *works*, dammit, and that's probably the real miracle. One French wine that's become kind of a staple around the house has the definite scent of grilled meat to it, and there's a subtle hint of the grill in the flavor, too. It's great with steak. Go figure.

Not having much of a life my own self, I started making lists of my favorite weird wine tastes and aromas as I encountered them in the critics' reviews. As we spent more time hanging around the wine shop tastings with all those swillers and sniffers, we frequently overheard them talking in these terms. We started doing it ourselves. God help us. These are the flavors that have become closest to our hearts.

10) Forest floor. Like wet leaves, moss, damp trees. Wine with flavors like this are far from spoiled. *Au contraire*, they cost a bundle.

9) Saddle leather. This is a very special kind of smell. Some wines have other types of leather aromas, and I've read serious critics who make the distinction between brown leather and black leather. I can swear I had a bottle once that tasted like my grandmother's sofa.

8) Horse sweat. Goes right along with the saddle leather.

7) Barnyard. Deb and I are both solidly from the city, but the bouquet of the chicken coop is unmistakable. Neither of us had ever experienced it firsthand, but we recognized it a lot quicker than we cared to admit. We learned that this flavor can come from the wine being affected by a fungus called brettanomyces, and a lot of people actually like it.

6) Smoke. This turns out to be a pretty common sensation in red wines like Zinfandels. Right around this time, we discovered a wine called Cigar Zin, and that's exactly what it smells like. Subtly, of course, not like that stogie my Uncle Morris used to fire up. More delicate. More sophisticated. A Cohiba, not a Tiparillo.

5) Bubble gum. I've never had a wine that tasted like bubble gum, but I'd certainly want to know if there are differences between Bazooka and Double Bubble. And do these bottles come with a little comic strip, or a baseball trading card?

4) Bell pepper. Red wines give off all kinds of pepper scents, and I'm darned if I know why. In addition to green pepper, some have a hint of white or black pepper, especially the Shirazes. Later, I learned that bell pepper aromas are usually considered a flaw.

3) Mothballs. If you like wine that smells like your grandmother's closet.

2) Pencil shavings. It takes you right to the second grade, and that gray crank machine screwed to the wall, full of wood and warm graphite smell. That's this.

1) *Pipi du chat.* I've been dreading this topic, feeling like the time I tried to explain human reproduction to a six-year-old, but it's one of those areas we had to explore if we wanted to know the truth about wine. Not to put too fine a point on it, but we went to our first major wine festival in Sarasota during this period, and had some white wines that smelled exactly like cat pee. And not new cat pee, either— the kind that's been in the litterbox a while. Not only that, but there are people who think this is a *good thing*. In my wine smelling kit, there's a little vial delicately labeled "Pipi du Chat," because even cat pee sounds better in French. We've been to white wine tastings where they served some extremely expensive Sancerres and Pouilly Fumes from the Loire Valley, and a discussion of this aroma was as spirited as it was lengthy. Hint: the more euphemistically-inclined refer to this distinctive fragrance as "boxwood." On a trip to Rome the following year, I found out why.

Boxwood is a low-growing hedge plant with small, shiny dark green leaves, and is used just about everywhere in Europe for landscaping. The Italians love it more than most. In the park above the Forum in Rome, right across the sidewalk from the Coliseum where young men get paid to dress up like Roman centurions and have their pictures taken with tourists, the stuff is all over the place. We love cats, but we couldn't stroll around the grounds for very long without getting overpowered.

A discovery during this period: there are two kinds of wine. There's the kind that tastes a lot like fruit, and the kind that tastes like fruit and just about anything else. Generally, the wines made in the Americas and Australia (the so-called New World wines) are "fruit forward." The ones made in the Old World (just about everywhere else on the planet) are not. They convey forest floor, black tar, and, sometimes, for those with more sophisticated senses, a little whiff of what Scruffy does in the box.

CHAPTER 6

The War
of the Ratings

There's a whole world of people who live and die by the 100-point system critics use for evaluating the quality of wine. Winemakers live in fear of this system, because it can quite literally either make them rich or drive them out of business. Wine lovers are divided between the followers of critic Robert Parker, and the legion of subscribers to Wine Spectator magazine, which pretty much rules the wine world. This is their story.

November, 1999

Debi was in her 6th year working for one of the local network television stations, which is how I knew that every three months, independent survey companies gather information on who's watching which TV shows, and who's listening to which radio stations. The results of the surveys are critical, because audience viewership levels determine how much the networks and local stations can charge for their advertising. Billions of dollars in revenues can rise or fall on the basis of these ratings, so passions run hot.

The instant the ratings come out, important broadcast and cable television executives, from their offices high above New York City, either praise the uncanny accuracy of the numbers or defenestrate themselves and hurtle to their deaths on the sidewalk right in front of horrified tourists in Rockefeller Plaza. Others whose networks come out on the bottom of the ratings may have a bit more to live for, and they pounce instead on the real or imagined flaws in the survey process, pointing out every hilarious inconsistency in the data, and casting aspersions on the parentage of the people responsible for such wildly distorted and comically inaccurate information.

Billions of dollars or not, the national outcry over television ratings is the merest whisper compared to how wine lifers feel about the way their favorite beverage is evaluated. The topic is absolutely incendiary.

The more we read and tasted, the more money we spent (and we did spend money), the more we realized that everything in the wine world is controversial. There are conflicting methods of grape growing, aging, filtering, how much oak, real corks or synthetic stoppers, there's not a single point that can't be contended. And all of them are, in many venues, at great length, and in brutal detail.

By the time the holidays arrived, I had expanded my reading beyond the *Wine Spectators* that arrived every three weeks or so to include similar publications that alleged to tell me what to buy, when to drink it, and how good it was. Being an English major, former college teacher, devout grammarian, and writer with a few modest publications to my credit, I continued to marvel at the adjectival escapades of the wine writers, and took their advice seriously. Slowly, almost imperceptibly, our wine budget had increased more during this year than in times past, and we were well into the $20-a-bottle range, so with the investment becoming more substantial, professional guidance was a must, and the opinions of the critics started to matter.

When we first started down the slippery slope, we made our buying decisions on the advice of friends, wine store clerks, point of purchase signs, and, on occasion, complete strangers. (I, a complete stranger, will often stop to offer unsought advice to an obviously bewildered and indecisive soul standing in the wine aisle at the supermarket). We bought what we discovered at the tastings, but still, one can sample only so much, and the wine world is a big place. We couldn't taste them all ourselves, though heaven knows we tried. So the guidance we needed above and beyond our immediate circle of new-found wine friends had to come from our confidence in the critics.

The difference between television ratings and wine ratings is this: television viewership and the resultant ratings are determined by semi-scientific surveys such as phone interviews, people who keep diaries of the shows they watch, and meters placed on individual TV sets that actually record data on every program the users tune in. Then all these numbers are subjected to mind-numbing mathematical manipulation that extrapolates, interpolates, and applies the "beta-binomial theorem" (whatever that is) to give advertisers some idea of how many people are watching what, and when, in every television market in the country, and there are 210 of them, last time I counted. The results are published, market by market, in thick books containing countless columns of numbers in very small type. They look impressively statistical.

But wine ratings are nothing like that. As soon as we got

seriously into reading the critics we learned the horrible truth. The numbers that can propel a wine to the top of the charts or consign it to eternal ignominy are determined, in most cases, by one single person, and occasionally by a small panel. They swirl, sniff, and sip, then assign points based on their personal opinion. As Emily Latella used to say on Saturday Night Live, "That's different."

Let's be sensible. Wine ratings are not a matter of life and death; they're much more serious than that. Even though we and our new wine lifer friends were willing to try just about any beverage that's made from grapes and comes in a bottle, box, or jug, we still had to rely heavily on comparisons and evaluations drawn by people who make a living at comparing and evaluating, and who are supposed to know what they're doing. Problem is knowing which ones to trust. Some people are willing to spend $20 or $30 to try a bottle they've never heard of, but we newbies wanted at least a little reassurance that the bottle we bought blind wouldn't make us gag and pour it, along with our money, down the sink. When we solicit recommendations from friends, it's not like asking whether the movie they saw last night was any good. A wine purchase is a much more emotional investment than a movie ticket. We found out pretty quickly that when a wine buddy tells us this bottle of Chateau la Dreq is the best thing since the stuff they served at the Wedding at Cana, there's still a good chance that our taste won't be her taste, and we'll wind up gagging and pouring it down the sink. We have to pay attention to the critics, but deciding which critics is a matter that can change lives. It's a question that deserves serious and lengthy debate in front of the General Assembly at the UN, or at the World Court in The Hague. Every critic, every wine rating authority, attracts both apostles and apostates.

Discussions about ratings keep the big wine magazines and newsletters cranking out pages, year after year, and the topic burns up the chat rooms on the Internet. As novices, even after three years of dedicated sampling, the rating point system had a major impact on our buying decisions, because wine stores slap little tags on bottles that receive good reviews, trumpeting the ratings from various critics and magazines. (In November of every year, *Wine Spectator* issues its list of the Top 100 wines of the year. During this particular November, an excellent Chilean Cabernet that sold for about $18 a bottle made it into this rarified realm, and the company *printed a new version of the label* to bring that distinction to the personal attention of prospective buyers). Gradually, we had become more familiar with the wine varieties and regions of the world, and had sampled enough to develop our own lamentably inadequate opinions. Then I'd spend my time agreeing or disagreeing with the critics, and arguing with everybody on the other side. The Internet makes it easy for anybody to air a screed or drain the main vein to a potentially worldwide audience of people who are just as inflamed as they are.

What could be more controversial than the matter of personal judgment and taste, except the discussions Deb and I have about how much to pay for a decent bottle? Nothing, that's what. But the critical evaluation of wines, the whole pass/fail system, the determination of which wines sell out and which are left to age forlorn and forgotten on the shelves, is concentrated in the hands (glasses, actually) of maybe fewer than 20 people in the world, and even that number is misleading, because some of them have far more influence than others.

Since we work for a living, the expenditure of our resources on wine had become, over time, an important issue, especially when we realized that the measly 100 bottles we'd accumulated would never be enough. We wanted to buy wisely, which meant going beyond the advice of the wine shop clerks and the hype on the shelf tags, and paying attention to what the critics said, more than how they said it.

The system in almost universal use assigns the wines being tasted a rating from 1 to 100 points. Actually, the numbers go from 75 or 80 points up, because any wine that scores below that will probably never be bought or drunk by anybody. So a bottle gets 50 points automatically, just for showing up on the tasting table.

But even a system so well-entrenched and well-accepted is open to argument, like everything else in the wine life. As we educated ourselves, we found out that some writers, like Hugh Johnson, used to advocate a 10 or 20-point system, because it allows for a more meaningful separation between a truly outstanding wine and whatever comes in second. He's not wrong. But over time, the 100-point system carried the day. Personally, I can't bring myself to believe that even the most completely absorbed wine lifer could really tell the difference between a 92-point wine and a 93-pointer. At that level, many people feel that the distinctions become meaningless. It really is astonishing that a multi-billion-dollar industry is at the mercy of maybe two dozen people in America and overseas whose happy task it is to make exactly those microscopic distinctions and publish them, to the benefit or doom of almost every wine on the market today.

We always try to keep in mind that ratings tell us one

person's opinion of a wine or a vintage, or sometimes give us the collective decision of a tasting committee that votes and averages their scores. Whether we actually like the wine or not is up to us. By the dawn of the new millennium, we'd been sliding in to the wine life for a little over two years, and had gone to enough local tastings (and the regional one where we learned about cat pee) to sample at least a few very highly rated wines, all of which carried price tags well beyond our beginner's budget. Some of them brought tears to our eyes, some just weren't to our taste, and with others we just looked at each other and asked why the hell would anybody pay $200 a bottle for this swill?

However, and there's always a however, ratings can be a good indication of relative value. Or not. As I read the reviews in the various magazines, I found hundreds of examples of wines selling for $75 a bottle that received 90 points from the critics, and others that sold for $11 that got the same score...or higher. So yes, we read the ratings all the time, and value-minded me tried to find not the 95 point wines that sell for $575 a bottle, but the 91 point wines that go for under fifteen bucks. They're out there.

The ratings published by various critics are also a huge sales tool in wine shops. Almost every retailer (as I've already mentioned) tags highly rated (88+ points) bottles with the numbers and reviews. Consumers who wander in needing a dinner gift for that night, or wine lifers looking to try something new, will pick a bottle that carries a rating over one that doesn't. At least there's some indication that somebody likes it, and even an individual's assurance of quality is better than none, most times.

I remember when I first started joining chat rooms on the Internet, back in the pre-Windows days, when there was Compuserve, before the advent of the GUI and the WYSIWYG, when the word "google" meant a one with a hundred zeros after it, and was spelled differently. I looked to the Internet for information to feed my rapidly-expanding obsession, and watched as the World Wide Web became a major adjunct to the wine life. Suddenly, it was possible for everybody to be a wine critic, and these days just about everybody is. Some of the more knowledgeable and absorbed wine lifers managed to turn their interest into a hobby, and their hobby into a livelihood, publishing newsletters and setting up subscription web sites filled with their personal recommendations and observations. (It is said that truly creative people make their own jobs.) Wine shops put out publications, too, both on line and on paper, hyping products that their sales force has tasted and found agreeable. But these people, however expert they may be, seem to have little if any effect on what happens at the top of the critic world.

I guess I've made it clear that the ratings had (and still have) an influence on our buying decisions, as they do on most people. Once the passion takes hold, it's inevitable that who the critics are, and what they write, will be important to a greater or lesser degree. And it's inevitable that the Internet will play a role as well. On the web, there are critics who dispense experienced opinions on certain kinds of wine, or certain regions. One newsletter publisher may specialize in Burgundy, while another is passionate about California Cabernets. But at the very pinnacle of the business are the amazingly few people who have the following, the platform, and the authority to make or break a particular wine, wine producer, or vintage, and they often do.

In one corner, from New York City, wearing the blue

trunks with white stripe, is *Wine Spectator*, published by Shanken Communications in New York. Marvin Shanken is the owner of the most widely-circulated consumer wine magazine in the country, if not in the world, and literally millions of wine buying (and winemaking) decisions are influenced by what his critics write. We'd been reading it faithfully ever since Debi bought me the surprise gift subscription, but to expand our education, and simply because we couldn't help ourselves, we gradually subscribed to other wine magazines in fairly high circulation, such as the *Wine Enthusiast*, *Food & Wine*, and many trade publications too, like *Wine & Spirits* and *Decanter*. But as far as I can tell, *Wine Spectator* has the greatest power over the consumer, especially over the beginning buyer, and thus over the market.

In the opposite corner, from Monckton, Maryland, in the solid white trunks, is Robert Parker. A writer for the *Los Angeles Times* called him "the most powerful critic of any kind, anywhere," which is saying quite a bit, and probably the reason why Parker proudly features the quote on his web site home page. How powerful is he? It is said that certain producers make their wine expressly to appeal to his tastes in order to get a favorable review. He's been at it for several decades, publishing a newsletter called *The Wine Advocate*, first in printed form, and later on the Internet. (As this book was being readied for publication, Parker caused a huge stir in the wine world by retiring, and selling the Wine Advocate name to a critic who has been working with him for several years.) There are several other well-known critics whose evaluations and ratings are valued by wine lifers, such as Steve Tanzer, and Burgundy expert Allen Meadows, who has been visiting the region and writing about the wine for over 20 years. But when the nitty meets the gritty, the real battle is between Marvin Shanken's faithful on one side, and Robert Parker's true believers on the other.

A really good wine is a really good wine, and quite often the *Wine Spectator* and Robert Parker ratings are within a point or two of each other. But the big difference is this: *Wine Spectator* is (as Parker followers nimbly point out) a slick, high-circulation consumer magazine which accepts paid advertising from the very winemakers it critiques. To some, this is cause for suspicion. Robert Parker prides himself on his independence, making his living from his newsletter, web site, speaking engagements, and a whole stack of highly-regarded books about the wine regions and cuisines of the world. His newsletters and web enterprises accept no advertising. Parkerites believe that *Wine Spectator* is a blatantly commercial publication pandering shamelessly to the common taste, whose ratings are not to be trusted because they're inevitably influenced by the crassest of commercial considerations. Every once in a while, a wine or vintage review in one of the publications will slip in a sly dig at the competition, but it takes sharp reading to detect it.

The critics at *Wine Spectator* are, of course, aware that they're treading a narrow and perilous path, and proclaim their objectivity at every opportunity. Frankly, I believe them, especially since they'll even review wines made by a vineyard that Robert Parker owns in partnership with his brother, and give them high ratings. Of course, unless a critic is tasting wine at a particular chateau or winemaking facility, he or she always tastes blind. Critics have no idea whose wine they're drinking, and that's what maintains fairness and objectivity. But perception is reality, as they say, and the folks at *Wine Spectator,* as scrupulous as their tasting procedures may be, are always exposed to the pointing fingers of the conspiracy theorists. The biggest dog is the biggest target.

Since we'd been subscribing to all these magazines for a year or so, and reading them from front to back, we became aware of the way the controversy violently boils to the surface right around the middle to end of every November, when *Wine Spectator* publishes its incredibly influential list of the top 100 wines of the year. The battle over the magazine's decisions is almost Miltonian in its intensity. All over the Internet, and especially in Robert Parker's chat room, the forces of good and evil line up on either side of the ratings, and screeds abound. How could they *possibly* rank *this* wine in the top ten? How could they ever pick *that* rotgut as wine of the year? I can't believe they overlooked *my* favorite Brunello or Burgundy. Insanity.

Part of the argument comes from the idea that even making a list of "top 100" wines is completely ridiculous by definition. For every wine that makes the list, there are dozens, equally as good, that don't. The selection standards are thus always in question. Another point of contention (among so, so many) is that critics rate wines according to different criteria. Some might base their critique solely on what's in the glass. Others take wider issues into account.

It would be reasonable to assume that the *Wine Spectator* committee compiles a list of all the wines they rated in the past year, and lops off the hundred that got the highest point ratings to publish in their incendiary mid-December issue. Two years earlier, I believed, quite reasonably, that the wines scoring the highest during the year would all be at the top of the list, but I supposed erroneously. Over the year, several hundred wines will gain a score between 90 and 100 points, and there will be dozens with the same score. How to decide which is the "wine of the year" and which languishes morosely at Number 89?

This is where the "wider issues" come into play, where the *Wine Spectator* crew applies its own version of the beta-binomial theorem, and where Robert Parker fans start foaming at the mouth. When choosing the top wine of the year, the magazine, according to its own meticulous explanation, "honors a wine that combines outstanding quality with fair price and wide availability." They also consider an intangible element they call the "wow factor," or the excitement that the wine creates among the tasting panelists. Nothing objective or mathematical about that.

Back to the Top 100. A 93 point wine might be in the Number One slot, while a 97 point wine could be five or six notches down the list. But there's an important consideration here. What good is a great wine if you can't get it?

Wine Spectator does that to me on a depressingly regular basis: as much as I like the magazine, it routinely calls my avid attention to a great wine that I'll never get my hands on even if I live forever. One of the things that always drove me nuts when I first started looking to the magazine for inspiration and information was—and still is—that they'd publish a rave review of a wine, rhapsodize about its aromas of forest floor, chicken fat, and antique saddle leather, give it 97 points, list the price at $18 a bottle, and then note "20 cases imported." Go ahead, yank my chain, get me all worked up about a sensational bargain wine that I'll never see in my life. What's the point?

Since I'm on the subject, I have to jump ahead just a bit.

In 2002, *Wine Spectator* picked as the Wine of the Year a bottle that's inexpensive, widely available, and rated only 93 points out of 100. The entire blogosphere went nuts, and all over the web, chat rooms erupted with venomous comments about the magazine, the selection process, and not a few uncharitable diatribes about Marvin Shanken's personal habits.

The annual revelation of the Top 100 is, at best, an ambivalent event. It does convey to the public a concise list of comparatively excellent wines, ones that do deserve attention and trial. But the morning after the list comes out, wine stores across America are mobbed by people willing to forcibly remove each other's eyeballs over a bottle of anything that made the cut. Retailers and winemakers smile until their faces ache, because they'd stayed up all the night before until the wee hours madly re-tagging bottles, upping the prices on every Top 100 wine they were lucky enough to have on the shelf. But that doesn't stop the wineries from cashing in a year or so later. For example—flashing forward one more time—in 2000, *Wine Spectator* chose as the Wine of the Year a red blend from California called Chateau St. Jean Cinq Cepages 1996. It got 93 points and sold for $28. The following year, Chateau St. Jean released their 1997 vintage of the same wine at around $60. Just as good, actually, but new and improved, with a lot more prestige, name recognition, and a higher price. The 1996, because it was the magazine's top wine, wound up selling at auction in the $100 range. The same thing happens to just about every wine on the list. Inexpensive and available today, high-priced and rare tomorrow. The transformation occurs literally from one day to the next.

Shanken's detractors will also point out that many of the

wines in the Top 100 are gimmes. In 2002 the magazine made effusive comments all year about the quality of the 1997 vintage in Italy, especially in Tuscany, and more especially in Montalcino, where the Brunellos come from. Best vintage ever, they said, and rated the vintage itself around 98 or 99 points. Result? Three of the top 10 wines of 2002 were 1997 Brunellos. I could barely contain my astonishment.

Another result? Try to buy a 1997 Brunello at anywhere near its release price. Even with a mere 100 bottles in our collection, some have doubled in price in under a year. Others that we read about sell for six times the original release price just a few years after the vintage date. If only my other investments would do that.

Many wine lifers who have been at it for a long time, who have extensive collections and consider themselves sophisticated, are "past" the kind of reviewing that appears in *Wine Spectator*. They consider Robert Parker, or one of the other specialized critics, to be the supreme authority, largely due to his long reputation for independence, and sometimes shocking forthrightness. Other sources of reviews, such as the Wine Enthusiast, are "too popular," not esoteric enough, almost vulgar in the true Latin sense of the word.

De gustibus non est disputandum, said the Romans, but Pliny the Elder is also supposed to have said in *vino veritas*. That's one of the pleasures of the wine life: critics be damned. We thought it all through, and decided that the only way to find wines we like is to sample widely, and seek our own truth.

CHAPTER 7

Wine and the Family Tree

ine has taken us places, geographically, intellectually, and spiritually. It has also expanded and deepened our relationships in unexpected ways. We agonized over our decision to attend our first annual Wine Experience. Had we not gone, we never would have discovered cousins we didn't even know we had. Actually, they found us...in the middle of a ballroom containing well over 1,500 people. Uncanny.

August, 2000

"If you're going to that thing," said Larry, "you're gonna have to learn how to spit." Since Larry got us hooked in the first place, and since he's had a continuing influence on our wine lives, I listened to his advice with special reverence. We figured he knew what he was talking about.

He was referring, of course, to our attendance at our very first Big Time Tasting, or BTT...the Wine Experience, a three-day swirling and sipping marathon sponsored by *Wine Spectator* on behalf of their charitable foundation. From Thursday night until early Sunday morning in late October, battalions of oenophilic enthusiasts including restaurant

owners, wine stewards both current and aspiring, and
plain old addicts like ourselves, would wade through
wine lunches, wine dinners, wine breakfasts, seminars,
workshops, grand tastings, mini-tastings, all involving a
daunting amount of wine, possibly worth more than the
hotel we'd be staying in.

I knew this because every year around August a two-page
full color ad would appear in *Wine Spectator*, seductive in its
splashiness, hyping this Wine Experience thing. Apparently
it had been going on for about 20 years entirely without
us. As soon as I saw the ads, they began to sing to me, but
unlike the hero of a Greek epic, I didn't have to lash myself
to the mast to resist the temptation. The *Wine Spectator*
folks were charging over $1500 a person to get in the door,
and that effectively extinguished any incipient arousal I might
have felt. Three grand was definitely not in the cards (or in
the checkbook) at the time. Still, there was this…beckoning.

Our attendance at the local wine store tastings had been
both profoundly educational and profoundly expensive. We had
sampled widely, asked deep questions of the distributors'
reps who poured for us, absorbed their knowledge of
winemaking, varietals, and regions. We rarely left the store
empty-handed, often requiring the assistance of more than
one employee to transport our purchases to the car. The
bottle situation had continued to get the best of us, which
meant another call to Larry, another trip to the warehouse,
and the carting home of two more wire racks, just like
the kind they use in neighborhood wine shops. Our back
bedroom started to look like a retail store, because the
racks all had colorful winery signs and logos on top. A
counter and cash register would have completed the effect.
The hundred bottles we'd counted earlier in the summer

had feverishly reproduced, and numbered half again as many. We were enjoying at least a bottle a night during and after dinner. But fifteen hundred bucks a person, plus air fare, plus hotel, plus meals? Wasn't gonna happen.

August of 2000 wasn't the first time I had longingly called Debi's attention to the Wine Experience ads. I'd salivated over them in years past, ruining several fine dress shirts, and showed her the dampened pages more as fantasy food than anything else. A "we should do this when we win the lottery" idea. Plus, we'd looked at other magazine ads for similar events, such as the Aspen Food & Wine Festival, and the wine weekends and auctions held by just about every charity in every major city. Washington DC has one. Telluride has one. Albany has one. Des Moines has one. There's a big Pinot Noir blast in Oregon every year. I wouldn't be surprised if they had one in Norman, Oklahoma or Yeehaw Junction, Florida. So we understood that there are people in this world who can actually come up with four or five grand out of their wine budget to buy their way in to these exclusive events. They drink wine for three days straight, discover new pleasures, meet fellow enthusiasts, and maybe learn a thing or two in the process. That's them. This is us. Not yet.

I can't deny it. The urge had built within me almost since Larry poured the Bottle That Did It. Winewise, we were, by that time, at least advanced novices, with around three years and one month's swirling and sipping experience. This sounds worse every time I think about it, in a conscience-bothering sort of way, but we had, over the past year or so, basically eliminated from our social lives anyone who didn't enjoy wine. Shame on us, but, in our defense, we weren't really aware that it was happening. We found out that we

could bring our own wine to certain tolerant restaurants, a
happy discovery, and since wine lovers enjoy sharing, it was
disappointing to open something nice and relatively elevated
in price for dinner companions who didn't understand
it, appreciate it, or who (heaven forfend) wanted to put a
few ice cubes in it. Over the previous year or so, we'd built
our circle of friends outward from people like Larry and
Charlene, people who shared the passion; we gradually
drifted away from people who didn't.

Ah, those ads, those big, colorful two-page spreads.
They beckoned like the painted, perfumed ladies on the
darker side streets of Amsterdam (the ones just across
from the Oude Kerk). I gazed at them over and over (the
ads, not the ladies), looking at the list of all the wineries
that would pour their wares at the big tasting sessions, and
the topics of the seminars they were holding. It was only
yesterday that we'd started with those $10 sipping trips to
the wine stores, made it to a few $100 tastings, even bit the
bullet firmly and paid for a couple of those $300-a-couple
wine dinners, where each course is matched to a specific
(expensive) variety and vintage. (Since Larry is a wine
salesman, he knows every bartender, chef, and manager at
every important restaurant in town, and has slipped us in
to some of the more elaborate wine dinners. More often
than not, we'd hang out after the event, when everyone had
left except the wine geeks. One restaurant owner in a very
exclusive section of town felt so friendly, and so generous
upon counting the take from selling a hundred dinners at
three bills a head, that he pulled out half a dozen dream
bottles from the depth of his cellar and opened them for a
few of his close friends, and for us, who were smart enough
to stay late).

But I stray. We really weren't ready to dig that deep, to spend the larger dollars on a weekend wine toot in New York. Not ready by half, but the compulsion had built to the point where resistance, as the saying goes, was futile. We recognized some of the wines on the grand tasting list, and aspired to them. The wines they were serving were on our "when we win the lottery" wish list. We were eager for one of those four day deals, a Big Time Tasting like the Masters of Food and Wine in California, the Aspen Food & Wine Festival, the Naples Winter Wine Festival.

There are considerations, here, spousal discussions must be held. Attention, as Arthur Miller once famously wrote, must be paid. We kept returning to the fact that committing to a BTT requires a significant investment of time and money. We had one out of two. Problem.

To put things in perspective, we had examined the ads for the different wine fests, and noticed that people who stage these grape juice jubilees always hold them in a sophisticated (that means expensive) milieu, like Sonoma or Napa Valley, midtown Manhattan, Hawaii, some achingly exclusive inn up in the rarefied Colorado Rockies, or at a Ritz-Carlton in South Florida smack in the heart of high season. But…what was *really* involved, here? We'd be buying plane tickets to get to New York, and enjoying a longish weekend in a five star hotel with room rates that would certainly blow a smoldering hole in our monthly wine allowance. (Didn't I mention? We established a wine allowance—a certain fixed and inflexible amount budgeted every month for wine purchases. It was just slightly less than our mortgage payment, and was customarily honored in the breach, not the observance.)

As we debated the pros and cons of signing up, totaling

the price of admission, travel, hotel, cab from the airport, all that, the actual cost became shamefully secondary (or even tertiary) to the historical density of what we were about to do. We were considering a Big Step, spending more than we ever had before on any kind of vacation, even our honeymoon in Madrid, which we had bought with flyer miles. This was just a four-day event, but the addiction had tied up and kidnapped whatever meager intellectual curiosity we happened to possess and frogmarched it off into areas geographical, historical, gastronomical, and touristical.

We tried, how we tried, through seemingly endless discussion and debate, to get our arms around the decision. Why was this event so special? I'd read enough by that time to understand the historical dimension, because the idea of Big Time Tastings is anything but new. The most famous (and possibly the most distinguished) modern BTT is staged each year at the Hospices de Beaune, a health care facility founded in 1443 (and since modernized) in the eponymous village of France's Cote d'Or in Burgundy. Since 1851, people have been wine weekending in Beaune on the third Sunday in November to benefit this hospital, taking only a few years off for wars, invasions and occupations.

Not to miss a trick, the Hospices de Nuits, another charity hospital up the road, holds its own wine auction. In both places, vintners and collectors donate their wines, having done so for hundreds of years, and some of them are worth large francs (or euros, I guess. Times change.) Since the Burgundians have been at this for so long, the auction and attendant festivities have soaked up a significance that not only keeps the hospital in business, but pretty much determines the worldwide market price of the vintage. We came to the realization that attending events of this type is more than merely a fun thing to do. It's practically a cultural imperative, a historical ritual, a *charitable act*. After talking around it for weeks, we reached the inevitable conclusion. We filled out the registration form and sacrificed the plastic on the altar of our obsession.

On the flight to New York, we were so excited that we didn't even think about why an event called the California Wine Experience was being held in a hotel in Times Square. We figured they knew what they were doing. The magazine has been sponsoring this event for over 20 years, and they've become very good at it. *Wine Spectator* editor and publisher Marvin Shanken, who has been described to me by one of his former employees as "very persuasive," somehow manages to cajole the most prestigious wineries in the world into donating hundreds of astoundingly valuable bottles. (Afterwards, I was told that during the event we'd gone through over 28,000 bottles).

In all fairness, it must be pointed out that the Wine Experience is, in fact, a charity event, like the Hospices de Beaune. It benefits a foundation that provides scholarships and financial support to students and other professionals in the food and beverage industry. So it's worthwhile, which salves the conscience a bit.

"Besides," said Debi, "we can write it off."

On that Thursday afternoon, we wandered to the registration desk and got our ID badges and goodie bags. The rest of the day was devoted to meditation, unpacking, looking around, and mental preparation for the evening's grand tasting and the 28,000 bottles in the 5th and 6th floor ballrooms, being attended to (and no doubt guarded by) hotel and restaurant sommeliers who came from all over the world at their own expense to work the weekend for free. I was sure that they felt a professional obligation to taste a bit out of each bottle, just to make sure it's drinkable. I want that job.

The doors opened at 6:30 for the first grand tasting on Thursday night, and that's when we really started feeling like newbies. We got off the elevator only to be confronted with a line of eager attendees that snaked all the way around the foyer and down the hall. The first people in the line, just outside the doors, were sitting on chairs, they had *provisions*, magazines, knitting, sandwiches, water, everything short of sleeping bags and Coleman lanterns, and had obviously been waiting there for hours, if not days. The rest of us would get in later.

In two ballrooms on two floors of New York's then-largest convention hotel, representatives from two hundred fifty wineries imprisoned themselves behind eight-foot-long folding tables, draped in impeccable white linen (the tables, not the reps), surrounded by exhibit-hall-standard pipe and drape walls. From 6:30 until 10:30 that evening they endured carpal tunnel syndrome and tennis elbow, pouring their best bottles for fifteen hundred enthusiasts who had been counting the evenings until this one since the same time last year. We swam in a sea of strangers.

I never knew wine glasses could be stacked that high. There were mountains of them, pyramidally glittering atop a long table just inside the doors, and heaps of buffet at the opposite end of the room, up three steps on a kind of stage, weighted with enormous platters of exotic cheeses shot through with veins of supposedly desirable microscopic life forms, breeding in colors that should never exist, breads and crackers of every national origin, and inspiring amounts of charcuterie, mostly Italian in recipe if not in actual provenance.

We were stunned at the magnitude of it, wandering from table to table, glasses extended eagerly for the next pour, literally not knowing where to start. All our careful examination of the room diagram that afternoon deserted us, and we wandered, not lonely as a cloud, but as children on a first trip to Disney World. Should we try the first growth Bordeaux? The small production wines we'd never heard of but wanted to discover? The California "cult wines" that we had definitely heard of but never expected to taste because they cost $750 a bottle and are never available to people like us?

"Excuse me." A voice, which I barely heard above the warm buzz that had filled the room from the moment the doors opened, came from behind, over my left shoulder. Not surprisingly, the noise level in the ballroom was increasing by orders of magnitude in proportion to the hour and the collective wine consumption. I turned to encounter a business-suited man in his mid-40s, about five ten, with short dark hair, staring at the name tag that was hanging around my neck along with the pack of credentials and "all access" passes we'd been issued earlier in the day.

"Jerry Greenfield," he read as he bent forward for a closer look. "I have a cousin named Jerry Greenfield. Are you my cousin?" Stunned, I realized, after a few moments, that I was.

The vaguely recognizable face belonged to Douglas Lasser. It took me a minute of intense thought, made more difficult than usual by the heavy and hurried sampling we'd been doing, but I finally placed him. Not easy, because he was actually my first cousin once removed, both genealogically and physically. I had lived all my life in Florida, and he was a lifelong New Yorker, so we were separate in more ways than one. I'd met him for the first time in my life, curiously enough, earlier that same year at an aunt's funeral in New York, and due to the emotional gravity of the event (she was a favorite aunt) I hadn't been in shape to remember removed cousins. I was in even worse condition (for different reasons) when he accosted me in the Grand Tasting ballroom.

He and his wife Cynthia were, like us, enjoying their very first Wine Experience, but, as the evening wore on (and that's just the right word), and as we got better acquainted, it became obvious that they were just as hopelessly captivated by (or captured by) wine enthusiasm as we were. In fact, they had something of a head start. At it a few years longer, with more bottles in their house than we had in ours.

Wine lovers love wine lovers, especially if they're family. We spent the rest of the weekend together.

Since we hardly knew each other at first, the conversation centered on the experience we were sharing. We compared the approaches we were taking to coping with the masses of wine in the room. The Wine Experience people had prepared not one table before us in the presence of our friends and relatives, but over 250, and our cups were running over. We felt a foolish obligation to try as many wines as possible. Bad idea.

Like us, Douglas and Cynthia had devoted an intense hour earlier that day to studying the ballroom diagram included in the convention goodie bag. Even as novices, we understood that with 250 wines to sample, careful planning and selectivity would be critical. First, we crossed off anything we already had bottles of at home, which wasn't much. Then, we crossed off most of the whites, because we're mainly red wine drinkers. Lastly, we got rid of any types we knew we'd never drink, like Ports and dessert wines. We wanted the heavy stuff.

Fortunately, the Grand Tasting was offered on both Thursday and Friday nights, in two separate ballrooms. It was obvious that the best plan would be to cover the fifth floor ballroom the first night, and the sixth floor the second night. As the four of us attacked the room together, Douglas unfolded his floor plan. He had meticulously marked off the location of the booths that had the rarest, most expensive wines, but, as we were to discover, the idea was not original with him. Some wineries were pouring vintages that were no longer obtainable, others had their highest-rated new wines presented for our consideration, and others were doling out dollops of "cult" wines so limited in production that they should have been serving them with eyedroppers. Our first stops. Everybody's first stops.

Gradually, as we sipped and elbowed our way from table to table, two things happened. First, we noticed that many of the people pouring the wine had their names on the bottle. It's a little intimidating to have somebody named Gallo pour you a sample then ask you how you like it. Then, as I had noticed when Douglas first approached me, the level of jocularity in the room had slowly swelled, the air vibrated, conversations got louder, more energetic, and by around 8:30, well, we were in the midst of a lot of very happy people. The crowd wandered from booth to booth, bouncing off the buffet on the way, introducing themselves to each other, making new friends, hailing and embracing table mates from previous years. I myself formed a close personal bond with two very earnest gentlemen from Taiwan, representatives of that nation's gourmet society, who had probably traveled for three and a half days just to be there.

CHAPTER 8

The Wines of the Cult

There are some wines in the world that are so good, and so rare, that nobody can have any. Is a single bottle of Screaming Eagle really worth over $1,500? Here's how to decide.

October, 2000

There were 125 tables of wine in that one room, so we had to keep moving. Douglas and I would taste down a row, get separated at the end, wander off in different directions, and join up again a little while later and a whole lot happier. We had no idea what had happened to Debi and Cynthia, but they had their own room keys, so we weren't worried. But as I visited each one of my carefully mapped destinations, I had a special personal goal in mind.

In the months before, this goal, this desire, was the elephant in the room, at least to me, and a determining factor in our decision to subject ourselves to the disastrous financial setback of coming to the Wine Experience. It was the urge to try wines that mere mortals just can't get their hands on. In my two years of obsessively reading nothing but wine books and magazines, there occurred a crux, or maybe a cusp. I continued to find articles about wines around the world that are so good nobody can get any, and especially not me. But in the ads for the Wine Experience, there they were, right on the list. We hadn't been compelled by the obsession for very long, maybe a year, when we started to hear those names...the wines that are so highly prized, so limited, that you have to be the winemaker's closest living relative to enjoy even a small sip. Anyone who is forced to hang out with wine lovers, or reads anything on the subject at all, sooner or later comes across this discussion, this debate, about "cult wines." Despite the way it sounds, these are not the wines we enjoy while waiting for the mother ship to take us back to the home planet. Nor have we ever carried them on our treks deep into the jungles of Guyana or Surinam en route to the commune where all of us will live together in love, peace and harmony, sharing our wives with Daddy. These precious liquids have nothing to do with faiths on the fringe, though some people who've tried them have experienced spiritual awakenings, or so I'm told. They are, however, more rare than nuns on a nude beach, and therefore priced in four figures, instead of two or three. I don't remember exactly when I started making a list of them, but it was early on, as I encountered the same names again and again in my reading. They were here, in this very room, and in the room on the floor above. All here, all circled on my floor plan.

There are, I suppose, wines considered cultish in many parts of the world, but in what I was reading at the time, the term was always applied to certain wines from California. They're almost all from Napa Valley, held in worshipful awe by a worldwide community of enthusiasts. I wanted to know why. What makes a bottle of wine worth $750 or $1000, when the perfectly satisfactory bottles we'd been carting home cost under $20? Do they represent some kind of monumental achievements in winemaking, being of stunning quality, possessing depth, dimension, complexity, and all the other rhapsodic descriptors that wine critics, lovers, and lifers can come up with? Is it that they're obsessively collectible, wines in the grand tradition, capable of aging (and gaining value) for decades? Will the bottles filled and corked today be ready to drink any time before the sun burns out? And if so, so what? There are dozens, maybe hundreds, of equally dramatic wines in the world, and they cost just as much. What makes one wine qualify for the cult, and another not? Is it just perception? The propagation of myth and legend? Marketing? As soon as I started seeing the names, as soon as I heard them in conversations with my more advanced wine life acquaintances, I knew this was a subject for further research and reading. I had to know the story. I had to try the wines.

In no particular order, most people agree that the major cult wines are Screaming Eagle, Harlan Estate, Colgin, Maya, Bryant Family, Marcassin, and Grace. Some would argue that there are one or two more, and they'd probably be right. But if I were to mention these names, or more foolish still, tell people I have some, my circle of friends would certainly expand, and everyone would show up at the house wearing a yummy look.

But I was trying to perspectivize these cult wines among the other famous wines of the world, the ones that take just as long to become drinkable, and often cost just as much. Like the five so-called First Growth wines from Bordeaux, for example, and others, equally as famous, from both sides of the river that cuts through the fabled region. The communes of Pauillac, Pomerol, Margaux, St. Estèphe, and

St. Julien positively wallow in their centuries-old reputations
as producers of the richest, biggest, most luxurious wines
you can buy. Made to age for decades, wines like Chateau
La Tour, Lafite, or Margaux have always inspired the bowing
of the head and the bending of the knee. They're made
in the most legendary wine producing region in the world,
demanded by kings and potentates throughout history,
(and more recently, by newly-minted Chinese millionaires)
and are officially classified by the French government as
grand cru classe which is French for "open your wallet."
Supposedly these chateaux make the finest wines in France
(and thus, according to the French, in the world), or so
believed the officials in Paris back in 1855, when they drew
up the list. The story just goes on and on, and every wine
lifer knows it by heart, and can quote chapter and verse.

By October of 2000, we'd enjoyed many quiet evenings
over dinner with new friends, and with old friends who
shared the obsession, most of whom owned more
bottles that we did, which was nice. And on more than
one occasion, someone (not us) would plunk a bottle of
something like 1989 Chateau Lafite or Margaux on the
table, just to see how far the eyebrows would go up. These
are names that everybody has heard of, even if not many
have tried. People drink them in James Bond movies.

But sorry, they're not cult wines, because there's too
much of them. The first-growth chateaux produce around
18,000 cases each a year, and while they're not cheap, at
least there's plenty to go around. I was told that once upon
a time, these wines and their lesser-classified counterparts
were sold only at premium prices, and only in the finest
shops. But by the turn of the millennium they had become
a commodity, displayed by the case at big box mass

merchandise stores. Historic, legendary, prestigious wines? Yes, sir, right over there on Aisle Six, about halfway down.

Sooner or later, every beverage magazine runs an article about the mythic wines of Burgundy, especially those from Domaine de la Romanée-Conti, which are prized possessions of any collector well resourced enough to have them in the cellar. One might think that their price and rarity would elevate them to cult status, because some of them can cost $3,500 a bottle new, and upwards of ten grand once they get a few years on them. But they, too, are pretty much available (mostly at the high-end wine auctions) if the old credit card will stand it.

So cult wines represent monumental quality and rarity? Yes and no. There's the availability factor, as well. If they're on the shelf, they generally don't qualify. Grand cru wines from Bordeaux are there for the asking in just about any decent wine store. In larger cities, Vosne Romanée and La Tache beckon from shop windows. But the real cult wines, the Screaming Eagles and Peter Michaels of the world, hardly ever make it that far. Each vintage sells out to the winemakers' seven hundred closest friends (and closest living relatives) on the highly privileged mailing list before the grapes are even ripe.

When I was about six, some cereal company or other had one of those offers where you could send in about a million boxtops and you'd receive an actual piece of land in Alaska. Well, I saved up the boxtops, sent them in, and, allowing six to eight weeks for delivery, received a very official-looking deed for one square inch of real estate someplace up there in the 49th state, though it wasn't a state at the time. Some of the cult wine vineyards in Napa Valley aren't much bigger than my domain in Alaska. Since

I knew that at least a few of the wines would be poured at the Wine Experience, I did my homework.

Harlan Estate has only 36 acres under vine, which doesn't exactly put them up there with Ernest and Julio. But then, the goal of the really fine wine producers is not to grow the most grapes, it's to grow the fewest. Overproduction dilutes the juice, so winemakers prune bunches off the vines. Their hearts break as the fruit hits the ground, but the pruning concentrates more flavor in fewer grapes. This is the opposite of abundance, and the very most a cult winemaker will produce in a given year is well under a thousand cases, and most of them are sold in three—or six—packs rather than twelves. Screaming Eagle makes five hundred cases, maybe. That's six thousand bottles for the whole world, which is not as much as it sounds like, considering that everybody wants some. The private collectors line up, of course, but so do the owners of the most amusingly expensive restaurants at home and abroad, who must have at least some of these wines on their list. Demand is, to put it mildly, frenzied and desperate, and far exceeds supply.

Okay, cult wines are expensive, and they're very limited in production. Got that. So that's where the mystique, the legend, the myth comes from? Not exactly.

One article lead me to the next, and to more sad news that I'd never get to taste the world's great wines, or even gaze upon a bottle of them, closely guarded, from a reasonable distance. Problem is, there are lots of producers in the world who make wine in comically small quantities. In Burgundy, the Napoleonic inheritance laws decreed that all property be divided equally among a person's heirs, instead of left in entirety to the oldest son. So the vineyards were subdivided again and again over the last century and a half until today, when a producer may be growing his fruit on a sixth of a half of a third of the original property, sometimes as few as three or four rows of vines yielding a few hundred fabulous bottles. Most of it never leaves the region, and if it does, well, I still can't have any.

Unlike the Burgundies, which are special because they come from single vineyards that have been blessed with just the right soil, sun exposure, and drainage, the cult wines are powerful, artistic blends of the most classic grapes. Like the wines from Bordeaux, they're usually made up of some combination of Cabernet Sauvignon, Merlot, Petit Verdot, and Cabernet Franc. Hard to find, but, as I observed, there are a lot of "limited production" wines that don't cost nearly as much. We have, somewhere in our meager hoard, four bottles of a 1998 Australian Reserve Shiraz of which only 500 cases were produced, and it cost about $60 a bottle. I figure that these four bottles represent a little under one per cent of the world's supply. Scary, but it still doesn't make it into the cult.

Flash forward: We would ultimately find out that Cousin Douglas, along with his wife Cynthia, who is my first-cousin-once-removed-in-law, are psycho golf crazies. They'd play twice a day if they could, and sometimes they do. (I'm getting ahead of myself, but there's a simile to be made here). A few years after we met, Douglas wanted to buy a new set of golf clubs. Not just any new set, but the new set. The ones he swore he'd never, ever spend that much money on. The ones that will be buried with him when he dies. He read about them for a year, every brochure, article, magazine review he could gather to himself, became an authority on them. Part of it was aspiration, fevered imaginings, whatever, but part of it was knowing that they would someday be his, and twenty strokes would magically drop off his score.

That was me with the cult wines. I aspired, I read everything I could find, and every time I dug up a new factoid, I'd tell Debi, until she made it clear that if I continued to plague her with further information, she would find it less than entertaining.

Since August, I had counted the hours until the night of the first grand tasting, because some of the impossible wines were being doled out, on a first come basis, in that very room. I had a wine glass, and I was moderately adept in its use.

Well, in later years when I discovered that Douglas got the clubs but didn't cut his handicap in half, I was reminded of that evening. Upon tasting the Wines of My Dreams, I didn't fall to my knees before a vision of the burning bush or witness the parting of the seas. The Blessed Virgin did not appear. Tears did not stream from my ecstatic eyes. The wines were wonderful, but they weren't a thousand dollars wonderful, which was disappointing, but not entirely unexpected. How many things in this world, I wonder, can live up to that kind of hype and reputation?

There's an up side. I found out what people thought "great wines" were supposed to taste like, which gave me a benchmark for future sampling.

Here's a confession. While doing my aspirational research on wines which are generally agreed to enjoy cult status, I read some pretty good stories. This is probably some people's idea of sick fun, but for my own amusement, I put together a cult wine compendium, and I don't mind sharing.

HARLAN ESTATE

Founded in 1984 by Bill Harlan, my first sample was a mouthful of huge fruit and solid structure. The wine has been made with the consultation of Michel Rolland, who was one of the first names I came across in my early infatuation. He is to wine what Elvis Presley is to rock and roll. They've made movies about him, how he jets and chauffeurs from one country to the next, flitting in and out of the wineries, consulting. The Harlan winery offers its output directly to "senior subscribers" on its list. If I were vain enough to put my name on the waiting list today, my grandchildren, if I had any, would still be waiting. ("They don't call it a waiting list for nothing," Debi likes to remind me.) It is rumored that to get to the top of the list you have to murder at least three of the people ahead of you.

SCREAMING EAGLE

Located on a rocky site in the Oakville appellation of the Napa Valley, the vineyard is only slightly larger than our driveway, planted with several of the classic Bordeaux varietals: Cabernet Sauvignon, Merlot and Cabernet Franc. While most winemakers' web sites contain several pages of information about the company, tasting notes on the wine, news from the barrel room and the friendly folks who work there, the Screaming Eagle web site is one page. No information. No about us. No links. No nothing. They don't have to. Some of the magazines that flood in every month list auction prices for collectible wines. At this writing, the most recent vintages are selling for well north of $1,500, though a bottle of the 1994 once sold for $3,500. In the highest-end restaurants, it can appear on the wine list for over $7,000 a bottle. For that price, I could buy an entire case of 1970 Chateau Latour. Or maybe even the Chateau itself. Is Screaming Eagle 12 times better than Latour? Only if you can't get it.

The thirsters in front of this table were even more rabid and frenzied than those who were clawing their way to Bill Harlan's attention. I was reminded of one of those zombie movies where the living dead climb up out of the earth, lurching toward the camera in their arms-outstretched stiff-legged way. The Screamer is possibly the most sought-after wine to come out of California, and while most cult wines are shipped to their adoring purchasers in boxes of six, Screaming Eagle lets their lucky wine club members have only three, or, in a difficult vintage, just two.

When I got to the table, people were crawling over each other like mice that sleep in a heap, glasses clutched in trembling outstretched hands, trying to get even the slightest pour. I was more determined than most, and besides, I was new at the event and figured I had an excuse for not following tasting protocol. I had heard about this wine almost since my very first sip, and I was not to be denied. With a few sharp elbows and an uncharacteristic degree of shamelessness I made it to the table, and noticed that the tabletop was strewn with Screaming Eagle corks. I asked the pourer if I could have one as a souvenir. He refused. Why? "Because people can use them to counterfeit the wine."

I would have paused for reflection at that, but the increasing physical pressure from people at my back reminded me of the Tokyo subway at rush hour. While I tasted the wine for the first time in my life in the relative safety of the corner of the room, I reflected on that incident. I'd have to find out more about this whole cork thing someday.

COLGIN

Ann Barry Colgin is one of the pre-eminent female vineyard owners in the world. Famed winemaker Helen Turley has been making wine from her Cabernet Sauvignon grapes since 1992. Two bottles of her 1997 Herb Lamb Vineyard sold at Sotheby's for $2990. Not bad, considering that it was released at $165 a bottle. Collectors have paid upwards of $16,000 for a case.

BRYANT FAMILY

Limited to about 1,100 cases a year, which is a flood for a cult wine, Don Bryant pulls monster grapes out of his vineyard on the eastern hills of Napa Valley. Of course, it doesn't hurt that the legendary Helen Turley (another name I encountered early on) makes the wine. Bryant's wines are compared by some critics to the most mythical Bordeaux of the century. It is said that those who taste a 1961 first-growth Bordeaux are simply not the same people afterward, and Bryant wines are said to have the same effect on the cerebral neurons. If I cared to have my psyche altered, which I do, the experience would cost at least $500 a bottle.

DALLA VALLE

Here's another case where the finest female winemakers team up with growers who really know what they're doing. Consulting winemaker Heidi Barrett, together with Naoka and Gustav Dalla Valle, put out a blockbuster bottle that drives people nuts. Their proprietary "Maya" label, named after their daughter, is made from more or less equal parts of Cabernet Sauvignon and Cabernet Franc. Their web site consists of a single graphic, the label of their 1999 Cabernet

Sauvignon, along with their address and phone number. For $400 a bottle, what more do you want?

GRACE FAMILY VINEYARD

Talk about tiny. Dick Grace's son Kirk seems to be happy producing only 250 cases of Cabernet Sauvignon a year, which is about all he can get out of his two acres of vineyards northeast of St. Helena. This wine is sold exclusively through a mailing list. It's like season tickets to a big NFL team. Places on the list are handed down, even though nobody gets more than four bottles. On release, the wines cost about $65 a bottle, but many of his customers turn around and put their treasure up for auction without ever opening the shipping case, and quadruple their investment.

ARAUJO

The Eisele vineyard owned by Bart and Daphne Aruajo is one of those blessed pieces of land that costs as much per square foot as the real estate on Broadway or the Champs Élysées. It covers 40 acres in northeast Napa Valley, and produces miniscule quantities of Cabernet, Sauvignon Blanc, and Syrah. Here, too, the feminine finesse is evident. This is another wine I'll probably die without trying. It's seldom listed at auction.

One makes lists only at one's peril. Wine lifers are a contentious lot, and will inevitably argue about exclusions and omissions. Some will say David Arthur wines should be included, and certainly his limited production "Elevation 1147" is a spectacular bottle, the kind of wine that very nearly renders people speechless when they taste it. Then there's Rafanelli Vineyards, something of an anomaly among cult wines because it's located in Sonoma Valley rather than Napa, and their fame rests equally on their Zinfandel and Cabernet. They make about 8,000 cases a year, which hardly qualifies as cult production, but do not sell at retail, ever. We were determined to make the pilgrimage to their tasting room at some point.

In later years, I would discover that there's a severe drawback to making wines that are this famous, or this highly rated. Debi and I were sitting on a veranda at the top of Spring Mountain above Napa Valley listening to a winemaker whose Merlot had been named Number One Wine of the Year by Wine Spectator. It turned into a nightmare for her and her husband, because people called them at all hours trying to buy some, or showed up unannounced at her gate with the same purpose. They had made a very small amount, and the would-be buyers were not hesitant to heap their displeasure and frustration on her, mostly through the medium of late night anonymous phone calls.

Myths and legends arise from the popular culture...and the critics. Let a Robert Parker or Bruce Sanderson give 98 points to some obscure wine from the middle of nowhere, and prices go into warp drive. Cult status is bestowed by serious wine lifers who got themselves on the mailing list 20 years ago (or didn't), restaurant owners, celebrity chefs, and otherwise normal people who share this particular passion. I sampled several that very first night in New York, and they were extraordinary enough. But life-changing? Is any wine worth $1,000 a bottle when we can buy three or four cases of something just as enjoyable for the same price? Do palates exist that are so educated, so precise, that their owners can truly tell the difference? It is a question that could take a lifetime to answer. I hope it does.

At ten thirty the grand tasting folded up and went dark. They were very insistent about shutting down on time and herding us out of the room, because otherwise everybody would stay there until breakfast. We didn't mind that our taste buds were tired. We were happy. We discovered new wines, new family, and we proved to ourselves that Larry was wrong. We didn't spit out a drop.

CHAPTER 9

The Experience Deepens

We had survived our first immersion in a grand tasting where over 250 of the world's finest wines were liberally poured into our eager glasses. What about the delights of the rest of the weekend, starting with our first glasses of wine at 9AM on Friday morning, and going happily downhill from there?

October, 2000

The morning after the Thursday Grand Tasting, we were made emphatically aware that the event organizers don't kid around. After an early continental breakfast buffet, the first tasting seminar of the weekend started at exactly 9:15. The ballroom from the night before had been transformed into a vast classroom, with a stage at one end where the vintners and critics would sit, and hundreds of rows of white cloth draped narrow tables spreading across the floor, split into three sections, laid out with places for 1500 people, laden with baskets of crackers, bottles of mineral water, and, at each setting, sixteen wine glasses, painstakingly arranged on placemats printed with circles and numbers, showing where each wine would be poured.

Panicked, I grabbed Douglas' arm.

"We're going to drink sixteen glasses of wine today?"
I asked. He consulted the program he'd pulled from his
goodie bag.

"No, we're going to drink sixteen glasses of wine before
lunch," he said.

Start sipping at nine in the morning, and the occupational
hazards, rather than becoming readily apparent, tend to
stalk for a while, then pounce. Even though the standard
wine tasting portion is a one-ounce pour, our morning's
work still involved putting away over half a bottle at a time
of day when we'd normally be washing down a double latte
and a whole wheat bagel with a shmear. We'd never had
the privilege of packing in that much wine before lunch and
would have been a lot more eager for the challenge had it
not been for the fact that the wines we had sampled the
night before were still singing inside us.

Surely, there are hazards inherent in overindulging in
wine, and we knew about most of them, but after the
morning session, we discovered a new one. It's called
Walking to Lunch on Your Knees. This was our first Wine
Experience, and it was obvious that we were amateurs of
the rankest species, rookies, newbys, neophytes, novices,
abecedarians, surrounded, we perceived, by seasoned
sunrise sippers, all of whom were settling in around us,
looking, with grave and critical regard, over the information
sheets that listed what we'd be sampling, preparing to make
serious tasting notes in the spaces provided. We didn't dare
risk falling down the escalator in front of people like that,
even if the steps did move by themselves.

The first disagreement of the day came from Debi, upon

her discovery of the small white cup she found next to the water bottle and crackers. She knew what it was: a Styrofoam spittoon.

"Spit this stuff out? Not a chance. You know how much these wines cost and they think we're gonna *spit them out?*" She went on to say that, in a circumstance such as ours, spitting is a first-degree felony if not actually a mortal sin.

"We came here to taste wines we won't be able to afford even when we do win the lottery, and vintages that will never again be available on the surface of this planet, and *you* want to *spit it out?*" Cousin Douglas came down solidly in her corner.

"I never spit," he said. Since he's an attorney, he could have said it in Latin—*nunquam spuemus*—but he didn't. I counted the glasses twice, thinking that if I swilled that much wine in one sitting, no matter how professional my intention, I would barely be able to sit upright and take nourishment. Voila, the little white cup, provided for my expectorating enjoyment.

Well, we got through four or five red wines from Australia, with the assistance of the people who made them, commenting in heavily-accented English, another four weird varietals that nobody ever heard of, and seven California Zinfandels, squirting none of it into the 8-ounce cup, though the more judicious attendees sitting next to us did. (This spitting thing, by the way, is a quiet and discreet procedure. It's considered unmannerly to go for distance).

As we smiled our way toward lunch, not yet on our knees, the atmosphere of the previous evening's grand tasting repeated itself. The tide of genial conversation in the room gradually increased, and the voices of the presenters on stage became lost in the overall mumble. People were blatantly ignoring the little white cups, and making lots of new friends. Besides, as I was belatedly discovering, even when I did spit, my mouth and tongue membranes absorbed enough alcohol to make me a moderately chatty lunch companion.

About that lunch. On both Friday and Saturday, there was a merciful break at 11:45, when we all made our way to a ballroom on another floor for the noon meal. Ten people at a table, five or six variously-shaped glasses in front of each, and ten different bottles of wine to pass around, sample, and compare. The lunches had themes, featuring cuisine from a particular region or of a certain style, and included wines paired with each course. Since they were all carefully selected by experts to enhance one of the lunch courses, we at the table (Cousins Douglas and Cynthia, and six of our new best friends, all violently—and violetly—smiling), were quick to agree that trying at least a little bit from each of the ten bottles was absolutely essential to the success of our educational experience. And no spitting.

After lunch, it was back to the ballroom down on the fifth floor for the afternoon seminars and tastings, which thankfully involved sampling only one variety of wine. Clearly, the worst was over, except that we were encouraged to try twelve glasses from twelve different years. "Piece of cake," said Douglas. "Besides, we have a break at 3:30."

Good thing, too. The women went shopping; the men took naps, because at 6:30 that night it was time for the second grand tasting, a repeat of the first night's experience, but in the other ballroom, with the other 125 wines.

After the first day, everybody at the Wine Experience walks around sporting purpled teeth, gladly exposing their indigo dentition for all the world to see. But there's more to the weekend than diving into rare wines. I'd mentioned that our lives had been hijacked by our passion into areas gastronomic, because fine wine and fine dining go together.

Which is where Emeril Lagasse comes in. He took over the stage on Saturday morning, commanding battalions of waiters who shuffled through the room pouring six different wines and gifting us with small plates of his gourmet inventions. Each of the wines was specially selected to complement the goat cheese tart, the Cajun shrimp, and the other little munchies. We had to taste the six wines several times each to decide which were best. Then we tasted them again. The rest of the day is something of a blur.

The weekend wine bash finished off, in characteristic fashion, with the obligatory Black Tie Gala. It was also the Night of a Thousand Plaques, when *Wine Spectator* hands out awards to restaurants with superior wine lists, and to industry professionals who have distinguished themselves.

From what I'd gathered, most Big Time Tastings include a formal event of this kind, since they're often held in conjunction with some charitable organization or other, and everyone feels compelled to give the women an excuse to dress up, provide dance music, and dole out honored recognition at the Black Tie Gala. We had the privilege of watching people we didn't know receive awards we'd never heard of.

On the flight home, Debi and I made up our minds about two things.

"Thing one," said Debi, "we went to two huge grand

tastings, where they served stuff like Ridge Monte Bello
1993, Screaming Eagle, Viader Cabernet, and other wines
you and I could never afford. We got two days of tastings
with even more completely unavailable wines, plus the
lunches and the Gala, so the price wasn't that bad."

"Thing two. We're never going to miss this again."

Even at upwards of $1,500 a person, hundreds are turned
away every year. In fact, immediately after we got home
from New York we received the forms to pay for the next
event, a year in advance, which we immediately did. Most
people do. In spite of the fact that the cost of admission
tickets edges northward each year, and in spite of the fact
that the event organizers sit on our money for eleven
months without paying us a dime of interest, over fifteen
hundred very nicely-dressed people show up faithfully, some
of them having attended for fifteen or twenty years, partly
because they get to drink wine that doesn't even exist in
most places, partly to indulge their senses at a very high
level, and partly because it's just plain deductible.

Fifteen hundred bucks a person. But we got a lot for
the money, especially since we lusted so desperately
to try those cult wines. At the Grand Tastings, we saw
people drink about as much Screaming Eagle as they could
stomach, and Harlan Estate, and all the rest of them. Not
many of them were spitters.

"Pay this kind of money and you'd better walk out
of the place smarter and happier than when you walked
in," observed Cousin Cynthia. She was right, and we did
broaden our horizons. Lesson: Some really good wines
need to spend time in the bottle, and some don't. Forget
those classic vintages, those bottles of Bordeaux and

Burgundy that have aged for as much as a century, and sell for the price of a Mercedes. We're Americans, and we want our gratification to happen a lot quicker than that. When we bring home a bottle of something tasty, we want to drink it tonight for sure, tomorrow latest. Most people, we're told, open their bottles of fine wine far too early, but there's plenty that's ready to drink as soon as it hits the shelves.

Two and a half days. Almost 28,000 bottles of wine. I had to ask how many glasses they used, and washed, and used again. I figure 1,500 people times 16 glasses at each session is 24,000, times four sessions, plus the two grand tastings and the lunches. Somebody at the hotel told me there were so many glasses that they trucked them from midtown Manhattan to Hoboken to wash them, but that turned out to be a lie. Sure, we found new tastes and new wines we'll definitely start buying as soon as I can convince my well-resourced and incipiently delusional grandmother to sign a power of attorney. And we ventured far beyond the wines we knew, discovering varietals that absolutely nobody drinks, like Lemberger, Teroldego, and Cattarato. Mostly, we made new friends. Start drinking wine at nine in the morning, and it's easy.

CHAPTER 10

Aftereffects and Consequences

We thought we were sick puppies before the Wine Experience weekend, but returning home, our obsession dominated our daily existence more severely than ever before. This is how.

December, 2000–June, 2001

It's not too much to say that going through our first Wine Experience changed our lives, at least as much as Larry and Charlene had done on that fateful first night, but in a different way. As soon as we returned home, we became even crazier, if that's possible.

Over the weekend, we had the chance to sample gallons of incredible wine that we vowed to search out and buy once we got off the plane in Florida. It didn't matter whether we had the money or not. More than once during the grand tastings, Debi and I looked at each other with eyes wide and said, "We gotta get some of *this.*" We wrote them all down. The other writing we did was on the sign-up sheets that almost every winemaker had on his or her table. We sipped, and we scribbled our names furiously, enlisting in every wine club and winery mailing list that would have us.

The inevitable consequence was that, once we got home, we faced a flood of correspondence and solicitation. We got dozens of letters and emails offering us dozens of wines, directly from the winery, before they were released to the public, if they were released at all. This is how we found out about the hidden world of the "wine club." The wine clubs at the local stores were one thing, but this…this was like looking at the wine world in Imax, instead of through a keyhole.

We knew we were sliding down to the bottom of the barrel when we realized that, even though there are wines on this earth available to only a Select Few, we could maybe be among them. What was hopelessly out of reach for us before was now, thanks to our participation in the Wine Experience, marginally attainable. Not the cult wines, of course, because we weren't *that* elite, but for other, only slightly less desirable products, like older vintages of Bordeaux and Burgundy simply not on the shelf at our friendly neighborhood wine merchant. To get them we needed to be on The List.

Actually, there are two kinds of lists: the ones kept by vineyards whose wine output every year is so small and so limited that it's measured in micrograms, like LSD, or milliliters, like experimental medication. They sell only to an infinitesimal base of subscribers, and if we wanted to be among them, we would have to wait until somebody on the list ahead of us died or we killed them ourselves. Sometimes there's a waiting list to get on the waiting list, but those were the lists we signed up for. And there are others.

The "others" are kept by people whose job it is to sell wine. Every local store has a wine club, which is how we got started, and since we faithfully went to the tastings and spent enough money to get the owner's attention, our phone often rang when something special came in. Revelation: a lot of the really interesting bottles never make it to the shelves, but go out the back door to so-called "private clients."

Lists are also kept by larger wine retailers in major cities who ship to customers all over the country. Eventually, our names appeared on those lists, too, because the more we bought, the more On The List we became. Here's what I mean.

There's a big wine store in New York that specializes in older vintages of impossibly rare wines, and new discoveries that aren't being imported into this country, but they get some anyway. They buy private cellars, and it's absolutely stunning how many of them there are, and how many major collectors want to cash out at any given time. I received ten or twelve emails a day from these people, deluging me with offers that included the personal collection of some Hollywood director or rock and roller or dermatologist to the stars who had accumulated about 35,000 bottles of vintages that are, for all practical purposes, extinct.

On a trip to visit Debi's mother in New Mexico during this time, we met a woman who came into the ownership of her husband's wine store because the man had recently died. She knew nothing about wine or the business of selling it, and wanted to dispose of the inventory. I generously offered my assistance. Never heard from her.

Dozens of emails a day, and that didn't include the ones I got from the wine store in St. Louis, or the one in San Francisco, or the private collectors who somehow found my name (could it be because they sold me something once?) or the two or three local stores who had me on their radar. Get thee behind me, all of you. When those offers popped up in my inbox, it was so easy to just hit "reply" and tickle the keyboard. "I'll take six bottles," my fingers sang as they pizzicatoed across the keys, "No, make that twelve." They already had my credit card number, they knew where to ship the stuff, just hit "send" was all I had to do. Please, somebody, break all my fingers.

Problem was, most of what they offered was merely a Powerball dream for most mortals. A dealer once inquired whether I had any interest in a magnum of 1945 Haut Brion for only $12,500, and a magnum of 1950 Pétrus for $15,995. I had the interest, I just didn't have the principal. Some of the other "parcels" they put out, consisting of six or twelve bottles of the rare, the precious, and the rapidly disappearing, went for the price of a beachfront estate in Hawaii, complete with a limo and driver. Given the fact that I couldn't seem to pick the right six numbers no matter how hard I tried, those "parcels" were uncomfortably and probably eternally out of my reach.

However, by the time summer of 2001 rolled around, we had succumbed to many of the wine merchants' less expensive importunings and damaged ourselves to a frightening degree. It was one thing to order a case and have it show up a few days later, and quite something else to keep ordering day after day and have nothing at all delivered for three or four months. Wine merchants won't ship during hot months of the year, because nothing boils a case of wine faster than a few hours in the back of a UPS truck on the sixteenth of July unless you live in Moose Jaw, Saskatchewan. We live in South Florida.

I spent the summer of 2001 caving to the e-mails, and so did Debi, when she saw them, ordering a few bottles here, half a case there, a case of that 92 point wine that costs only $7.99 a bottle, and then October came in like a lion, bringing the realization that we'd run through over seven grand without even knowing it. One day late in the month, just before our next Wine Experience, a guy in a brown outfit rolled a brown truck up to the front of my office, wrestled a handcart through the door, and said, "Fifteen cases. Where do you want them? Sign here."

That offer of the mag of Pétrus brings my thoughts neatly back to the two kinds of lists, and how exclusive all this rare wine commerce can be. (There is structure here, after all). Early on, I read *The Wine Bible*, in which author Karen MacNeil traces how a bottle of a certain priceless juice gets through the system to the elite wine lifer. First of all, according to Karen, only about 700 cases of this particular wine make it to the United States, which sounds like a lot but is the entire output of a California cult wine like Screaming Eagle or Harlan Estate. In Karen's words, the importer offers the wine to "a small, select group of wholesalers" who dole it out to a "small, select group of their best customers" like high-end restaurants and wine shops. The wine shop will, in turn, "offer the wine, often by telephone, to a select group of customers." Are certain words beginning to make an impact, here, such as "small" and "select?" "For average wine drinkers," writes MacNeil, "it can be next to impossible to break into this loop."

Being small and select, being *in the loop*, can be immensely profitable. Even though I might languish for years on a waiting list before I get on *The* waiting list, it can be done, and it can bring in a lot of ridiculously easy money, whether it's Pétrus or one of the California cult wines. A serious and well-resourced wine lifer I know somehow managed to get himself on the Screaming Eagle list, which is a tribute either to his persistence, his connections, or his ability to commit murder without getting caught. The winery sells him and the rest of the fortunate few three bottles of each vintage for around $750 a bottle, or only two bottles in an off year. But aforementioned friend has never tasted the stuff, has, indeed, never even taken it out of the box. It's in the door, it's out the door to a private collector or restaurant, and he triples his investment.

(Confession: I myself have done the same. My friend Tom, who brings $300 bottles to the restaurant when we go out to dinner, is on one of those "small, select" lists. Every year, when he gets his allocation, we go partners on the three precious bottles in the luxurious wood case. By the time we receive it, I already have it sold to some guy in California, who already has it sold to some guy in China).

When wines like that appear on the open market through auctions or private sellers, people are prepared to dig deep, because they go for a good $1,500 a bottle and up—way up—depending on the vintage. It's hard to argue with a 300% markup, not if you believe in a free economy, supply and demand, the profit motive, and Truth, Justice, and the American Way. Restaurants sometimes manage to get a cult wine from outside normal channels, putting it on the list more as a symbolic gesture than anything else, because they'll ask $5,000 for it, hoping that some trifecta winner will stumble through the door in a celebratory mood. This is especially true in Las Vegas.

Being on a list and receiving offers from a small boutique winery is both a good thing and a bad thing. Once we started inscribing ourselves, I received a letter from a winery in Napa that I'd never heard of. They got my name from another boutique winery whose list we'd put our names on the previous October. They're making 167 cases of purportedly outrageous Cabernet, and did I want some, six bottle minimum, for $75 a pop. Sure I did. But the bad part is if we're on the list and we don't order, we get purged. The list regurgitates us, and we never get another offering. Once we were on, we were required and obligated to buy the juice every time they sent us an order form, and to buy as much as they allow. If we buy less than our allocation, the next letter will offer us less than before. If we pass on the offer, we might as well consider *seppuku*, because we'll never hear from them again.

Flash forward to an even worse situation. Internet marketing has made possible new selling methods that allow wineries to gouge their customers in ways that were hitherto unheard of and unthinkable. My friend Tom received an email from a winery whose list he'd been on for years, telling him that his allocation was ready, and if he wanted to order, he should click on *this* link which would take him to *this* web page. So he did. When the page popped up, it informed him that he would have fifteen minutes to place his order, or it would be cancelled. The clock was ticking. "Those bastards," he yelled to me over the phone. He thought the practice was abusive and uncivilized, and I agreed.

But it gets worse than that. We have made friends like Tom, wine lifers all, who are on other lists than ours, and if they can't take their allocation they want us to pick up the slack so they don't get dropped. Tom sends me faxes all the time with offers for this or that allocation, because after living in San Francisco for over 25 years and spending more time in Napa than he did at home, he's on every list there is. He's buying less wine these days because he's having intimations of mortality and knows he'll never drink his whole collection before he dies. (I told him to have his wife put it in his drip at hospice. If he likes it he'll blink once. If he doesn't he'll blink twice). When offered a case of big juice that costs $250 a bottle, some wine buddies may not want to suck it up for the entire amount, so they try to unload three or six bottles on their dearest friends. I grit my teeth and write a check. They'd do the same for me.

Back to the autumn of 2001. After Debi and I put away the fifteen cases that the UPS guy unloaded on us, we headed toward our second Wine Experience weekend, and it became ever clearer that the keys to a successful wine life are lots of taste and lots of money, with the latter being more important. A prominent wine magazine did an article once on people of that ilk, how they developed an interest in wine, what did they drink, what did they collect. They interviewed this pediatrician, that bond trader, this mutual fund manager…we got the picture. Come to think of it, several of the people I've met who are sitting on collections numbering ten thousand bottles and up *are* bond traders, mutual fund managers, etc. As my mother used to say, rich or poor, it's nice to have money.

On the bright side, many dedicated wine lifers don't feel the need to go big time and stock those $200 bottles, because the wine world is broad enough to give lots of delight in the $15 to $30 range, and that's a bit more within reach. Larry, for example, has excellent taste in wine and can certainly afford some of the big stuff, but he has never invested in the elaborate accoutrements of the collector.

His tiny wine refrigerator nestles under the kitchen counter, holding maybe 30 bottles, and he's never had the impulse to refrigerate a closet. I don't think he's even on any lists. He has a great time with the economical bottles, and knows how to pick them at the under-thirty-dollar level. Too, dedicated wine lifers are always alive to a bargain, educating themselves, reading widely, knowing what things cost, so they'll recognize the real values that jump off the shelves from time to time.

These discoveries can happen in the least expected ways. During the summer of 2001 we were at a small restaurant on one of the resort islands off our Florida coast, and they had Chateau St. Jean Cinq Cepages 1996 on the wine list for around $45. It happened that Cinq Cepages 1996 was the wine served at the Night of a Thousand Plaques banquet we'd attended the previous October, and was *Wine Spectator's* Number One Wine of the Year. We loved it at the banquet, and spent months afterward trying to find it. Even though the original release price was $28, the stores wanted to violate us for $75 or $80 because it was famous. So at $45 in a restaurant, where the usual markup is three times retail, it was a steal. I asked the waitress how many bottles they had (four) and could I buy them right then (yes). I scurried to my car with the bottles clasped tight, expecting to be detained and questioned on the way out, but I got away with it.

CHAPTER 11

It's All in the Glass

Among wine lovers, the type of glasses used for sniffing and sipping is a Very Big Thing. A glassmaking company like Riedel (in business for the last 500 years or so) makes a different kind of glass for every kind of wine. Grape geeks are compelled to buy them all. They're $90 each, and they shatter if you look at them funny.

July, 2001

I spent almost all my life in South Florida, where the air is so humid that small children often swim in it, so when I moved to Ohio for career advancement, I was totally unprepared not only for the cold weather, but for the total lack of moisture. The skin on my lips started falling off in November, and didn't stop until May. That's when I discovered Chap Stick, which apparently everybody but me knew about.

I also discovered that those little tubes of lip moisturizer, when left to themselves in the pockets of an overcoat, will become fruitful and multiply. Not only that, but as they spawn, they migrate. By the time the leaves came back on the trees in Columbus, I had eight or ten of them, distributed in the hidden depths of every pocket of every winter coat I ever wore.

Wire clothes hangers from the dry cleaners are equally fertile. In the dark of the closet, they perform unimaginable acts of procreation, increasing their numbers slowly and imperceptibly, until one day I slide open the doors and am confronted with having to untangle and remove hundreds of the things, without ever realizing where they came from.

This is all leading up to the point that wine accessories do that, too, only worse. As a result of our inspiration at the Wine Experience and the subsequent shopping spree, the bottles piled up, and so did all the little stuff that went with them. I should have foreseen the inevitability of it, because sliding into wine made us Do Things. I'm not talking about obeying the Voices, though it's probably a blessing more people don't share that particular compulsion with me. Mostly, the Doing Things drove us to accumulate (not entirely on purpose) a wide range of wine merchandise, or, as the French call them, tchotchkes. Some of these tchotchkes are items we had bought for ourselves, like stoppers to preserve a bottle on the extremely rare occasion when we didn't finish it. The others, the more heinous ones, were holiday gifts from friends and relatives who got sick of hearing about our wine addiction very early on.

Sure, other passions have accessories and merchandising and items you can buy when you're absolutely stuck for a birthday or holiday gift. My friend Rick has played every major golf course in the Western Hemisphere, and his collection of bag tags proves it. But wine carries centuries of experiential and cultural baggage, so friends have considerable latitude to inflict gifts upon us and other wine lifers that derive from all manner of human experience, and far outnumber anything one could buy for a golfer. I lived in Spain in the early 1970s, and visited lots of castles. There weren't many 12th–Century tapestries depicting the act of sinking a chip shot from 30 feet off the green from an uphill lie, but every old stone building, castle, or palace in Europe had the walls festooned with richly-woven fabrics that illustrated, in somewhat faded detail, harvesting of grapes, letting the juice go bad, and getting happy off the result. Tapestries, hell. On a trip to Sicily a few years later we would visit a well-preserved Roman ruin called the Casale Romana, with hundreds of square feet of priceless, highly detailed mosaic floors dating back 2,500 years that showed exactly the same thing.

People who study matters like this (and I'm sure there must be at least one), often divide the tchotchke topic into two categories: (1) items that bear directly on wine as a beverage, which includes its purchase, storage, and consumption, and (2) everything else.

If *only* it were that simple. The buying, storing and drinking parts would seem to be pretty straightforward, but such is not so. It's the hardest, because it takes money. Buying is the first thing we had to do, and we did. Everything, it seems, is easier when money is no object, so strictly for entertainment purposes, I'll imagine that our funds are unlimited.

Buying the bottle was just the first step. It sat on the kitchen counter for a brief time, waiting to be opened and enjoyed. So we needed something to open it with besides our teeth, and we required a glass, unless I cared to sip it out of Debi's slipper, which I would not recommend until well into the second bottle.

Sidebar: I did see a YouTube video that instructed me how to open a bottle of wine with the heel of a shoe, but I never tried it.

Early on, our wine lifer friends had instructed us and demonstrated the phenomenon that the shape and quality of the glass have a lot to do with the experience of the beverage. This was actively reinforced by the glasses we encountered at the Wine Experience lunches—all shapes and sizes. And we had accumulated a small assortment of glassware during the past four years, some as a result of gifts, others through attrition. But as soon as we took up investigation of the crystal alternative to the slipper, we found ourselves peering over the edge into the Abyss. Again.

Like almost everything else connected with wine, glassware is a much more divisive topic than one would think. For starters, some people (like the glass manufacturers) would have us believe that we need at least eight different kinds of glasses, because each shape, each configuration, is crafted especially to be used for the kind of wine we happened to be enjoying at the time. Best to have lead crystal, mouth blown, of course, because that tacky machine-made stuff simply will not do.

Naturally, the people who sell fine wine glasses would like us to purchase as many as possible, and they have insidious ways of accomplishing that.

First, they insist on a complete assortment of differently-shaped glasses for each specific kind of wine we pour. There are dozens.

One for young Bordeaux and Cabernet Sauvignon

One for vintage Bordeaux and Cabernet Sauvignon

One for Burgundy and other Pinot Noir

One for Cognac, if you drink the stuff, which we don't

One for Champagne, which we do

One for vintage Champagne, which we'll never be able to afford, no matter what

One for vintage Port

One for Chardonnay and Chablis

One for white Burgundy.

(Okay, hold it. White Burgundy is Chardonnay, which even I knew by the middle of 2001, but they say we need a separate glass, and they're supposed to know.)

One for Sauternes

One for Malbec

One for Grappa

We decided to pass on the grappa glass, because speaking from experience I can state categorically that brandy distilled from grape seeds and stems is an acquired taste, enjoyed by a twisted few. Most of us buy grappa to give as gifts because it comes in bottles that are true works of art, even nicer than perfumes. We never expect anybody to drink it.

History (at least the way I read it) tells us the Italians dreamed up grappa to get back at the Mexicans for tequila. It's such a reasonable recipe, though. If I'm going to distill me up some brandy first thing I'd throw in the vat would be grape stems and seeds. Surely, anyone else would do the same.

People have been making glass ever since they got tired
of bundling up against the chilly wind that blew through the
big square holes between the stones in the parapets. There
are plenty of wine glasses around, but apparently the Riedel
(rhymes with "needle," and is frequently mispronounced)
family is the go-to bunch in this department. As soon as I
found that out, I had to get the story, because they charge
a fortune for their products, just like almost everything else
in the wine life, and I wasn't going to spend $75 on a wine
glass made by people I didn't know.

The Riedel clan has been making fine glass for 300 years,
which, if you ask me, is a long time for a family to be doing
any one thing. The business cranked up about the year 1700
or so, in a town north of Prague, its founding credited
to Johann Christoph Riedel, a glass merchant whose
name lives to this day, and not just because he was foully
murdered during a business trip. After Johann's regrettably
early passing, there have been nine generations of Antons,
Johanns, Carls, and Leopolds, all of them Riedels, and all of
whom furthered the company's reputation for glassmaking
technology and hence the family's personal fortunes. In our
era, the scion of the family has been Georg, whose son (I
believe) is Maximilian, fondly known as Max. (Flash forward:
In 2006, Max showed up at the Wine Experience in San
Francisco accompanied by a statuesque fashion-model-type
woman whose stunning beauty almost caused me to sit
down involuntarily.)

Back to Georg. Guess what he did.

People have been using different styles of glasses for
various kinds of wine practically since forever. But according
to Georg Riedel, the specific shape and structure of the
glass directs and channels the flow of flavors to different

parts of the tongue. Who knew? Georg maintains that, since our tongues register different flavors in different places, the way in which the liquid flows into the mouth, where the wine first hits the receptors of flavor, becomes somehow important. For example: we taste sweet at the tip of the tongue. Drink a fruity wine from a glass with a slim bowl and narrow rim, and it puts the beverage onto the tongue right where it does the most good. Other wines, which tend toward other flavors, need differently shaped glasses to put the right flavors in the right places. This is not my wine wisdom saying this. It comes straight from Georg, who found a way to fine-tune the lowly wine glass into an artifact, nay, into a kind of highly-fragile instrument of tasting technology.

There are other fine glassmakers, such as Spiegelgau (ultimately acquired by Riedel) and Schott Zweisel, all of whom happily supply most of the sizes and shapes named above. Many of them are extremely fine, and I'd be proud to own them, and penniless. But Georg showed up in the wine world, standing confidently on his family's 300-year history in the business, and told people that, after about 2,500 years of wine drinking, someone (him) had, after all that time, finally tweaked the shape of the glass for each kind of wine based on how the aromas are released, how the vapors are channeled to the nose, all of that. Furthermore, his conviction was so robust that he was able to aver that if one were to drink a certain wine out of a normal ordinary shaped glass, and then out of a Riedel, the difference would become immediately obvious to anyone, even if they'd had their taste buds shot off in the war.

Well. Such boldness, in the wine world or anywhere else, must be either validated or ridiculed. Which is to say everybody thought Georg was nuts. When he challenged the late Robert Mondavi to take just such a Riedel challenge, people were afraid he'd truly become a danger to himself and others.

Mr. Mondavi: (many years before he kissed Debi on both cheeks): Let me get this straight, Georg. I drink some of my limited production $250 a bottle To-Kalon Vineyard Cabernet out of your glass, and it tastes better than out of my glass?

Mr. Riedel: Correctamundo.

Mr. Mondavi: How long your family's been making glass?

Mr. Riedel: Almost 300 years, Bob.

Mr. Mondavi: And you're telling me this *now*?

By the end of the conversation, Riedel had Mondavi completely unconvinced. A taste test was in the air. Sell Mondavi on the idea, and there's a hell of a credential.

I don't even want to think about the kind of wine collection the Mondavis have, but I'm sure they felt the test deserved a bottle of something that would cause at least temporary respiratory arrest in many of us. Georg poured, Robert sipped, Georg conquered. The rest was easy. Today, just about every wine expert, critic, and sommelier in the country swears on his or her corkscrew that wine tastes better in one of Georg's cunningly-shaped vessels, a perception that makes the company's competitors cry into their pillows practically every night, and assures Georg's place on the family portrait wall.

The only other family dynasty story I know of that's the least bit comparable is that of the Zildjians, who have been making cymbals (somebody has to) for hundreds of years, and they're pretty much the only game in town, because any percussionist you ask will tell you that Zildjian cymbals sound better than anybody else's, and that's a proven fact. A dear friend and fellow writer who plays percussion for the Los Angeles Philharmonic backs up this story, and she should know. The formula for the alloy the family uses in making its products is a more closely guarded secret than Col. Sanders' eleven herbs and spices, very literally handed down from one generation to the next, and from what I'm told, only one family member at a time knows the secret recipe. If he gets hit by a bus, the whole clan is out of business. They should get to know Georg.

There are people who keep a set of Riedels in a padded carrying case, and actually take their *own glasses* to restaurants. A poll of wine drinkers indicated that only 16% actually do this (without Debi and me, it's only 15%), but over three-quarters say they demand a decent glass when they dine out. It doesn't have to be a Riedel, but it should be shaped as much like one as possible.

As the wine life took us ever closer to a greater appreciation of food, it struck me as absolutely amazing how many restaurants will put an insanely killer wine list on the table right next to those heavy little 3 ounce glasses that come in green racks and are built to withstand the punishment of large-scale high-volume food service. Every single one of them, it seems, is made by Libbey, and they're so ubiquitous that the brand has become the generic name for this type of indestructible wine glass. ("You're not going to make me drink that out of a Libbey, are you?") In fact, when the apocalypse occurs, and nuclear winter gives way to nuclear spring, the only thing left on earth will be all those Libbeys, manhole covers, and possibly Wayne Newton.

It's rare for a restaurant to put Riedels on the table, although the $50-a-plate places almost always do, but the people who notice, notice. Debi and I had dinner in Santa Fe one night, and the waiter placed a pair of Georg's finest in front of us. We noticed. If a wine lover's glassware expectations are shattered, they go out to the car and bring in their own damn Riedels. We hadn't started doing that in October of 2001, but it wouldn't take long.

We had to find out if the Mondavi story was true, even if only in principle, so we conducted our customarily extensive tastings using as many different glasses as we could find, with inconclusive results. We did make one discovery: Aside from the scientific shape of the drinking vessel, there is one goblet-oriented factor that really does enhance the wine drinking experience. The thinness of the glass.

This may be one of those mystical things that history blesses us with, because the making and quaffing of wine is such an ages-old human pursuit. In times gone by, around the Mediterranean, they drank it out of terra-cotta amphorae, as they sailed their quinquiremes from Nineveh to Ophir. Later, God help them, they sipped it out of lead bowls, causing complete and unexplained mental incoherence, learning-disabled offspring, unpredictable mood swings, and some really interesting dinner conversation. They never had the thin-glass experience. But drinking from a restaurant glass, even one that's more or less the right shape, is not as pleasant if the thickness of the rim gets in the way. It's a mystery.

Here's the other, more insidious way the Riedels, Spiegelaus, and Schotts keep us as a loyal repeat customer. The stemware is hilariously fragile. It didn't take long to discover that the damn things would explode into glittering nonexistence if we didn't greet them properly in the morning. This does not keep my friend Ron from installing special Riedel racks in his dishwasher. He says if you wash them by hand, you'll sooner or later smack one against the side of the sink, and watch it instantly disintegrate. I've done it three times, and we lost number four because I woke up grumpy one day. After watching several of them burst in a very short time, Debi and I made a rule: never wash the glasses the night we drink out of them. The diminution of dexterity that results from sipping through half a bottle of wine is a real danger when trying to wash glasses that can barely stay together on the best of days. Just a gentle tap against the countertop or faucet, and we kiss them (and our $65) goodbye. I've actually seen them self destruct, spontaneously, for no reason at all. It's a comfort that the used ones are always waiting for us next to the kitchen sink the following morning.

Back to the slow and almost unnoticeable accretion of (I) merchandise and other goodies that directly relate to wine and (2) all the rest. The glass, the corkscrew, and the bottle fall into the first category, because of their indispensability. Everything else belongs in Category 2: decanters, wine racks, refrigerated storage cabinets that hold 24 bottles under the kitchen counter to whole freestanding rooms that display 2,600 bottles to glorious advantage. Really. They'll ship you the entire structure. I know someone who has a complete wine room that arrived flat packed in a number of boxes. He put it together inside his guest bedroom. Then there are the cooling units, racking systems, and other wildly expensive paraphernalia. Plus the coffee table made from the trunks of 100-year old vines, the furniture crafted from halves of used wine barrels, software to track the thousands of bottles in the collection, bar code generators and scanners for bottle tags, shirts with vine leaves printed on them, and the wine bottle stoppers with little doggie figurines on top (choose from sixteen breeds).

I've heard nasty rumors about people who actually stop drinking before the bottle is empty. For those few, there are these little sucky rubber stoppers that help preserve wine in the bottle for a period of time, which is never long enough, but they do come in handy. There's a valve on top that looks very much like an epiglottis. A small white manual vacuum pump fits on it, and with a few ups and downs, all the air comes out of the bottle. Well, most air. These devices became essential to us in the early stages of our condition, because we were still in that pathetic phase where we actually left some over. It didn't last long. We got past it, and gave all the sucky stoppers we owned to a friend who wasn't quite as far gone.

Decanters. I'd place these items about halfway between the two categories, because once we started buying wine that was good enough or old enough or expensive enough to decant, our tchotchke collection was the very least of our concerns.

Also in category (2), we have the special wine glass washing soap, the previously-referred-to dishwasher wine glass racks, specially shaped washing brushes for every type of wine glass, little spray bottles of potions that take wine stains out of your carpeting, upholstery, Donna Karan blouse, and lighter colored house pets, handcrafted individual charms that clip around the stem of a glass at the party so you can tell which one belongs to who, because people at wine parties do lose track, and an "antiqued" wall plaque that says, "We will drink no wine before its time. It's time!" In Italian. We have one.

We also had the doormat that said "We Serve Only Fine Wine. Did You Bring Any?" And decorative colored tiles that read "Wine Drinkers Make Grape Lovers." And funnels to pour our wine from the bottle into the decanter, because no, the white plastic one from the kitchen drawer that we used for olive oil and Gatorade and bug spray simply would not do. It had to be pewter, with a little screen in the bottom to detain any escaping sediment. Please shoot me.

One we saw how viciously all this crap had piled up, we struggled to get back to the basics. We needed a bottle, a corkscrew, a glass. That's it. No nitrogen gas system to keep our leftover wine fresh, no tasting table handcrafted from the trunks of hundred year old Zinfandel vines. Wine can be tasted off any kind of table, though many prefer drinking it from a glass.

We've gotten all the way down here, and never talked about the other Category 1 item that's a must have, and will be discussed in exhilarating detail a few chapters from now. This, after all, is the wine world, and the subject of corkscrews is not more twisted than we imagine, it's more twisted than we can imagine.

CHAPTER 12

The Mayor of America

*arvin Shanken, the publisher of
Wine Spectator magazine, is, not surprisingly, very
influential in the wine world. His juice in the larger
universe was stunningly demonstrated at our second
Wine Experience, in mid-October of 2001. The ruins
of the Twin Towers were still smoldering at the time,
but the event took place as scheduled. Nobody
cancelled. At the black tie banquet on Saturday night,
Marvin pulled off a coup that brought all 1,500
awestruck attendees to their feet, and very nearly to
their knees.*

October, 2001

The Wine Experience of 2001 turned out to be three
days of odd disquiet. It was held at the usual time of year,
the end of October, and Ground Zero was still smoldering.
We know, because we went to see it, and we cried along
with everyone else. I remember encountering a woman who
just stood there on the sidewalk in front of St. Paul's Chapel
on Broadway and Fulton handing out tissues to anyone who
needed them. She went through boxes and boxes.

Predictably, a pall hung over the gathering, as thick as the smoke that continued to billow up from that horribly violated ground. The organizers absolutely surpassed themselves in the choice of wines and tasting seminars, but in spite of that there was only one topic of conversation for three days straight, and nobody was disposed to the kind of revelry we'd enjoyed the year before. When glasses were raised, as many were, it was to the victims.

At the traditional Saturday night gala, Marvin, in his address to the group, told us that the staff had seriously considered canceling the weekend, but decided to go ahead. Out of the 1,500 people who had registered, only four requested a refund, which is a testament to the power and importance of the event.

To conclude his remarks, Shanken said, "The only thing that would make this evening more complete is if Rudy Giuliani were here." He was setting us up, but we never saw it coming. At that point, right on cue, Rudy Giuliani walked out on stage.

Ever since the attack, Giuliani had been arguably the most famous man in the world, his face and voice on the news every minute of the day somewhere, as the media covered the tragedy wall to wall. And yet, for a brief shining moment, he stopped into the Wine Experience. Score one for Marvin.

Everybody in the room had just spent a solid hour at a Champagne reception, liberally sampling some of the world's most precious sparkling whites. They were ready for almost anything, but not for this, and the stunning significance of Giuliani's appearance was lost on no one. When the Mayor of America strode onto the stage to thank us for supporting the city during that terrible time, we were stunned. As one, we vaulted to our feet, and the applause was as thunderous as it was prolonged. We couldn't have been more impressed if the Holy Father himself had flown in specially from Rome to lead us in a blessing.

CHAPTER 13

In French, They Call It "La Cave"

Every day, we thought our involvement with wine could become no more intense, no more obsessive or all-encompassing. We were wrong. We were compelled to build a wine room in our house. Our first. Not our last.

November, 2001

When the delivery guy with the brown truck wheeled the 15 cases into my office, it was early in October, and we had not yet been subjected to the Giuliani Surprise in New York. Fifteen cases is 180 bottles, but nobody goes out and buys that much wine all at once. It had snuck up on us during the previous four months. June: an email from a wine store in New York, and a two case order. July: another message from that high end purveyor in California, another case. August: two or three from wineries who had us on their list, and we had to take the allocation. And so it went.

It took us three trips to haul them all to the house. As we unpacked them it became obvious that, with the couple hundred bottles we'd already gathered unto ourselves, our

collection had overwhelmed the capacity of the wine racks
Larry had given us. We had nowhere to stash the new
shipment, so instead of worrying about it, we went to dinner.

A new restaurant had opened right next to my office, and
while we'd been in there a few times, we'd never dined in
what they called the "Opus Room." This was a smallish dining
room right off the reception area, decked out in fine wine
style, with pin racks on all the walls and fancy large-format
bottles on display. I can't say that Debi and I had the idea at
the same time, because she's usually ahead of me in these
matters, but as soon as we saw the racks and bottles and all
the atmospheric loveliness, we knew what we had to do.

We found the names of the people who had built the
"Opus Room" in that restaurant, and got them on the
phone. There was a third bedroom in our home we weren't
using, and it was perfect for the idea that had snuck up
on us. In a flash, terra-cotta tile replaced the (expensively
upgraded) carpeting that we put in when we built the place,
dark brown and roughly timberous but totally cosmetic
beams were glued across the ceiling, the walls were
concealed behind floor to ceiling bottle racks and bins, there
was a tasting table, and scattered wooden wine boxes on
the floor, just for atmosphere. In the corner stood a half
life-size painted wooden statue of Albert Einstein, solid
white hair flowing back, serious mustache, and monocle.
I've never seen a picture of the real Einstein sporting that
particular type of eyewear, but ours did. Long story short,
we turned the whole room into a combination study, home
office, and wine locker. We couldn't afford any kind of
fancy refrigeration system, so we ordered one of those
100-bottle wine refrigerators that comes in a box (cheap at
only $999 plus shipping). I am proud to say that it took me

a mere three weeks to put it together, and I managed to keep most of my fingers.

When the whole project was finished, I counted the racks and found that we had room for exactly 514 bottles. I stood in the doorway next to Debi, marveling, when she asked me, "When the hell are we ever going to own 514 bottles of wine?" She will certainly forgive me if I say that, in the entire history of our species, a sillier question has never been asked.

Open up one of those impossibly upscale architecture magazines where they advertise watches, jewelry, and private cruises that absolutely nobody can afford, and you won't see a picture of that wine room. It wasn't that impressive, and it certainly wasn't full. If we had any kind of extravagant personal resource, we'd be living on one of those luxury ocean liners that they've converted into floating condos, and where to put our wine wouldn't be a problem. Such, however is not the circumstance. I didn't think the room had anywhere near the kind of décor that would get us held up for societal admiration in the fancy house section of our local Sunday paper, but I was wrong. A friend tipped off a writer from the regional lifestyle magazine who was doing an article about people exactly like us. Well, ours was certainly no custom cellar, scrupulously maintained at 55 degrees and 70% humidity, but she was interested. We invited her over, opened the obligatory bottle, then another, and before we knew it we were the subjects of a two page spread in the Fall issue. This wine life crap was getting us into the media. It was time to step back a pace or two and take stock. The unexamined life is not worth living.

CHAPTER 14

Our Friend,
Mister Cork

*There are three plants on the planet that are
essential to wine, and two of them are oak trees. One
for the barrels, and the other, of course, for the corks.
Of the two, the cork tree is the more troublesome.
Herein, a brief reflection about why wine corks are in
grave danger in our modern world.*

August, 2002

The accumulative nature of the wine life offers a virtual
panoply of surprises, mild and severe, and most of them are
quite agreeable. It wasn't that much of a shocker when we
noticed how much more of our floor space was being taken
up by wine racks, bottles, and a few wooden wine boxes
that Larry had given us, just to enhance the vinous décor.
It was those boxes that called my attention to the serious
subject of wine corks, because as we opened bottles,
we threw the corks in the boxes, along with the ones
we'd collected in various containers over the years. It's no
surprise that they filled up at a shamefully rapid rate.

Frankly, we weren't even all that astonished as we

watched more and more kitchen cabinet shelves yield to, sag beneath, and nearly buckle under an ever expanding inventory of German and Czech wine glasses in all shapes and sizes.

And, God help us, we gradually got used to the other wine tchotchkes, too, the ones inflicted on us by well-meaning friends. But one night, as we were opening another bottle in the wine bedroom study, Debi made an observation.

"There must be two thousand corks in those boxes."

"And?"

"Boy, do we drink a lot of wine." I reminded her that the cork collection was the result of six years of dedicated, consistent effort, and the only reason there were so many is that we finally had them all in one place. "We didn't drink it all at once."

Even so, two thousand bottles represents 1,500,000 milliliters, which translates into a little under 400 gallons. That's a lot of wine, and even if some of those corks came from multiple bottles we opened at parties for multiple friends, we sort of had to step back and ask ourselves some serious questions.

The damn things just…piled up. We never planned to collect them. Who in their right mind would, except for dedicated handicrafters who make cute little *objets d'art* out of them? (Debi sews, paints, and creates all kinds of useful things from scratch, but in the six years we'd been trapped by our wine enthusiasm, I never saw her get artistically inspired by corks).

It started innocently enough. At first, we threw them in

a cut glass vase encased in some kind of loose wrought iron filigree floor stand. There was a certain old-world feeling to it. But one thing, as with all addictions, leads to some other damn thing, and the floor of our rudimentary wine cellar gradually became next to impassable with wood boxes full of imprinted stoppers made from the bark of the *quercus suber* tree. At least half of them had come to us all the way from Portugal by way of France, Italy, Spain, California, and Washington State.

The other surprise, of the more pleasant variety, came when we found out that we could make money from them, thanks to the cork crafters cited above. Even though Debi had never been impelled to get crafty with corks, there are people who do, bless 'em. Over the years, our names had shown up on the national direct mail database, search criteria people who buy anything to do with wine. So we received every wine tchotchke catalog on the planet, each issue blossoming in our mailbox crammed with all manner of gadgets and accessories. Cork crafts were always well represented, although I didn't see a whole lot of imagination in the product offerings. Even the best minds in the world (with one or two exceptions to be mentioned a bit later) can't figure out what to make out of wine corks except bulletin boards and trivets in various sizes, and if those aren't some of the biggest clichés in the handicraft world, I'll put on a dress and change my name to Shirley. But it's a fact that certain kinds of handicraft people need corks, and if they don't lead an active wine life, they have to get them from somewhere else.

Debi, being an inveterate eBay shopper, found a ready market of corkseekers who had some surprising requests, and was delighted to find out that she could sell 100 of them for $10, plus shipping, so she did. One woman was having an Italian-themed wedding and wanted only corks from Italian wines, because she was going to use them as place card holders at the dinner. Another told us she was covering an entire wall in her bathroom with them, which sounds like substantial grounds for divorce or the invocation of the Baker Act, but she did help us whittle down our oversupply, and pick up a few bucks in the process.

Sidebar: Some people really do have an imagination when it comes to wine bottle stoppers. In 2002, *National Geographic Adventure* magazine reported on two men, John Pollack and Garth Goldstein, who built a two-ton, 27-foot long boat out of 165,321 wine corks (with a little help from their friends), and sailed it 165 miles down Portugal's Douro River. I couldn't believe they had consumed that much wine, and was thinking that the poor guys were going to have to donate their livers to the Smithsonian, but it turned out that Pollack, a former speechwriter for President Clinton, had put together a wine cork stash of some 70,000 pieces, which he had been collecting since childhood. Apparently, he descended into the wine life much earlier than we. Then, somehow, he convinced a major wine cork supplier to donate the rest, which is a pretty good sales job, because even the cheapest ones sell for about a quarter each, and the supplier donated 100,000 pieces. They took two years to put the boat together, finished it off with a wood deck and a couple of oars, and in a Thor-Heyerdahlesque adventure, off they sailed.

Funny stuff, cork. But as benign as it seems to be, it has a dark side which, like so much else in the wine world, embroils us in controversy, disagreement, and injured emotions.

CHAPTER 15

The Teflon Worm

Corkscrews. Another Very Big Thing in the wine world…especially in the last few years, as more and more winemakers opt for the extremely controversial screw cap instead of the time-honored cork. We have our own thoughts on the subject.

September, 2002

WC Fields once remarked about a camping trip he had taken: "We lost our corkscrew and were forced to live on food and water."

In Spanish it's *sacacorchos*, which, literally translated means "cork taker-outer." In Italian it's *cavatappi*, but just about everybody has a word for this indispensable device.

There's an important realization, here, and it's this: By the end of our third Wine Experience, and the beginning of our forays into Napa Valley, we had opened our share of bottles, and collected (and sold) our share of corks. Drinking a bottle a night (and two on Saturdays and Sundays) will do that. So it was only natural that I would pause for a moment while extracting a cork, regard the unusual little tool in my hand, and wonder what it was doing there.

There are basically two standard ways to get a cork out of a wine bottle, and one of them requires a sabre, a supple wrist, and considerable practice. The other is the application of the corkscrew. I wouldn't recommend the shoe method.

I apologize for not mentioning that our corkscrew inventory had expanded at the same exponential rate as the bottles, corks, and other tchotchkes. Over the course of six years or so, the supply, and the variety, in the drawer seemed to increase every time I opened it. Some were purchased, some were gifts, and most were giveaways from various wine events, since they're a favorite promotional item for wineries and distributors. Most of the hardware in the drawer was inscribed with names of various wines, and it all begged for attention.

As I looked at them, in their various shapes, configurations, and mechanical workings, I thought that perhaps we don't give enough regard to the small things we use and depend on every day. Who invented the fork? The little plastic tips on the ends of my shoelaces? What about the incredible design of my garlic press? Maybe it's better not to know, because paying attention to any small detail of the wine world is always fraught with confusion and the temptation to go, intellectually, down a road less traveled. When we take up the subject of corks and removal of same from wine bottles, there are…implications.

I started at the beginning. When our ancestors graduated from putting wine in amphorae and carrying them across the Mediterranean in boats rowed by galley slaves, they started putting it in bottles. It happened around the 12th or 13th century, and we can probably thank the Venetians, because they got the whole melt-sand-produce-glass thing

figured out way before anybody else, and in the ateliers of
Murano they still do a swell job at it. Once bottles came
on the scene, the problem was keeping the contents from
dribbling out the hole in the end of the neck. It's safe
to conclude that people experimented with all kinds of
stoppers, wax being a likely choice, though the Romans
stuffed the openings of their amphorae with oak. Gradually,
they began to understand that (A) exposure to air makes
wine go bad, and (B) if it sits around for a while and
ages, sometimes it tastes better, so they started looking
for a seal that would be almost airtight. Some unknown
Portuguese genius scraped the bark off one of his country's
overabundant cork trees, and had one of those "aha"
moments. His countrymen were delighted, because at the
dawn of time, during the initial distribution of our planet's
natural resources, Portugal, for some reason, got no oil,
coal, minerals, or other major marketable resources. But
they did wind up with more cork trees than anyone else in
the world, and figured that if they just sat around for a few
millennia, sooner or later they'd find a way to make them
pay off. During that same early epoch, some trees were
carelessly spilled into Spain, Italy, and Sardinia, but today,
about 50% of the world's cork comes from Portugal. The
Centro Tecnológico da Córtica, which translates to "the
one place in the world where all the smart cork people
work," is located in Oporto.

Like I said before, funny stuff, cork. According to those
who know, it makes wildly effective wine bottle stoppers
because its cells are tiny 14-sided polyhedrons, and I haven't
seen one of those in forever. The spaces between the
cells are hollow, and it's this characteristic of microscopic
porosity that allows miniscule amounts of air to reach the

contents over time, which, it is believed, ages and develops the wine in the bottle and causes it to mature. The air trapped in the cells also makes cork float beautifully, which is important to some fishermen, and to those cork boat captains I've already introduced.

If cork had aspirations, it would want to be stuffed down the neck of a wine bottle, because only the very finest grade cork is used for this purpose. Poorer grades are used for cheaper wine, and the rest gets made into insulation, flooring, bulletin boards, and (unkindest of all) engine gaskets.

Once the people Back Then started using corks, it didn't take them long to understand that stuffing a cork into a bottle was a lot easier than getting it out. An ancient text does relate the (almost certainly apocryphal) story of one Guy L'homme Blanc, who may actually have been a real person. Maybe not, since his name translates as "the man in white," but who really knows. Having finished corking over 200 bottles of Petit Verdot, Guy suddenly realized he would die of thirst if he didn't invent the corkscrew, and darn quick, too.

The history of this tool as I tried to dig it out is long, complicated, and, spellbinding, at least to some of us. To others the story may be mind-numbing but I had to know. Supposedly, the twisty part, called the "worm," was inspired by an implement called a bulletscrew, which soldiers used to extract stuck bullets from rifle barrels. This is also probably false, since we probably had bottles well before we had rifles.

Those who delve deeply into the subject (esoteric as it is, there are those who do), learn that there are four types of corkscrews. There's the basic direct pull idea, which is the kind normally found rendered in white plastic in moderately-priced hotel rooms, with the lodging's logo on the side. I tried one once, twisting the worm down into the cork, holding the bottle between my knees and pulling up until my groin gave out. I herniated myself and fell backwards, opening up my head on the edge of that round table with the tourist magazines and room service menu they always put right in front of the window. The assisted pull variety, a definite step up, less dangerous and not as physically challenging, applies some kind of extra mechanism to make the pulling a bit easier. Some corkscrews use the principle of torque, and have a collar around the worm that sits on the lip of the bottle. When the worm is screwed down (terrible as that sounds), the cork comes up.

Then there's the kind on the shelf of just about any supermarket, the ones with levers on each side, where you pull down on the two handles to pull the cork out. Wine purists scoff at the entire idea. In public.

The clear winner, thanks to Archimedes, is the leverage model, which is the form of instrument most people are familiar with. Screw the worm down, clip the folding piece to the rim of the bottle, and it serves as a fulcrum when you pull up on the handle. Elegant in its simplicity. It's called the waiter's corkscrew since most restaurant people use it.

Human ingenuity through the centuries has known no limits in the quest to get the cork out of the bottle with ever less effort, and ever more style. Some of the assisted pull mechanisms in the books and museums (of course there are corkscrew museums…there would have to be) are worthy of a da Vinci or even a Rube Goldberg. People collect these, and with a passion, making many antique versions worth more than my car. The Abraham Russel corkscrew, patented on January 21, 1862, sold on eBay for over $13,000. There aren't many wines that cost that much.

This just in from the I'm Not Surprised Department: even as there are supposedly superlative brands of wine glasses, there are supposedly superlative brands of corkscrews. And, like wine glasses, they come from the Old World, France in this case (which is absolutely no surprise), and from a company that's been making them since almost the beginning of recorded history. Again, since some kind of corkscrew manages to find its way into my hand at least once a day, every day, I set off in search of the truth.

La Maison du Laguiole has been in the knife and corkscrew business in the Aubrac region of France for over 200 years, which makes them look like newbies alongside the Reidels and Zildjians, but so what. Their quality and craftsmanship are world-renowned, and their corkscrews, shaped in elegant curves and adorned with boxwood, olive wood, or real cow horn, sell for hundreds of dollars. Not quite in the same league as Abraham Russel's, but maybe someday. Even the simplest piece undergoes, they say, 109 separate operations in its manufacture. The more complicated models are subjected to around 200. Their logo is a kind of abstract honeybee, and no purported Laguiole is genuine without it.

Laguioles are elegance in action, the Platonic ideal of grace in design, with a heft in the hand that inspires confidence, but the one thing they do not have is a Teflon coated worm, and that's too bad. Many corkscrew manufacturers coat the worm with Teflon, or some other friction-reducing goo. This makes the act of screwing in much easier, though it has no effect on the act of extraction. We learned that when the worm is the same color as the inside of a frying pan, that's a good thing. Larry gave me a Laguiole corkscrew that he won in a sales contest, and it's a treasure, Teflon or no.

In the last few years, however, technology has transformed corkscrew design to an alarming degree. The basic principle of the fulcrum and lever still applies, but the mechanisms are almost unrecognizable. The most minimally developed among us can look at a normal corkscrew and say, "Uhhh...corkscrew." But the first time I saw a Screwpull or a Rabbit, I thought it was a plumbing fixture, or a tool used to subject terrorism suspects to physically demanding interrogation.

The Rabbit has two horizontal handles shaped like (yes) rabbit ears that clamp on to the neck of the bottle, another handle that sticks out at an angle that drives the worm down into the cork, and the opposite motion pulls the cork out. Flip the handle up and down one more time, and the cork comes off the worm. These monster machines are engineered like pieces of industrial equipment (though the design is quite modish), cost up to $100 each, and weigh six and a half pounds. Unfortunately, like most industrial equipment they rob the cork-extraction ritual of all elegance, grace, and style. Squeeze, push the handle down, pull the handle up. It is a brusque, almost brutal act.

The tchotchke catalogs are filled with cork extraction devices that are "perfect for the wine-loving friends on your list," and we thank our assorted deities every day that nobody has given us any. There is an electric one that contains a rechargeable battery. It looks like a long cylinder with a button on the side that lights up. The user places it over the top of the bottle, pushes the button, there is a silly buzzing sound, the worm goes in, the cork comes out. We have some friends who actually bought one, and I just can't bring myself to use it.

Now that the subject has been covered in inspirational detail, the whole issue may well become moot, because all these elegantly designed devices are even now on their way to obsolescence. There's Trouble On the Way for the makers of cork and corkscrews, and there was a realization on the way for me.

CHAPTER 16

Our Enemy, Mister Cork

he cork may be near and dear to wine lovers, since the ritual of opening a bottle certainly has an undeniable frisson of romance. But the venerable stopper is in danger. There is a modern winemaker stampede toward alternative closures, and what does this phenomenon mean to the wine world?

October, 2002

By the end of 2003, it was obvious that a fundamental change was taking place in the world of wine. I didn't have to go far to see it—just looking at the bottles on the shelves screamed the story at me. This was not a revolution, but a slow, incremental, creeping transition that had been going on for a while. But it was gathering steam, and attracting attention.

The same vintners (or their descendants, actually) who gloried in the discovery of the cork bottle stopper had become increasingly disenchanted early in the 21st Century, and it was apparent that if things kept keep going like they were, the entire country of Portugal would be out of work in a very few years, along with the corkscrew crafters around Aubrac.

I probably wouldn't have cared all that much, at least not at that stage of the obsession, if it hadn't been for the little episode about the Screaming Eagle corks at that first Wine Experience. While that situation involved counterfeiting wine (who knew that people did such things?), this problem was—and is—a lot more serious.

It's a phenomenon called cork taint, and until the turn of the Millennium, it was like the weather...often discussed but rarely acted upon. The revered traditionalism of the wine world is both a blessing and a curse. They've been at it for so many thousands of years that customs and lore have evolved in every aspect of winemaking. The blends, the ancient vineyards, the practice in the cellars. Cork is one of these traditions, and tough to escape.

Back to the reference books, and the Internet. Winemakers have been stuffing corks into wine bottles for over seven centuries, and everybody accepted all along that some percentage of them would leak, letting air into the bottle and turning the wine into mediocre salad dressing. If that didn't happen, there was always a chance that the cork (which is only tree bark, after all) would harbor a certain mysterious compound which relatively recently, winehistorywise, was identified with the ominous name of 2, 4, 6-trichloroanisol, mercifully abbreviated as TCA, that makes the wine taste...well, corky.

Coincidentally, it was right around this time that we went to dinner with our friends Ralph and Trish, whom we had met years earlier (surprise!) at a wine tasting. We each brought a bottle, since the restaurant didn't have a very good list, and the one Ralph opened was not only corky, but embodied the very Platonic ideal of cork taint. I'd never tasted anything like it, but all my reading and research told me that what came out of Ralph's bottle was cork taint in the most classic sense. Wet newspapers, cardboard, and some other aromas that are indelicate to contemplate, or even mention.

Either leakage or cork taint happens in about 3% to 5% of all wine bottles, and when it does, we have to pour it down the sink, whether it cost $24 or $2,400. Leakage is a problem, but cork taint is a lot more serious, because it can thrive and reproduce not only in cork, but in the environment of the wine cellar itself, on wooden surfaces like pallets. Some researchers say that humans can detect 2, 4, 6-whatever in quantities as low as five parts per trillion, which is like tasting about ten grains of salt in an Olympic-sized swimming pool (not from the kiddy end, please). The spoilage doesn't always make drinkers spew the offensive liquid from between their violated lips. Mostly, it just makes the wine taste a little "off," eccentrically-flavored enough to spoil an often expensive and long-anticipated experience. In more extreme cases, TCA imparts the already-mentioned aromas and flavors of wet cardboard and newspapers. In any case, it's so much of a problem that one famous Northern Italian vintner sued his cork supplier over the spoilage of a heartbreaking number of bottles from an excellent vintage of Nebbiolo. He was awarded a settlement thought to be in the half-million-dollar range. Just one more topic of Much Debate in every corner of the winemaking world.

It's amazing that cork should harbor any weirdness at all, considering what it goes through to become a bottle stopper. In a normal cork processing plant (and we know where most of them are), forklifts dump the bark of the *quercus suber* tree into huge vats where it is boiled for an hour. Then it's boiled again to make sure it's nice and moist. After that, the proper shapes are punched out of the sheets of bark and dunked in chlorine, washed again, and immersed a third time in a solution like oxalic acid that neutralizes the bleach. Back in the old days, the corks were put in net bags and dipped in these solutions by hand, but technology has caught up with this end of the business, too. There are stainless steel vats, computerized control systems, and milder chemicals. Since I became so raptly engaged in the research, I found out that today's corks are washed in hydrogen peroxide, potassium metabisulfite (whatever that is), and good old chlorine. Great to know.

I couldn't help thinking that TCA must be some kind of strapping sickness to survive a bath like that. If bleach and peroxide won't kill it, and the nuclear solution is not an option, we either have to live with it or (dare I even say it) find a replacement. This is where things get bloody.

The evidence on the shelves in early 2003 proved it. Bottles appeared that were sealed with…screw tops. Just like the awful mass-produced wines of the "Hearty Burgundy" and "Pink Chablis" days. Apparently, the movement was afoot to find Alternative Closures, but this quest is not without its own strong nostalgic apron string. Who does not treasure the festive sound of the popping Champagne cork, just before it destroys the chandelier? That sound may soon fade, and not very gently, into the past.

As Debi listened to my discourses on corkscrews, not always with her characteristic Mother Theresa equanimity, she pointed out that wine people are heirs to millennia of tradition, and are deeply conservative, at least in the Old World. Many New World winemakers have roots back across the ocean, too, and are also loathe to fix something that's only a little broken. Those who talk about replacing the time-honored cork, the bottle stopper of the ages, should look over their shoulders, because Big Names were lining up on several sides of the question, and nostalgia, as important as it may be, is the least of the debate.

There's another side, and on it are the more adventurous and experimental North and South American vintners, the South Africans, and the Australians, who'll try anything once and if it hurts, they'll try it twice.

These people say what this planet needs is something to close a wine bottle tight and keep it that way for fifty years or more. Obviously, the more expensive the wine, the more likely it is to be cellared for long periods of time, so I thought it would stand to reason that the makers of huge Bordeauxes and Rhônes and Burgundies and Ports, whose products are often kept for that long, would be in the forefront of the Alternative Closure Movement. I was embarrassingly mistaken.

The answer, one of them, anyway, is plastic. The more adventurous winemakers, like the American Randall Grahm of Bonny Doon, switched to plastic stoppers years ago. Same shape, same size, same bottling machinery, but the plug they stuff in the little hole is a kind of soft plastic that behaves like cork (they think), springs back into shape after compression, creates a tight seal, and yields appropriately to a corkscrew. There are three or four major varieties, and they've been used primarily on lower-priced wines that are meant for drinking within a few years. They come in colors to match the labeling and artwork on the bottle, which is a clear marketing advantage over cork, but pink stoppers look kind of stupid.

As far as I can tell, the wine world has little faith in the plastic stopper as a long term solution, because there's another candidate waiting in the wings to replace the cork. It's your basic everyday screw top. Nobody puts ginger ale or Coca-Cola in a cellar for fifty years, but many testing laboratories have reported that good screw tops will keep air out of a bottle until every event in the Book of Revelations comes to pass, and for a few days after.

When that same Randall Grahm announced in the middle of 2002 that his Ca' del Sole wines would henceforth be sealed with a screw top called the Stelvin closure, it was another, earlier, spur to my compulsive inquisitiveness. Replacing the 17th Century technology of the cork, the Stelvin cap requires only opposable thumbs for opening, so almost all of us have been carrying around our own wine opening device since birth, and never even knew it. Grahm isn't the first to use screw caps, but he is the first to do so on a "bet the farm" basis. Plumpjack, a California Cabernet that goes for around $135 a bottle if it reaches the stores at all, got some PR mileage a while back for bottling a portion of its production in screw top bottles, and other wine estates have dipped a timid toe or two into the same murky waters, but none have jumped in with both feet. However, at this writing Grahm was bottling all his production, around 80,000 cases, with the Stelvin closure, and if it doesn't work, he's up the excremental waterway with no means of propulsion. True, his wines, excellent as they are, don't sell for $100 a bottle, and it's unlikely that anyone will cellar them for enjoyment by generations to come, but it's a big gamble no matter what.

Jumping ahead a bit, I once spoke to Paul Pontallier, estate manager of the Grand Cru Chateau Margaux, at the Florida Wine Fest in Sarasota, and he wasn't buying it. I asked him about screw caps and he said, "Would you gamble the entire production of your chateau on an unproven technology?" Well? We won't know if screw tops will preserve wine for fifty years until fifty years from now, and who's willing to risk all that fine wine on a bottle seal that we don't have any long-term experience with? At least, he says, we've been using corks for so long we know what to expect, and if we lose a couple of bottles, well (he shrugs his shoulders in that inimitable Gallic manner), c'est la vie.

Jumping ahead again, Pontallier's boss, Corinne Mentzelopoulos, announced in 2012 that Chateau Margaux was bottling a few cases of their current vintage under screw caps as an experiment. Results to come in 10-20 years.

Incredible Irony Department: Paul and his compatriots in Bordeaux and Burgundy may be arch-conservatives on the matter of corks, but the company that makes the up-and-coming Stelvin closure is extremely French, definitely non-traditional, and has over 300 plants in 50 countries. They've been testing this particular screw-top technology for more decades, now, but I'm afraid it will take a burning bush, parting of the seas, the Second Coming, or a surprise visit by creatures from beyond the stars to make Paul and the other producers of ultra-high-quality wine shift their thinking.

Still, Pontallier had a point. Changing the closure system could easily bite us in the butt 20 years down the road, when we unscrew a bottle of $2,000 Bordeaux and find out it's only good for rinsing out the garbage disposal. But this movement is more than a groundswell, and it's swelling.

In South Africa, several producers have banded together to research and develop screw cap closures. They're following the lead of New Zealand in the effort, and other national associations aren't far behind.

There are other, less obvious, consequences of the movement away from cork. For one, winemakers have taken to imprinting all sorts of things on their corks, as a sort of extra merchandising message to the consumer. Many, of course, just stamp in their vineyard logo, thus the counterfeiting fear of the Screaming Eagle people, but others are of a more imaginative and puckish sensibility. The Frog's Leap winery puts the word "ribbit" on each cork. The wine corks from Justin carry marketing messages to each of us who pulls the cork from the neck: "Just fine, just fruity, just fabulous," and similar phrases to assure us that we've made the right buying decision. And, supposedly, that the wine is authentic. Some corks have toll-free numbers or web site addresses. On others, the vintners just say "thank you" for buying their product. We may be losing a small but important channel of communication between the winemaker and the customer.

There is one other (outside) contender to replace the venerable cork. It's the "diamond cap," and the more mature of us remember it as the old-time crimp-edge bottle cap that came on soft drinks, and had to be popped off with a church key. They're absolutely impenetrable, and are used by all major producers of Champagne-style wines to seal the bottles until it's time to disgorge and cork them. They're so tight and secure that they can contain the six atmospheres of pressure inside sparkling wine bottles, but nobody actually believes the diamond cap will happen.

The owners of the cork orchards aren't sitting in their estates outside Lisbon, calm and unconcerned, drinking Port and watching the sun set over the Tagus River. They've suddenly found themselves on the run, and are making multi-faceted attempts to stop the Screw Top crusaders before they gather too much momentum, and before average consumers reach the point of no return in their acceptance of the new cap. They've tried treating their corks with more compounds to supposedly neutralize that 2,4,6 stuff, but nobody's sure whether or not the compounds themselves will have a long-term tainting effect on the wine.

More recently, in Portugal, Spain, Sardinia, wherever cork is grown, they're developing new types of cork technology (if I can get my thoughts around "cork technology") trying composite stoppers made of compressed and molded cork granules in the middle, with sold cork circles at each end. And they're doing the most important thing of all— advertising. Full page ads in wine trade and consumer magazines trumpet the superiority of our friend, Mister Cork, loyal servant of humankind, and how wonderfully he's worked over the past 700 years. Proven. Tried and true. Tell that to somebody who's waited five or ten years to open that special bottle for their 25th anniversary and wound up gagging in disgust.

But there's always the proverbial rub. Randall Grahm makes several kinds of wine, and he didn't put all of them in screw top bottles. Why? Because nobody is sure how the consumer will accept it. Wine drinkers are only slightly less traditionally-minded than wine makers, though there is every evidence that those attitudes are changing as younger people get hip to the juice. They're drinking Champagne "pops" out of tiny bottles, with a straw, and may not be bound by the same ritualistic, ceremonial impulses that afflict older customers. Still, there is the inescapable, well-conditioned association of screw tops with the $7-a-gallon jug wines of the old days. The Stelvin people (and the Aussies) are hoping we'll get over it.

Personally, I'm desperately concerned not for the vintners or the cork producers, but for all those people we've sold corks to who devote their lives to covering their bathroom walls with them, and who may have to find another hobby pretty darn quick. There are thousands, yea, tens of thousands of these cork crafters around the country, and they're an active, vocal, dedicated bunch. There are in this world, astonishingly enough, a flood of cork crafts web sites, where artists who have chosen *quercus suber* as their metier show the latest wreaths, wall coverings, tiny animals, and other creations that are possible only because somebody somewhere opened and enjoyed a bottle. And guess what—they buy our corks and don't give a damn about cork taint. What will become of these people?

The screw cap debate has raged for quite some time. (Flash forward: The controversy was a cover story in *Wine Spectator*, maybe in 2008 or so, with editor Jim Laube taking the screw cap position, and now-former editor Jim Suckling standing up for the old-fashioned ways. All of Laube's points in favor were practical—longer wine life, better seal, no TCA—and all of Suckling's were sentimental: no ritual of opening the bottle, no examining the cork before pouring, no joyous "pop" of celebration.)

Cork is dead, long live the screw top? Must we say a bittersweet farewell to the sweet rituals Jim Suckling holds so dear? The presentation of the wine at the table by the sommelier, the deft extraction of the cork with a few poetic yet economical twists of the wrist, the careful examination of same. Above all, that festive sound.

Will we lament? Time will tell.

CHAPTER 17

Wine Lifers Extraordinaire

Wine takes us places...to new locations and new people. Our world was broadened considerably when we met Miles and Tony at our third Wine Experience. Through them, we got Inside the Wine Life.

October, 2002

One of the best things about the wine culture is that it's especially amenable to being examined in dualistic terms. Reds and whites. New World and Old World. Dividing a few thousand years of human culture into two parts may seem overly simplistic, but it's a small step toward embracing the subject. However, in learning as in life, this half-and-half way of considering reality can be dangerous.

Taking the this-or-that approach does work well both when considering the people who make wine, as well as the wine itself. There are some winemakers, quite successful ones, who make it in industrial quantities and put it in boxes and jugs, pulling 12 or 13 tons an acre off their square miles of California Central Coast vineyards and cranking out twenty million cases a year from facilities that look like oil refineries, only cleaner. They'd never do that if the demand didn't exist, so somebody's drinking it, which means that the industrial producers are leading a lot of people toward wine appreciation, kind of. Gotta start somewhere.

While the 20-million-case companies certainly make their product to meet certain standards of acceptability, I'd bet that somebody like Fred Franzia of Bronco Wines doesn't spend a lot of time in the winery dragging hoses around or stirring up the fermenting grapes to extract more flavor. (Coincidentally, Fred is the nephew of Ernest Gallo, who's been known to ferment up a gallon or two himself).

Not that the large producers don't take the craft seriously, but the second kind of winemaker works in a smaller venue and looks at the process from an entirely different perspective. They take the tasks of winemaking not only seriously, but personally. Some, having been smart and lucky in business, find themselves drawn to wine country as if by tractor beams, so they gather up their resources into one huge pile and haul it up the coast from LA or San Francisco, along with romantic notions of glamour and the urge to become gentleman farmers and return to the soil. A few succeed, a few produce three or four vintages and give up, some don't make it at all. Those who have the dream but not the pile feel just the same pull, and they, too, find a way. We've been fortunate enough to meet some of both, and therein, as is said, lurks a narrative.

We first encountered Miles and Tony as we stood in a very long line with cousins Douglas and Cynthia, waiting to check in for the 2002 Wine Experience in Las Vegas. Long story short, one hello led to another, the six of us stuck together all weekend, formed a secret society, took blood oaths, and have continued the practice every year since.

Miles and Tony are attorneys in California, and ever since we met them they have had a Burnsian effect on our slide down into the wine life, every bit as significant, in its own way, as Larry with his bag of six bottles.

Tony is from Los Angeles, Miles lives in San Diego. There's more to know about the San Diego connection, but in a minute. They've been friends since they roomed together, by chance, in law school, and they're way out in front of Debi, me, and practically everyone else when it comes to being marinated in the wine tradition.

Sidebar: The movie *Sideways* would not come out until January of 2005, but reminiscing about how we met Miles leads me into a flash-forward line of thinking. In *Sideways*, the misfortunate wine lover played by Paul Giamatti is named Miles, and he's from San Diego. This caused our own Miles to suffer a nearly-unconscionable ration of (mostly) well-intentioned ridicule because he, like us, has no friends but wine friends, and all of them saw the film.

In the movie, Miles is a dejected, somewhat morally bankrupt junior high teacher and angst-ridden aspiring novelist. The real Miles experiences no angst at all. His life is much more interesting than his counterpart's in the movie, and that's all I'll say about it.

About Tony. He's proof of the fact that wine is primarily a guy thing. His wife Patty, lovable as she is, would rather suffer through a case of monkey pox or Crimean hemorrhagic fever, or be trapped for a week in the Beijing Museum of Tap Water than sit around all evening drinking wine and talking about it. Debi, as mentioned, has a hedonistic and gustatory fascination, but Patty's interests lie far afield. Tony makes his wine pilgrimages alone, and he and Miles room together on their wine weekends. Just like old times.

It didn't take long for us to discover that Miles and Tony, between the two of them, were personal friends with dozens, maybe hundreds, of winemakers from even the most obscure wine regions of California, all of whom were at the opening Grand Tasting that Thursday night. Having met Tony only hours before, I trailed him around a Venetian Hotel ballroom the size of a dirigible hangar, watching him wave to, stop and chat with, or enjoy huge embraces and double-cheek air kisses from people whose names I recognized only from reading bottle labels at the wine shop. The big bottles they keep in the cold room, locked up and video surveilled. I could barely speak.

"Is there anybody in this room you don't know? Who are you, really?" I was so stunned that I asked him if he had ever killed anyone because it wouldn't have surprised me, but he was off for another series of long-time-no-see clinches behind the tasting tables.

Our new friends were practically honorary citizens of Napa Valley, so it seemed, traveling up there for weekend visits almost once a month, attending (and donating to) the St. Helena Catholic School auction as well as other charity events, and making lots of friends. They'd been doing it for years.

The next impression of how cozy they felt among the wine worlders came in the spring of the following year when we joined them for what was to be our first real trip to wine country. We'd been there once before, in August of 1997, spending a few days driving up and down

Sonoma Valley clue-deprived as to who was who and what was what. Larry—who else—had set us up for a tour and tasting at a few of the area's more prestigious wineries, but it turned out to be the weekend that Princess Diana met her unfortunate fate in that tunnel under the Pont l'Alma, which is why I remember the date, and not much about the wine we drank. Strange how so much of our wine travel coincides with tragedies and disasters.

Miles and Tony had bought an item together at a Napa charity wine auction the previous year, which turned out to be dinner for ten people at the home of winemaker Delia Viader, who donated it. That was another name I knew, even then. Critics consistently gave her wines zillions of points, and her Cabernet blend, which sells in the $80-$100 range, has been in the *Wine Spectator* Top Ten more than once. Since Miles and Tony are only two people, they needed to come up with eight more dinner guests, and we, among others, got the nod.

Sidebar: When I lived in northwest Florida in the late Sixties, I somehow became a hockey nut, chancing on the NHL game of the week on television every Sunday afternoon at two, and getting sucked in. Back then, it was Old Time Hockey, anything but a gentleman's game, and I loved it. Watching the game turned into a ritual, and like most people who observe certain rituals on Sundays, I was religious about it. But upon my game day spirit squatted the heavy gray certainty that I would never in my life actually attend a major league hockey game. I lived in Niceville, Florida, population five plus me, where ice skating was not the number one sport, and watching the Canadiens skate at the Forum, or the Rangers at the Garden, well, that was a dream that would require more than one pipe. I was in

Niceville forever, far as I could tell. Funny how things work out.

Thirty-four years later, I wound up at the Stanley Cup final game in Tampa just a few months before the 2004 Wine Experience, watching my beloved Lightning skate around kissing a great big silver bowl on a pedestal, mopping up the salt water that fell from my eyes. I had been at the very first practice game they ever played, and the very first everything else they'd ever done, and there they were, Lord Stanley and all. Long way from Niceville.

Dinner at Delia's was like that. A place we never expected to be, high on a mountain we never expected to attain. Her home offered spectacular vineyard vistas in every direction, and as a lagniappe, a glistening lake below. Her son Alan's fiancé Mariela, a classically trained chef, slapped one Michelin Three Star dish on the table after another, whap whap whap, and they were so beautiful that everybody took pictures before they ate. All the other guests, except the dentist from St. Helena, were winemakers, and, soon after, new friends.

The wine world, global though it may be, is very small, and the world of Napa or any winemaking valley smaller still. It's maybe 30 miles long and three miles wide, and everybody meets everybody sooner or later. They have associations for exactly that purpose. Winemakers, and wine world people in general, are notoriously convivial and interconnected, so after being introduced to one or two, our circle of acquaintances expanded outward.

The dinner guests couldn't have been more assorted. Chuck and Anne McMinn made some highly profitable decisions early in the dot com boom, gaining the resources

to make the journey north from Palo Alto and build a
winery that would make any Star Trek lover swoon. It puts
one in mind of the engine room of the Starship Enterprise,
glistening with ethereal inner life, and looking every bit as
though it runs on dilithium crystals or beryllium spheres.
Chuck had it built so that the whole place produces its own
power, and the heat from the propane generators goes
through an exchanger that refrigerates the fermentation
tanks. He's off the grid, as well as off the charts.

Apparently, Miles and Tony had developed a tradition
with Chuck and his winery office staff long before we
met. Any time they visit, they bring lunch. On subsequent
trips, we became part of the lunch bunch, and started
contributing, which made the people at Dean & DeLuca
very happy.

Sidebar: For those who are not familiar, to call the
Dean & DeLuca location in Napa Valley a market or deli
falls so short as to be an affront. It's more like a temple
of gastronomy, fine wines and fancy food in all directions,
at every one of their locations. So we raid the cheese and
charcuterie counters of the store on St. Helena Highway,
throw in a few baguettes, and head up the hill to break
bread, knowing that Chuck, generous as he is, will open a
bottle or two to go with.

Sitting across from the McMinns, taking pictures of
Mariela's creations along with the rest of us, were Steven
and Sue Parry. They nestle in a lovely white-porched house
on Silverado Trail landscaped in the traditional Napa Valley
motif, which specifies two or three acres of primo Cabernet
Sauvignon vines in the front yard. I think the county levies
fines on homeowners who don't have at least two rows
of vines on their property. The Parrys produce 250 cases

in a good year, which Steven sells to his mailing list, and to restaurants in San Francisco and beyond. In my way of thinking, he should sell the wine along with his recipe for short ribs, because the pairing is uncanny.

After that evening, we encountered other winemakers in equally unexpected ways. Like Rob Fanucci, who is so close to the Zinfandel he makes that he puts his home phone number on the back label, and take calls from his customers and fans pretty much no matter when. That's how Cousin Douglas found him a few years later. Douglas tried a bottle of Rob's Monte Rosso Zinfandel, liked it, and called the number, catching the Fanuccis at breakfast. Next trip, Rob was on our must-visit list, where he graciously demonstrated his winemaking techniques.

Rob falls somewhere between the McMinns and the Parrys. An attorney in St. Helena, he makes killer Zinfandel in the basement his grandfather used as a winery before Prohibition, and probably during. It's below an old clapboard house in St. Helena, with shutters on the windows, low bare-beam ceilings, the smell of sweet musty old wood, and gallon jugs of wine along the walls that have been there since the time of Al Capone. Rob conducts his fermentation in open vats out in his driveway, which alarmed me when I first saw it, but have since been a guest at wineries where wine, Zinfandel especially, is made in similarly simple ways. No Starship Enterprise for Rob. He's hands-on all the way, and pretty much all by himself.

As time went on, one thing led to another. Douglas and Cynthia went to a wine dinner one night somewhere in New York, and shared a table with a couple named Chris and Pauline Tilley. Nice to meet you, says Chris, we just completely gave up our (remunerative) careers in law and banking to follow our passion for wine, we're moving back to St. Helena where I grew up, and building a winery where we're probably going to bust our butts working seven days a week, ever day of the year. You should come visit. (And by the way, when they bought their property, Rob Fanucci handled the deal).

I have to admit to a small selfish thrill. At first, we were both amazed and gratified at the way Miles and Tony slipped us in among so many of the winemakers. But it took only a year or so for us to develop our own friendships and make our own discoveries, and begin introducing *them* to the people *we* knew.

Perhaps our experience was unique. I can't say. I only know that when we talked to these unfailingly gracious and welcoming people, and showed even a glimmer of understanding about what they do, and an appreciation of the effort they make, a bond developed. Wine. It takes us places and brings us people.

CHAPTER 18

A Whack on the Head

It's very easy for a wine lover to turn into a wine snob, as personal passion becomes excruciatingly boring for everyone in the immediate vicinity. I found out that it was happening to me, because I have a relative who is all too happy to smack me on the head when I get too insufferable. But she's more than qualified to do it.

July, 2003

One of the dangers—among many—of falling into the wine life is a practically inevitable propensity to become a grape geek. A cork dork. Some people call them wine snobs, and write books about how to be one, or how not to be one, but any hobby, passion, or obsession we pursue takes up a chunk of our lives, and when we get jacked about something, we want to share. Friends who love to work on cars drag us into their garage whether we will or no, and smother us with details about the installation of their new double overhead split-cam gazoom pipes. Those who succumb to and pursue the intellectual component of the wine world sooner or later become the same way. Only worse. And I didn't even know it was happening. I did know that when people came to visit, I would drag them off to see the bedroom/wine room/study before they'd even taken off their jackets.

Wine as a beverage—or a food, in some places—appeals to and involves our hedonistic sensual side, which is seldom a bad idea. But all along I had sensed that there was more to it, and that's what led me down the path. Wine is a cultural artifact, made by certain people in certain places during certain times, and I wanted to understand that. But it required me to learn geography, history, a lot of stuff.

Matt Kramer, a wine writer I much admire, once wrote, "In order to understand what a fine wine has to say, you have to bring to it almost as much as it brings to you. This is where knowledge comes in, where context is essential and ultimately, where travel to a wine's geographic source but also to its originating culture is vital." Which is a much more richly textured way of saying something I've said all along: wine takes us places.

We can enjoy a bag of Cheesy Poofs without knowing how they're made (and it's probably better if we don't) but by the middle of 2003 we'd been inside more than one wine cellar, at more than one winery, swirling, sipping, and spitting with winemakers. The experience gives the next bottle—especially if it's one of theirs—a whole new meaning.

From the beginning, I sensed that the wine world was a very big place, and voyaging through it would offer many rewards. That inkling has proven itself more than somewhat in our travels. While Debi is completely enchanted by the aromas, flavors, and sensory experience of wine, and has never met a wine she couldn't deconstruct, I needed to know what was inside those weighty wine encyclopedias and beginners' books like Wine for Abysmal Morons. Debi is less than mesmerized by those aspects of the pursuit, and if I enthuse to her about the elevation of the vineyard or composition of the soil, I do so at considerable risk of personal injury.

A lot of people don't care, but it's only because they didn't have a crack at the revelation or epiphany. There are plenty of things that can turn someone into a borderline grape geek.

As Kramer says, wine is the kind of thing that makes you care, and takes you to geography, history, sociology, geology (if you get really hooked), but sadly, to most people it's just a big so what. Cork dorks who discourse over dinner about the 500-year history of what's in the bottle or say Thurberesque things like, "It's a naïve domestic Burgundy without any breeding, but I think you'll be amused by its presumption" get smacked on the head sooner or later, often sooner, multiple times, and hard, by multiple people. Sometimes they experience gunshot wounds.

When I have the occasional need to get smacked, I count on my closest living relative. Cousin Annie provides much-needed perspective, because she was born with (or developed) a deliciously quirky take on life and a skewed view of the essence of the universe, a quality which she brings to her exceptional creative work. I long ago learned to respect and cherish her otherworldly understanding of behavior and relationships among our species. She gives me percussive perspective when I ask for it, and sometimes when I don't.

One major thing that differentiates grape geeks from those who chase after other passions is that we tend to elaborate rhapsodically on our obsession in mind-numbing detail after the second or third glass, and sometimes before. We need someone like Annie around to call our attention to the fact that we're becoming socially disabled, a burden to those around us, and possibly a danger to ourselves and others.

We were in New York on a visit, celebrating the sixth or seventh anniversary of the fatal glass of Sauvignon Blanc when I got a whack from Annie. The impact jolted into focus the danger under discussion. One day in the middle of a chat about wine, she called my attention to the one-sidedness of my conversational technique. I was discussing, but nobody was listening. I was being boring and insensitive, or drunk and boring, or drunk and insensitive. Memory is unclear. She would never use those words, because she loves me, but when it came to my ardent babbling on a subject nobody in the group gave a crap about, her level of tolerance sort of scraped bottom.

It's not news that wine has an alcoholic dimension, and it's a good thing, too, because back in the Old Days, wine was the only liquid that was safe to drink. Water was deadly, milk could kill, but wine, thanks to the miracle of fermentation, kept everybody safe and happy. Still does, and that's where part of the dorkiness comes from.

There are other faults of the wine life, of course, including the always-present risk of going broke buying the next discovery, the inevitable purpling of the incisors, canines, and other dentition, ripping out rooms in the house to accommodate a part of a life that's insanely out of control, selling the children, that sort of thing. But the one act that most quickly compels my friends to leave me out on the ice to die is when I come to close to being a grape geek. Boring. Insensitive.

Sometimes, it's hard to resist. After four years of going to Wine Experiences, six years of tastings, and reading everything I could get my hands on that had anything to do with wine, I had accumulated a bit of knowledge, most of it, apparently, of absolutely no interest to anyone but myself.

Like that friend in the garage, or the one who shoves us down the stairs into the rec room where he's built a full scale computerized video game driving range, and compels us to try out his sixth new set of golf clubs, but we don't play.

Talk about it, spread it around, gain a few converts, maybe. There's certainly an element of proselytizing among wine lifers, arising from an admirable and altruistic desire to share with others the usually expensive delights we've discovered, and urge everyone toward those pleasures. Problem is, not everyone wants to be shared with. Or urged.

I have some very good friends who are bridge players, and they're insufferable. Personally, I never got around to learning the game, because with my mentality, I sensed that the attempt would be both misguided and futile, in that order.

But these bridge players. They spend two-three nights a week at the club, play in tournaments, do the quiz in the newspaper. I've been close to choking the life out of them more than once when they guffawed about how South should have led low from dummy when she pulled the second round of trumps because it was obvious that the spades broke three-two. The weird thing about bridge players is that none of them ever remember being beginners, and they don't remember learning the game.

They have a talent for it, an interest in it, and they've been doing it for so long that it's all so obvious to them, but not to you and me. Same with wine.

Cousin Annie likes to tell an old Hollywood joke. The movie star is out to dinner with a writer and the star says, "That's enough about me. Let's talk about you. What do you think of my work?"

There are, basically, two kinds of wine snobs. The most insufferable kind wears a tastevin around his neck, like that lumpy man who dangled his at the neighborhood wine shop tastings. He drinks only what he considers to be the very best, whether it's first growth Bordeaux or some obscure varietal from the Rhône. He cannot hide his disdain for consumers of white zinfandel, or any other kind of wine that you can buy at a convenience store. If the bottle at hand doesn't meet his criteria of quality, rarity, or obscurity, his lip curls, and he can barely conceal his contempt.

The other type is the cork dork, and becoming one is much easier. Anyone can do it, because it doesn't take all that much knowledge. It's the perfect example of that old "a little learning is a dangerous thing" proverb. I believe it's more or less axiomatic that you don't have to be much better than everybody else to be better than everybody else. The difference between the gold and silver at the Olympics is often a tenth of a second or quarter of an inch. With wine, I didn't have to know much, because so many people weren't interested enough to know anything.

It doesn't have a lot to do with the kind of wine or the price, though cork dorks, when they see people pulling gallon jugs of white zinfandel off the supermarket shelf, will often run up to them, grab them by the lapels, and box them about the head and shoulders, yelling "What the hell is wrong with you? Don't drink that crap!" Same for those who order a glass of Pinot Grigio in a restaurant out of simple unawareness of the delights some other decent and relatively inexpensive choice can offer. Cork dorks are boring and insensitive because they love wine no matter how much they've actually learned about it, they talk about it, shop for it, read about it, play with the bottles, collect corks, surf the web for information. They even try to write books. This often causes them to lose sight of the fact that most of their friends aren't nearly as agog about it all as they are.

Avid golfers, and I know a few, have friends who share the passion. They travel together to play distant courses and collect bag tags and logo balls. Same with my bridge friends, or anybody who develops an interest that bursts into his life and hijacks it.

Those who do not share a special fervency often have at least the basic decency to tolerate, out of simple courtesy, those who do. They will marvel (for a moment) at all the meticulous painstakingness performed on that enormous, highly-detailed model train village down in the basement, or make appropriate exhalations of wonderment (for a moment) at the collection of 458 pre-Civil War thimbles, but only to a point, and only once or twice. Keep talking, and there will be glassy eyes, slackened jaws, and occasional abrupt upward jerks of the head. And possibly gunplay.

Wine lifers hang out with other wine lifers, whom they meet at tastings and seminars. They go to dinner with them, invite them over for food and drink, share their latest discoveries, pass along information about which wine shops have what, and who charges how much. They form cute little tasting clubs and meet once a month to drink and discuss. And since it's endlessly fascinating, they never get tired of it. My friend Ron, who married the wine store manager's daughter, sends me an e-mail every Monday morning with a list of what he drank over the weekend at the bar mitzvah or wedding or restaurant or Chaîne des Rôtísseurs banquet. And I don't find him to be the least bit boring and insensitive for that reason. He's boring and insensitive for lots of other reasons. Not long ago, he sent me a list of the oldest vintages in his extensive collection, and I read it like a novel. Others might not read with the same avidity.

Likewise Cousins Douglas and Cynthia. They live in New York, so wine tastings and dinners are all over the place, and they go to a lot of them. Right after I read the summary from Ron, I read the description of all the wines and vintages they sampled over the weekend, and their point ratings.

Caution is essential. We still have friends whose palates and consciousness are elsewhere, and we want to preserve the relationships. I vividly remember the 1993 Ridge Montebello I tried once, the 1998 Masseto, and one or two other special bottles. I also have to remember that nobody else cares. They should, but they don't.

CHAPTER 19

Trinkets and Wampum

he makers of wines and spirits are not above shamelessly promoting their products with what the marketing industry calls "specialty advertising" or "promotional items." This category includes a virtual cornucopia of hats, bags, mugs, beer coolies, and even articles as elaborate as wall hangings, beach umbrellas, and entire pieces of furniture. I have them all. Here's how—and why.

March, 2004

Since 1997, Larry had happily shared my wine discoveries over the years, and I his. But his contribution to our relationship turned out to be much more far-reaching. His innocent initial act contributed to a broadening of my gustatory sensibilities and interests that was as panoramic as it was unexpected. But he also had an influence on the composition of my casual weekend wardrobe, and the décor of our home, far beyond the dreams of a Gucci or Coco Chanel. This all dawned on me, belatedly, almost seven years after it started. Sometimes, it takes that long.

When I moved my business to a new building next

to a doctor's office, I couldn't help noticing that she was constantly visited by what are called "detail people." Sales reps from the drug companies walked in and out all day long bearing gifts. Clipboards, ballpoint pens, and coffee cups, lots of coffee cups, all splashily imprinted with the polysyllabic and unpronounceable name of the medication they're intended to promote. The drug companies throw tons of money at this stuff, and they put a lot of wildly creative effort into the trinkets they spread around to the doctors and nurses. But compared to the wine and spirits people, they are mere infants, gone missing in the forest, lost and alone.

Wine and beer are recreational, and prescription drugs, for the most part, are not. That sort of puts a nasty fence around the promotional possibilities Big Pharma can exploit. But the liquor people? Well, by the time I realized what Larry had heaped upon us in the way of "promotional items," it was apparent that they had carte blanche, the freedom and license to conjure up giveaways with either direct or peripheral relationships to any sport, any pursuit, any locale. As a marketing person myself, it was evident that the wine and spirits companies employ battalions of unconventionally-minded individuals who do nothing with their lives but envision a cornucopian cascade of bangles, gewgaws, baubles, novelties, curios, ornaments, and knickknacks that inflicts hyper-ventilation upon all who stand before its majestic expanse. After almost 40 years in advertising and marketing, I've bought and received my share of them, and I can't even begin to stifle my shock and awe at what these people come up with. It's like standing on the rim of the Grand Canyon for the first time. The panorama is so vast that the mind loses all sense of distance, perspective, and scale. The landscape, due to its sheer magnitude, flattens out.

These trinkets and wampum items may include, but not be limited to, hats, shirts, ice buckets, bags, jackets, scarves, coffee cups, mugs, jugs, wine glasses, wine carriers, corkscrews, church keys, headbands, neckbands, armbands, kinky leather wristbands, socks, golf towels, beach towels, cheese boards, patio umbrellas, tablecloths, wall hangings, beer can coolies, pens, bottle stoppers, underwear, posters, clocks, plaques, table displays, placemats, bar mats, floor mats, beach towels, golf towels, bar towels, and all manner of logo apparel. I always wondered why Larry parked his car down the block from his house and it was because his garage was so full of this bounty that the space was no longer navigable. He couldn't give the golf shirts away fast enough.

Gradually, I became a head-to-toe walking advertisement for Johnny Walker Scotch, Tommy Bahama rum, and a multitude of wineries, and we shouldn't even go near the topic of the glasses, Champagne buckets, and dummy double magnums displayed in various nooks and niches around the house. Debi is similarly arrayed. But, since the possibilities of this industry are so immeasurable, Larry also had an impressive stock of dipped-in-testosterone wall décor within easy reach. Some of it is perfect adornment for a beach condo: tropical motifs, like bamboo-framed rum logos printed on what looks like old wood, but most is aimed directly at the questionable artistic sensibilities of the tavern traveler, and it's all just the most fun. Sports scenes, glow-in-the-dark beer logos, clocks, plaques, posters, wall hangings. If not for Larry the interior of our billiard room would never bathe our guests in the hearty masculine Gemütlichkeit that comes only from the distilled spirit world.

As I mentioned, Larry's largesse, and the catalog of items available from the Burns Collection, have, gradually and over time, clothed us and, to some extent, furnished our lives. He watched, amazed and perhaps a bit pitying, as we sank ever deeper, and planned the construction of a real wine cellar, upon which his imprint was to become clearly visible.

CHAPTER 20

Wine on the Web

*The Internet, as it has changed every aspect
of our society, has also changed just about everything
to do with wine. Here is the art of buying and selling
wine on the web, chat rooms, and wine geek goodies
that have never been available until now.*

April, 2004

Much too late, I was made aware of a wine world saying,
in the pseudo-Confucian style: Man who build wine room
double collection in one year. Couldn't happen to me, I
thought. But it did. The back bedroom had been sacrificed
to the obsession.

We started spending all kinds of money on all kinds of wine
because of one single circumstance. Of all the temptations
that beckon the hard core wine junkie, none is more
insidious, more vicious, more cynical in its manipulative
cruelty, than the Internet. We had been buying wine in
helpless, compulsive response to email solicitations for a
while, but the Internet found new ways to grab us by the
collar, pull us in, and cause us to double our collection and
halve our savings. I can't say we weren't warned. Whether

it's hand-made copper kitchen sinks or photos of Brazilian transvestites, the Web has made the pursuit of every enthusiasm, compulsion, and fetish quick, easy, practically free, and overwhelming in its offerings of information and advice. Wine lifers are certainly not proof against its blandishments. It was only a matter of time before we discovered that every single winery had a site where we could learn more about their products than anyone would ever care to know, right down to the barometric pressure and relative humidity on the day the grapes were picked.

There are hundreds of sites, thousands even, and from the time we built out the back bedroom, around Christmas of 2001, all through the following year, I'm sure we looked at most of them. Our stash of some 200 bottles, which we thought was so rich and overwhelming, made no impression whatsoever in the new room; indeed, our paltry collection was lost among the 514 allotted spaces. There were really even fewer bottles in sight, because half of them were in the wine refrigerator I had assembled with my own two badly-scarred hands, so every time I stared at the empty rack spaces along the walls, they cried out to me like abandoned children for fulfillment and completion. Hard to resist. Practically impossible.

Some winery web sites are intellectual, others, like Randall Grahm's Bonny Doon site, are funny as hell. Every wine magazine and publication has a site, some free, some by subscription, offering wine ratings (of course), recommendations, history, articles on winemaking in some obscure Chilean highland, food and wine pairings, restaurant reviews, recipes, links to wine retailers, just type in a search word and be whisked away.

Then there are sites by the critics themselves, such as

Robert Parker's Wine Advocate, Steven Tanzer's site, and others set up by individuals who want to impart their considered opinions on a particular type of wine or region, and will share their knowledge for a monthly fee. I signed up.

Naturally, there are wine stores on the web, retail sites that list and sell their wares, offering those of us in the boonies access to wines that may not be available locally. One such specializes in discounting closeout lots of wine, and sends me five or six emails a day, with offering after tempting offering.

But the very worst kind of web enterprise, the lowest, most subtly menacing, the road to hell paved with the foulest of intentions, are the wine auction sites, damn them. The fact that auctions are seductive is no news, but I never suspected that being seduced was going to lead me to study some serious issues in the Constitution of the United States. Wine takes you places.

One goes to wine auctions (whether live or on the Web) because most rare or desirable wines are available nowhere else, not even in the largest stores. There are the cult wines, made in yearly runs of 500 to 1,000 cases, that never trickle down to ye olde wine shoppe, or the rare French and Italian wines, of which maybe 50 cases will be imported into the United States and sold to those "special select" people we discussed earlier. That's twelve bottles for each state in the union, or maybe thirteen because most of it never gets to Alaska. I bought a bottle in Ketchikan one day and it was so awfully spoiled that I barely got the cork out of the bottle before reeling in disgust and staggering backward.

There are other wines in more plentiful supply, but sometimes the critics go ballistic about a particular vintage, as happened in the case of the 1997 Brunello di Montalcino, and the California Cabernets of the same year. As soon as the ratings came out, the bottles vanished from the shelves, no matter how many cases were originally produced. The prices of many 1997 Brunellos have more than doubled or tripled since the wine was released, and even if I were willing to pay the heavenly prices, there was only a slim chance I'd ever find any, and then only in the most complete wine stores, in the largest cities.

But the auction sites? Well, the rare and unusual wines are all over the place. Bottles of 1874 Chateau d'Yquem, 1945 Lafite, the mythical 1961 vintage of Bordeaux, legendary labels and obscure vintages abound.

Note to self: stay off the wine auction sites. Ah, if only I could, for the sake of sanity if not economy, but they are succubi, sirens beckoning us to financial wreck and ruin on the shoals. Auction sites are kind of like wine porn, page after page of photos of labels that make me open my eyes wider, lean closer to the monitor and say "ooohhh." They are well outside community standards, appealing as they do directly to the prurient interest. It took a while, but we gradually summoned enough collective willpower to limit ourselves to two of them, because each has its own advantages and disadvantages, which we discovered only through hard experience, and trial and error.

This is worth a word or two, because even though the two sites have much in common, they operate (and charge) very differently.

Just like eBay or any good online store, the sites have a graphic format for displaying the wares of the seller. There's room for photos, reprints of wine reviews, the scores the

wines were awarded, a place where users can post their
feedback about their experience with the seller, search
features that allow the lookup of wines by name, region,
type, year, etc., and a way to flag and track the items as the
auctions progress. But that's where the similarities end.

The first kind, typified by winebid.com, is much like a
regular auction house. Headquartered in an anonymous but
well-refrigerated warehouse in an industrial park just south
of the city of Napa, they accept lots from sellers, store
them, evaluate them, collect and disburse money and ship
to buyers. For so doing, they charge a commission on the
"hammer price" from both buyer and seller. At this writing,
the commission was around 12% to 13% on each end.
Add to that the cost for the seller to ship it to the regional
warehouse (Winebid has several around the country), and
then for the auction house to ship it to the buyer (a case
of wine weighs around 42 lbs., and costs a bundle to ship
since it pretty much has to go overnight or second day air, so
that it doesn't wind up boiling in some shipping company
warehouse for a week), and the cost gets kicked up by a
significant amount. With all those front end and back end
commissions and extra charges, what's the benefit to
the buyers?

Basically, the wine comes with some reasonable
assurance that it's not crap. The biggest risk in buying wine
at auction is the provenance of the product. (When it
comes to wine, the French have a word for everything.)
Provenance basically means "where it comes from" but
like most French words, means a little more than that. It
embodies both the storage conditions (proper temperature
and humidity, kept away from light, stored horizontally)
and the condition of the bottle itself. Is the label clean and

in one piece? Is it moldy? Is the level of the wine up to the neck of the bottle? Is the capsule intact? The last thing any collector wants to do is pay $5,875 for a single bottle of 1947 Chateau Pétrus and discover that the seller stored it in the trunk of his car in July in Las Cruces, New Mexico.

When Winebid receives bottles and cases from sellers, each is inspected for condition and ullage (the level of the wine in the bottle, since the contents of older bottles diminish over time). The seller "represents" that the wine was kept under proper conditions, but that's pretty much anybody's guess. At least Winebid says it's in good shape, and it's stored well once they receive it.

When I win an auction (should I be mentally disturbed enough to bid), Winebid rapes my credit card and ships me the lot. Voila, I've easily bought desirable wine from the comfort of my own computer, and it was quick, clean, and (except for the payment) painless.

The second, and somewhat homier way to buy wine is through Wine Commune. The name "commune" is aptly chosen, because the feeling here is more like a community of wine lovers sharing their interests than it is the Sotheby's-like online image of a Winebid. There are three differences between the sites, and they're major. Allow me to consider two of them here, and the third a bit later, because it's huge.

First, sellers do not send their products to be evaluated, or kept in the custody of the auction house. Wine Commune exists entirely in cyberspace. Buyers place their bids on the site, and if they win, they contact the seller directly to arrange payment and shipment. The downside is that there's no guarantee that you're not dealing with a phantom scam artist who, like Matilda in the Harry Belafonte song, will take your money and run Venezuela. Wine Commune guards against this much the way eBay does, by providing a "feedback" section, where buyers post their opinions of the seller, and evaluate the quality of the transaction. So it makes sense to buy from people who have lots of favorable comments. The sellers with unfavorable reviews disappear sooner or later. Darwinism in its purest form.

(I had only one semi-negative experience shopping in this way. The seller sent me the wrong wine, but it was better than the stuff I originally ordered, so I kept it.)

Second, since the company doesn't actually handle any product itself the overhead is minimal, so they charge the seller 3% to list a lot, and the buyer nothing. Suddenly, the cost of the wine I buy has dropped as much as 24%, plus the 6% or 7% I don't pay in sales tax, miscreant that I am.

The third factor, to be discussed later on, is how the wine gets shipped from the sellers to the buyers. There is a controversy about direct shipping, and it quite literally involves very deep, and very interesting issues of Constitutional law. In 2005, the Supreme Court struck down individual states' laws against direct shipping, but the states are fighting back. Virginia, for example, allows out-of-state wineries to ship to its residents. One bottle at a time. Some other states are just as restrictive, but that's a topic for another chapter. Soon.

CHAPTER 21

Fulfilling the Obsession Yet Another Way

It's the wine cave again, but this time it's serious. When we had the opportunity to build a new home the sickness once again made itself felt. Worse than before.

August, 2004

The next step was perhaps the most critical phase of the obsession—the one where we irrevocably surrendered to the unyielding urges that had gripped us for the past eight or so years. It happened when we got the opportunity to build a new home. First time in our lives, and I left the entire project (except for one thing) to Debi, who designed it from scratch and supervised the year-long construction, breaking into tears only twice. The wine room was my job.

A wine room in the new house? If ever a conclusion was foregone, this was it. As I mentioned, I had already been told (warned is a better word) during our first venture into wine room installation that when one builds a wine room, the collection doubles in a year. We had experienced exactly that phenomenon. Clearly, strong measures needed to be taken.

After several years of attendance at the Wine Experience,
I had met many collectors who, out of vanity and necessity,
had built similar facilities, and asked them for advice. They
all told me the same thing, in mostly the same words: "Make
it as big as you can." (Miles, the poor soul, built one wine
room in his house, then a second. Then ripped out half his
basement and put in a *real* cellar.)

Tearing up the back bedroom gave us a taste of it. But
then, with the new house, we got the opportunity to kick
the silliness up more than a notch, sort of like my friend
Rick. For him, it's the satisfaction of having played golf at
seven of the ten most famous courses in the world. Maybe
more by now. Pebble Beach? He did it twice. St. Andrews?
He has the bag tag. For us, it was the Vision of a wine room
like the kind they have in restaurants. Thermo-glass doors.
Maybe a glass wall. Over a thousand bottles. A ladder on
rails so we could slide it around to reach those obscure
bottles all the way on top. A tasting table with a painted-
tile mural of the Tuscan countryside on the wall behind it.
Wooden cases stacked on the floor. We got most of it, but
had to do without the ladder and glass wall. I also resisted
the temptation of installing those showy shelves and display
racks, because they reduced the overall capacity. "Make it
as big as you can."

The process started late in 2004. The original 200 bottles
that the back-bedroom wine cave had absorbed and
concealed so easily had new neighbors in the pin racks.
I had made contact with a company that designs custom
racking systems, traveled three hours to meet with their
representative in St. Petersburg, and was waiting for her to
send me some drawings, proposals, and (gulp) price quotes.

Meanwhile, we had added a new dimension to the

preparations for our annual wine orgy in New York, and to our collecting activities, which required us to take even greater pains, and we suffered them gladly.

Since discovering each other in 2000, Cousin Douglas and I had evolved a tradition of dragging each other's wine purchases around the country. He would find deals and bargains and buy them for me, and I for him. Pretty soon I was holding a case or two of what he bought, and he was in the same condition, the other way around.

Back in the days of paradise, before people tried to bomb airplanes with their tennis shoes or tighty whities, when we could travel with liquid in our carryons, it was no big deal. Douglas and I had each acquired identical roll-on wine carriers as gifts from our respective wives: small padded suitcases on wheels that fit conveniently in the overhead, with cushioned compartments that cradled 12 bottles. It took a bit of work to hoist up there, since a case of wine weighs about 50 pounds, but it was good exercise. Those days were over.

In order to keep the tradition alive, Debi bought me a SkyCrate. It is not merely a wine carrier on wheels; neither can it be tritely described as a wine carrier on steroids. It's much more than that. It is built to (I think) military combat specifications from impenetrable molded fiberglass in a depressing grey color with dull chrome metal fittings. It is squat, rectangular and menacing. If someone wanted to transport a tactical nuclear device or a few pounds of Kryptonite, they'd put it in a SkyCrate. When I wheeled it to the check-in desk at the airport for the first time, I could actually see the security people perk up like a bunch of meerkats, those cute furry mongoose-like critters who live in the Kalahari desert and spend most of their time sitting up on their hind legs, staring with huge black eyes the size of silver dollars. For TSA personnel, the sight of this thing must have been a shot of adrenaline right to the heart. I thought I could see them start to drool.

Inside, the Skycrate is solid soft foam, with scalloped holes cut to cradle and caress each individual bottle. If it somehow fell out of the airplane at 35,000 feet, nothing would ever break.

This particular piece of luggage is an embarrassing indication of how serious things had become in such a pitiably short time. We traveled with wine, and not just a couple of bottles. Cases. We brought our own glasses to restaurants, geeks that we were.

Sidebar: Speaking of restaurants, Bern Laxer, the late and much-lamented owner of Bern's Steak House in Tampa, Florida, is known to have assembled over 500,000 bottles and 6,800 individual labels in the restaurant's cellar(s), making it one of the largest restaurant wine collections in the world, right up there with the Tour d'Argent in Paris. Bern didn't have to hide his cellar from the Nazis the way André Terrail did, but his restaurant has a special place in our hearts, not the least because the wine list is published in a hardcover edition the size of the Moscow white pages. It take three strong waiters to lift one, and for some reason they chain them to the tables. The wine lists, not the waiters.

Early in the obsession, we discovered that the wine selection at Bern's is so impenetrable that the best thing to do is put ourselves into the hands of one of the sommeliers and beg for mercy. When we met Douglas and Cynthia, they let us know that they had made more than one intentional journey from New York to Tampa, just to eat at Bern's, and when we finally joined them, we invariably applied this tactic: decide on a wine budget, tell the sommelier "we have X dollars for the wine, we want a white and two reds, and you pick 'em." Always been surprised, never been disappointed. (In fact, Bern's has become a new family tradition for dinner on New Year's Eve).

The restaurant is famous for its wine list, its steaks, and its décor, which reminds most first timers of a 19th Century Parisian bordello, but not quite as classy. Nonetheless, its place in our hearts and our relationship originates from other, more emotional reasons, one minor and one very major.

In 1971 and 1972, I lived in Spain, and then in Israel. Coming back to the States and starting all over again in Tampa was something of a relief, but a few years later I saw a notice in *Advertising Age* magazine that a marketing firm in Bangkok, Thailand, was looking for a writer and creative director. The urge to get out of the country hit me anew. My hands were not my own; autonomously, they wrote an application letter despite all the solid reasons why packing up and leaving again for a job fourteen time zones away wasn't a good idea.

One of the job requirements was "proven ability to live in and adapt to foreign cultures." Well, that was me. Even though I was sure that the differences among Madrid, Tel Aviv, and Bangkok would reach far beyond the merely linguistic, I had that qualification, so I made the cut for interviews.

The agency, instead of flying all eight or nine finalists to the Orient for a look-see, wisely and economically sent one of its executives over to travel around North America and conduct the face to face on the applicants' home ground.

When he came to Tampa and called me, I asked him what he would like for dinner.

"A good piece of fish and a nice bottle of wine," he replied.

"Which is more important?" I asked. I hadn't even met him yet.

"The wine."

"We're going to Bern's."

I must not have impressed him, because I didn't get the job. He was, however, so overwhelmed by the wine list that he plunked down $35 and bought one to take home. This was long before I had taken that fateful first sip, but even then I could see that there was something to this wine thing, after all.

Then, in 1993 when Debi and I started dating, we lived about 150 miles apart and would join up on weekends. Early on, to show her what a suave urbane sophisticate I was, I splurged on Bern's one night, and while the dinner and wine selection didn't completely close the deal, it did get me to second base.

Then, a year later, it was Bern's again. After the second bottle and halfway through dessert, I struggled down to one knee next to the table, took Debi's hand and asked the Big Four-Word-Question. That time, I got the job.

CHAPTER 22

Wine and the Sports Hero

The wine world is a magnet for celebrities. We've been to tastings hosted by some of the most famous winemakers in the world, and sipped alongside celebrities from sports, television, and film. As we developed our taste for wine and started attending ever-larger and ever-more-expensive events, we became haunted by the appearance of a Hall of Fame baseball player. Since then, he's been everywhere, and we can't get rid of him.

December, 2004

The wine life takes us places. We explore, we quest, we thirst. Long ago, the impressive yet still limited selection at the local retailer ceased to arouse. We'd either worked through them all, put aside the ones we were sure we wouldn't like, and tried to ignore the ones we couldn't afford. Most of them.

We wanted different. New varietals, new vintages. Wines so rare or so laughably expensive that we'd never buy them on our own unless we got up the nerve to murder Grandma and take over her charitable foundation.

That's what made me salivate on those ads for the Wine
Experience, drove us there, and then took us beyond, to
the world of bigger time tastings: the charity auctions.

Some big time tastings are staged at fancy restaurants
and sponsored by a particular wine store, which is common
in the larger cities. Cousin Douglas has paid well over $300
a person to go to tastings where only California cult wines
from the 1990 vintage were served. Considering that the
bottles are worth up to $700 each, he thinks it's a bargain.

Some are organized by private bands of aficionados, like the
Wine Berserkers. I have no idea who chose the name, but
he or she was a genius, because they hold wine happenings
all over the country, all year around. Go on the website,
find out the location of the next event, and show up with
a couple of your favorite bottles.

Still other tastings are larger, more elaborate, and go on
for days. Just about every city and town in America has one.
There are "wine festivals" in places as diverse as Boston,
Washington DC, Albany, Omaha, and the Florida Wine
Fest every April in Sarasota. They have become a favorite
fundraising tactic of the "party with a purpose" crowd, who
look for the most enjoyable ways to raise money for charity.
Some of these bashes are so pervasive, and so elaborate,
that they rate a whole separate chapter, which I'll get
around to sooner or later. Maybe even next.

Big time tastings are important not only because they
raise millions for people who need it, but because the wine
life is especially adept at reeling in celebrities. Not so much
at the annual Wine Experiences, though every famous
winemaker in the world is there, and in past years, Francis
Ford Coppola could be spotted in the crowd. I doubt that

the average person would recognize celebrity winemakers Piero Antinori or Angelo Gaja on the street, except for the exquisite Italian tailoring of their suits. Maybe Robert Mondavi had attracted a glance or two when he was still with us, but most of them, no matter how wonderful their wines, pass unnoticed.

But as I said, the charity juice jubilees stand a good chance of being patronized by movie and television notables, the rich, the famous, and sometimes both.

Enjoying wine is a lot like being a polo fan. We can pay to watch the matches, but if we don't have the money, we'll never get to ride the horse. So we splurge on the long-weekend big time tastings not for the celebrities, but in hopes of tasting wines so rare or so insanely expensive that we, as non-dot com millionaires, would have absolutely no chance of getting our hands on in the normal course of our lives unless we cashed in our children's college fund, and don't think we haven't considered it.

The really big events cost a fortune, but the wines they pour are so legendary and so hard to come by that for some people the experience almost justifies the price. Almost. For some people. They often surpass the Wine Experience, not necessarily in terms of quantity, because no private charity auction can summon 250 wineries to a grand tasting as persuasively as Marvin Shanken, but since many of the sponsors and trustees of these charity to-dos kick in bottles from deep in their private cellars, one often finds astonishing wines from fabled vintages on the table.

Although the larger wine events attract celebrity chefs, owners of famous restaurants, yacht captains, jurists with their own television shows, movie directors, and sitcom actors, they also attract sports stars, and that's what worries me the most. Very soon after we tumbled down the hole into wine wonderland, in fact at our first Wine Experience, we started having visions of actors, television personalities, and all-star baseball players. Not current ones, either—just guys who haven't been on a ball field since around 1971. Specifically, Rusty Staub. Le Grand Orange himself.

Flash forward: in July of 2006, we attended our first Wine & Food Festival in Aspen, the trip and our admission to most of the private to-the-trade events facilitated by (guess who) Larry Burns. The first day there, as Deb and I hurried past the main square, we heard people saying, "Hi, George." "How's it going, George." Looking to our left, Debi spotted the obsessively bronzed loveliness of George Hamilton as he ambled, and while he ignored my remark about how much I'd enjoyed his performance in "Love at First Bite," he was quick to put his arm around Debi and clasp her unto himself for a photo op. And a bit less quick to release her, if I remember. She didn't mind.

The baseball player sightings were as alarming as they were frequent. I suspect that everyone who populates the wine life has similar visions, though I can't prove it because nobody ever talks about it. I further suspect that each of us can see a baseball player or other sports figure who, like our own private Harvey, is invisible to the rest of the world. I'm not sure, though, if the players are assigned to our particular sight by reason of the position they played (I was hoping for a third baseman), how they match up with our own personalities, or if it's just a matter of blind fortune. Maybe it depends on how old our souls are, or our worth as an individual, measured against some kind of cosmic spiritual yardstick that's beyond our understanding. I think some people might see Phil Rizzuto or Whitey Ford. Me, I see Rusty Staub. Debi sees him, too. Cousin Douglas catches a flash of Bert Blyleven sometimes, but it's not a regular thing, and it unsettles him.

After discussing the phenomenon at length, we honestly can't figure out what causes this. Deb thinks it's lucky for us that Rusty's incognito skills are not exactly well-honed, so he's pretty easy to spot. He's not a small man, and he does, in fact, have that eponymous hair. I've never been a baseball fan, but if I'm going to have visions of ballplayers, I want one I can at least recognize. Thankfully, our personal major league hallucination is comfortably obvious.

Thinking back, I realize that our Staubian sightings didn't actually occur until we'd started going to some of the bigger wine events in major cities. We went to ten tastings at Crazy Bernie's Discount Liquor Barn, got our frequent buyer card punched, and were never blessed with a vision of Mickey Mantle. Baseball legends have not generally manifested themselves in the Super Tuscan section of our favorite wine stores—we've been watching—except in certain Arizona or Florida cities like Clearwater or Fort Myers when said municipalities are awash in Spring Training. Those times, we could stand at the cash register next to Mark McGwire or Jose Canseco, and be thrilled, if we knew what they looked like.

The initial apparition of Le Grande Orange was at the first New York Wine Experience we attended, in 2000. The sightings were repeated for years, which is what led to the realization. Given that Rusty made his appearance just after we'd sampled our eighth or fourteenth glass of wine, we shouldn't have been too startled. As visions go, it could have been a whole lot more disturbing, like having Nuestra Señora de Guadeloupe float before our startled eyes, or Dennis Rodman. Rusty is okay as apparitions go (Lord knows I've seen worse), even though some sports writers have described him as "leading the league in idiosyncrasies." At least he belongs in the wine tasting environment, being something of a gourmet chef and owner of a restaurant on the Upper East Side of Manhattan. Short walk to the wine life from there.

I was a little disappointed that Rusty wasn't a private vision, because Cousin Douglas saw him too. "Rusty Staub and Ty Cobb are the only players to homer before age 20 and after age 40," he whispered at our first shared sighting. "Willie Mays missed by 23 days. He's the only major leaguer to play in 500 games for four teams, and get 500 hits for four teams. He also set a Mets record for RBIs in 1975."

"That's pretty exciting." Douglas is a Mets fan, and at the Wine Experience, he follows Rusty around.

Staub won't go away. Less than a year after our first sighting, he appeared to Debi alone, an apparition once again confirmed by Cousins Douglas and Cynthia. The three of them were doing a Burgundy tasting at the ultra-fashionable W hotel in midtown Manhattan, and there he was.

"Never guess who I saw at the tasting tonight," said Debi, reporting back to me, a sudden indisposition having prevented my attendance.

"Dennis Rodman?"

"No."

And then it happened again, not long after, at the Naples Winter Wine Festival. Blue blazer, red hair. No mistake. I'm hoping that we'll start spotting him at other, less major wine events. I've kind of gotten used to him.

CHAPTER 23

Wine Friends, and Friends of Friends

hanks to our love of wine, and our willingness to spend silly amounts of money buying it, we've met people who have been invariably gracious, welcoming, warm, and interesting, and we treasure the relationships. We have eliminated from our lives anyone who doesn't drink. Shame on us.

January, 2005

There's a program on cable TV called Dirty Jobs, or Disgusting Occupations, or something like that, about people who support their families by spending their days as roadkill collectors or chicken busters or catfish noodlers, or some such. It makes me think about all the things that I would not do for a living, even under threat of slow starvation or fatal violence, or both.

By the beginning of 2005, we'd been to five Wine Experiences, Miles and Tony had shown us wine country from the inside out, and we'd grand toured most of the tasting rooms, if not all. Those travels brought me to the understanding that there are things I'd love to do for a living

—wine things—if I weren't writing and doing marketing. In our travels, I met people who have the best jobs in the world, instead of the worst. Like Bruce Sanderson, with whom we've spent many happy hours. Bruce is Senior Editor of *Wine Spectator*, and we met him a year or two after we first started bankrupting ourselves by going to the Wine Experience.

Bruce used to have the best job in the world, traveling through Burgundy, Champagne, and Germany, sampling and critiquing and writing. Flash forward: As I write this, he's been forced out of that position to the best *best* job in the world, now being responsible for sampling and critiquing and writing about the wines of Italy and Bordeaux. I'd take his place on the Burgundy beat, if they'd let me.

Another person in the wine world who has a good job, in a different way than Bruce's, is Neil Aldoroty, who was creative enough to invent his own profession. He built a wine storage facility in St. Helena, smack in the middle of Napa Valley. With his wife Karen, they own a vast warehouse, carefully maintained at 55 degrees Fahrenheit and 70% humidity, where collectors store their wine, and wineries send their orders for reshipment to buyers. That means Neil knows just about everybody who grows grapes, makes bottles, prints labels, imports corks, crushes, ferments, drinks, name it. If they have anything to do with the wine business, the Aldorotys know the names of their kids. Fortunately, Neil is generous enough to give smaller wineries a boost by tipping off his subscribers to the Next Big Thing. Right after our initial revelatory Napa trip with Miles and Tony, we inscribed ourselves on his mailing list, much in the way that Jewish people pray to be inscribed in the Book of Life every Rosh Hashonah.

Every so often, he sends an email blast to people who store their wines with him, recommending a new discovery that absolutely nobody has ever heard of. People who produce maybe 150-200 cases a year, doing it for love and fun, growing or buying the best grapes, tapping into talented winemaking consultants, and turning out classy Cabernets and memorable Merlots that will never, never appear on local wine store shelves.

That's how we found Gary, Ricardo, Walter and Joan.

"There's this new winery called Garric Cellars," was the sense of one of Neil's emails. Gary Ochwat and Ricardo Cajulis, it turned out, were two doctors from Chicago who had bought a home in Calistoga and were Following the Dream, making some excellent high-end Cabernet. Garric Cellars. Gary and Rick. So I ordered six bottles from their web site, and emailed them to ask if they would hold them for us, since we'd be in Napa a few months later and could come by to pick them up.

Well, I called Gary just before the trip to arrange a visit to the winery to get the bottles.

"We don't have a winery," he said. "Why don't you just come over for lunch?"

Huh? This is the kind of thing that takes one aback, and truly exemplifies the seductive charm of the wine life. Why would someone not only invite a complete stranger to his house, but offer him sustenance, besides? For all he knew, I could be the leader of a gang of mother rapers and father stabbers, rampaging through wine country leaving horror, devastation, and bloody dismemberment in our wake. I guessed that being a customer of Neil's confirmed our bona fides, and that was good enough for Gary.

So Deb and I went, accompanied by Miles and Tony, who had never heard of either the two doctors or their wines. We knocked, and Ricardo opened the door.

"Wait!" exclaimed Debi. "I know you." So did the rest of us. We'd been seeing him and his partner Gary at the Wine Experience for years, but had never personally met. Conversation never lagged as they grilled our steaks and opened their bottles, and we've been friends ever since.

Same thing happened with Walter and Joan. Another email blast from Neil and another Hot Tip, this time about the Teachworths, who, like the two doctors, had also followed the dream and were making killer high-end red somewhere up on Diamond Mountain. We called to find out about picking up the wine, and next thing we knew we were sitting on the balcony of their house, admiring the sweeping panorama of the mountains and the valley below, eating their food and petting their dog, whose name was Asta, because Walter had been a big fan of the famous "Thin Man" movies of the 1930s.

And so it went, one life event after another, drawing us closer to the places wine comes from, and the people who make it. Near our house, I'm guessing it was around 2005, a chef named Preston Dishman opened a restaurant called Dragonfly, and it was sensational. Not expensive, with great food and atmosphere. Debi and I went there on an extremely regular basis, and it's where we met Tom and Sandy. I've mentioned Tom before.

"There's this couple I want you to meet," Preston said one night, hovering over our table. "They're in here all the time and they really like wine." Hell, we'll meet anybody who likes wine.

"I'll bring them over."

Preston bustled to a neighboring table, said a few words to the couple seated there, and herded them over to us. When Tom sat down, he put a bottle of Sine Qua Non Grenache on the table. I'd never had it, but recognized the name because that wine had been a dream of mine for years, but it cost $350 a bottle and was so rare that it made the famous cult wines look like tap water. When I saw them edging their way between the chairs to join us, I whispered to Debi.

"Anybody who brings a $350 bottle of wine to dinner is my kind of guy."

Preston operated the restaurant for a little under two years, then was offered another opportunity…as partner in a very well known establishment in the town of Sonoma, handing us yet another connection to the area.

To paraphrase Kurt Vonnegut, we were the victims of a series of accidents. Happy ones.

CHAPTER 24

Big Time Tastings

It's inevitable. As we developed a taste for wine, we graduated from the monthly tastings at the local wine store and started traveling to larger-scale wine events that cost a lot more money. And boy, do they ever.

January, 2005

Got a bit off track, there, so I'll try this again.

Around the end of 2004, as we sank ever more deeply toward the bottom of the barrel, there was a peculiar sensation of moving up and down at the same time. It had been about eight years since the Cloudy Bay Revelation, when we took that transformational sip, dashed past the rabbit with the waistcoat and pocket watch, and found ourselves, like Alice, in a seductive, confusing world, where new interests bloomed like those flowers with faces in the Disney version of the story, and new discoveries lay as a lush carpet under our feet. When it comes to hobbies and interests, some are born to the cat fancy, some achieve model railroading, and others have the wine life thrust upon them. The awakening happens when unrealized predisposition meets unexpected circumstance.

I recalled that, in the aftermath and wreckage of Larry and Charlene's departure on our fateful first evening together, several empty bottles were resting in the recycling bin and we were resting on the kitchen floor. Later that week we started buying more than one bottle of one thing at a time, becoming initiated quickly into the miraculous Case Discount, by which we could save a lot of money simply by spending more. It was the beginning of the end. We felt warm pulses of perverted personal accomplishment and spiritual completion with every case we brought home, and wouldn't have been surprised if our friends had attempted to carry out a court-ordered intervention by licensed and certified mental health professionals. But we didn't understand what being devoured by the wine world was really like until Larry asked us to volunteer.

"We need help at the Winter Wine Festival down in Naples," he had said a few weeks before the New Year. "You and Debi want to work?"

Well, hell yes. We had just come back from another Wine Experience where Debi had taken her fifth annual photo with Piero Antinori. I can't imagine he really knows who we are, or recalls us from year to year, but he smiles uncomplainingly for the camera every time Debi hugs up to him. Anyway, it seemed to me that being a volunteer at the richest most successful charity wine event on the planet wouldn't be much like real work. Since Larry works for a wine distributor, and since they were very heavily involved in supporting charity events, he had something of an inside track.

The Naples Winter Wine Festival, as it prepared for its

annual event in February of 2005, had become, in the few very brief years since its founding, the pre-eminent wine weekend and charity auction on the entire surface of the earth. Raising literally tens of millions for community causes in Collier County, Florida, it attracted an annual pride of luminaries from the stratospheres of wine, food, and entertainment, as well as the very rich but not very famous, many of whom like to spend their winters in the balmy humidity of Southwest Florida, playing golf and smoking cigars. Not for them the glitz of the Palm Beaches or Hobe Sound, or the private enclaves along the Florida Atlantic coast, but rather the very laid back and anonymous world of Naples, with its Port Royal, Millionaire's Row, and radiant beaches fronting the tepid waters of the Gulf of Mexico, an easy yacht ride to Key West.

Some weekend wine events, like the Wine Experience, are for tasting only, and don't provide any opportunity to buy what's being poured. Too bad, because they could move a lot of cases if they let us take it home. It's as inevitable as the Black Tie Gala…we sample 200 wines in three days, and even though the flavors, like our mental processes, start to melt and run together after a while, two or three of the samples do grab us in our intimate places and spirit us away. At tastings like that, where we shuffle from table to table holding out our glasses for the next pour and the next, we're lucky if we remember anything at all. So under those conditions, when we taste a wine we do remember, we'd nuke the Amex for it on the spot, but sorry, it's not for sale. At one Wine Experience, Debi tasted something that transported her so completely that she excused herself, rushed up to our room, fired up the laptop and ordered a case online. Cost us $3,600.

It's at the other big time tastings that wines are actually available for purchase, but not at retail, or anything close. They're being auctioned off for noble charitable purposes, and we think more than twice about making a bid. The ante, shall we say, is up there where supplemental oxygen is required for everyone on board, and the stars shine during the day. These events raise gratifying amounts of money by receiving donations of rare wines, trips, and other life experiences, organizing the donations into auction lots, then putting them up for bid. Some, like the Florida Winefest & Auction held in Sarasota, which we started to attend around 2003, are relatively reasonably priced. Relatively. Even we could go, even back then, and we did, for about three years. There were a few grand tastings, a wine lunch and dinner, and a Saturday afternoon brunchie sip and snack thing, followed by the auction. Those who conduct such events want to make sure that (A) they host the weekend someplace obscenely beautiful and expensive, and (B) the attendees snack a little and sip a lot, because while ancient history tells us there is truth in wine, there is also astounding generosity. Give the group enough samples of enough wines, and the credit cards quake in trepidation, then run for cover.

The toll for the thing in Sarasota was about $600 a person, which we could almost afford as long as the cats didn't eat for about a month and we walked everywhere we needed to go. The tariff included admission to the brunch and charity auction, the inescapable Black Tie Dinner and Dance, and a few other activities. The hotel was on us. Attending the supplemental sessions, such as the conducted tastings and off-premise wine dinners at the city's finest white tablecloths, set us back an amount that would not be appropriate to mention. And that was cheap, as long as we behaved ourselves at the auction and didn't suffer a fatal attack of paddle twitch when the Big Reds came on the block. Better to stick to bidding on the silent auction items, where emotions run quite a bit cooler.

As big time tastings go, the Florida Winefest didn't hurt our meager credit line too badly, and it was a relatively tame event. But it was the first time, even though we'd been going to the Wine Experience for five or six years, that we were able to chat with winemakers like normal people, because there weren't fifteen hundred swarming wine lifers packed together in that fifth floor ballroom, nudging our elbows and giving us the occasional Burgundy baptism.

This was more up close and personal. At dinner we sat with Christina Mariani May and her father, John Mariani. Since John had experienced no little success in importing and selling Reunite Lambrusco to the US in the mid-seventies he was well resourced enough to buy a real castle in Tuscany, and their Castello Banfi wines set a new (very untraditional) standard for Tuscan winemaking.

I guess we knew most of that when we met them, and had certainly tasted Castello Banfi wines, but never understood the scope of who they were and what they did until years later, when we spent an afternoon at their place near Montalcino. They own a *castle*, with turrets and crenulations and everything.

The other personage who caught my attention in Sarasota was Paul Pontallier, who I have mentioned a few times already. He is the estate manager for Chateau Margaux, and was standing all by himself in the middle of the Saturday afternoon buffet lunch (and tasting) with absolutely nobody going near him.

Gadzooks, I thought, or something like that in Middle English. This man makes one of the most famous, most historic wines on earth, he's the Beethoven of the barrel room, the Velasquez of the vineyard, standing on the highest peak of his profession, and he looked like he was in quarantine, the flow of munchers and sippers eddying around and past, as though he were infected with kwashiorkor or some other loathsome disease. I didn't dare try out my French on him, but he was amenable to conversation in English. I told him we'd met before at other events, and he listened to my questions and suffered my ignorance with Gallic courtliness and noble grace.

This was an out of body experience. I stood next to myself and thought "NASCAR." I'm not a fan myself, but I'm told that one of the major appeals of high level motor sports is that the drivers commit themselves to being completely accessible to the fans. Anybody can walk up to the biggest names in racing and have a friendly talk. M. Pontallier showed me that winemakers do the same thing. So did the castle owner at dinner the previous night, who treated us like his next door neighbors. And there next to me was the maker of one of France's five first growth Bordeaux, asking me, "Est-ce que vous habitez ici?"

So, a discovery. We'll probably never meet a winemaker we don't like.

When Larry asked us go help out at the Naples event, we signed up, despite the advice to the exact contrary regarding volunteering by my Army veteran father. I didn't care. The NWWF, like a few other charity wine jubilees, was famous for being less reasonably priced than the weekends we'd enjoyed, and less restrained. We could never afford to be real attendees.

Another wine blast that falls into the less-restrained category is held every year in Napa Valley, peopled by everybody who's anybody in the wine business and the world of entertainment, dashing men wearing Hong Kong custom tailored sport coats that cost as much as a small airplane, and glittering women gliding beneath hats that hover above them like flying saucers. They all bring money, they auction entire barrels of wine, and they all support the cause. The Napa big time tasting has long been the top charity auction in the country, raising upwards of $6 million a year through the sale of donated wines and other items. But the NWWF didn't take long to raise the bar. A lot.

CHAPTER 25

Wine Festing in Naples

*here ain't no bigger wine life event than
the Naples Winter Wine Festival, held in Southwest
Florida at the end of January. It has become
the richest charity wine auction in the world,
attended by the superstars of the wine, sports, and
entertainment world (including Judge Judy, Regis Philbin,
Kyle McLachlan, and, of course, Rusty Staub.)*

February, 2005

Naples is one of those hushed enclaves that attracts
seasonal residents who stroll 5th Avenue South in blessed
anonymity. Tom Cruise's aunt. Jerry Seinfeld's mother. The
drummer for AC/DC. Unrecognized, they go from art
gallery to art gallery on Naples' answer to Worth Avenue
in Palm Beach or Rodeo Drive in Beverly Hills, but every
once in a while, their famous offspring come to visit, and
there is a celebrity sighting. Mostly, in the October-April
"season," the street is choked with very nice-looking people
nobody would ever look at twice except for their exquisite
clothing and lovely cars.

The reason we were excited about volunteering is that

admission to the Naples Winter Wine Festival runs about $8,500 per couple. Those who attend can afford to put their hundred foot yachts on barges and ship them to the Mediterranean so they can spend a week cruising the Greek Isles.

Once attendees wrote the admission check, assuming that they were granted access, because there's a very distinguished waiting list, they got a lot for their money. The trustees of the NWWF herded celebrity chefs from all over the country onto their private jets, aviated them to southwest Florida, and treated them to deep-sea fishing expeditions and golf games at very private courses. They plied them with Cohibas, two-hundred-year-old Port, and other entertainments, then installed them in mansions all along the beach, where original Renoirs adorn the walls, and where they cooked private dinners for 20 or 30 guests each. Thomas Keller cooked. So did Todd English, who was Bon Appetit's Restaurateur of the year, Eric Ripert, chef and co-owner of Le Bernardin in New York, and Luciano Pellegrini, who wrangles the kitchen at Piero Selvaggio's legendary Valentino restaurant in Los Angeles.

But that's just the tease. Each chef was paired with a world class vintner, so for eight and a half grand attendees could admire Chef Keller's tour de force in the kitchen of some 15,000 square foot mansion on the beach while drinking Harlan Estate and exchanging appreciative comments with Bill and Deborah Harlan their actual selves. It's too good.

Not done teasing yet. The vintner dinners were on Friday night. On Saturday, those who had struggled their way back to consciousness were hungry, and ready for the buffet lunch on the lawn of Ritz-Carlton's golf resort in Naples, overlooking the Tiburón Course, designed by none other than the Shark himself. They arrived early, to inspect the lots of wine and other goodies they'd be bidding on (ha!) later in the day. Then they strolled out to the golf course for the buffet lunch under a glistening white canopy, prepared by even more celebrity chefs. Under another tent were the tasting tables, where volunteer sommeliers (like us) poured wines donated by the vintners, trustees, and others who had ransacked their cellars for some older bottles. Most of these free-flowing vintages went for around $150 a bottle, and it was an open bar. Then, when everyone had had enough to eat and nearly enough to drink, the auction started, over seventy lots on the list, and it went on until the early winter shadows sent cool fingers across the fairways.

About those lots. Most of the items up for bid are wines, and the room where the lots are displayed before the auction is like an adult bookstore full of wine porn. A 16-bottle vertical of Opus One, starting with the 1980 vintage, a 3-liter bottle of Burgundy from Domaine de la Romanée-Conti, which means "really expensive wine" in French. In fact, almost everything in French means "really expensive." Then, of course, there's that box containing six magnums of Screaming Eagle, and the case of 1961 Chateau Latour, sitting over there in the corner, which would go for a disappointing $120,000. Ten grand a bottle. We might want to save one or two for a special occasion.

But rare and ancient wines aren't the only treats up for bid at the Naples Winter Wine Festival. The proceeds benefit dozens of children's charities in the area, so attendees bid freely on a 9-day wine safari in South Africa for two couples, including six 5-liter bottles of wine, round trip business class airfare and other luxuries. The winning bid was $340,000. The people from the charities cheered.

Or consider the week-long Mediterranean cruise on the MS Katharine, a 177-foot floating palace that's considered one of the top yachts in the world. Worthy of a Greek shipping magnate or Saudi prince, the immodest vessel is staffed by a crew of 12, and stuffed to the gunwales with satellite TV, wireless Internet, wave runners and, according to the description in the auction catalog, "every kind of water toy you can imagine." There might even be a recreational submarine, but the catalog doesn't mention it. Below decks, there is a private collection of original French Impressionist paintings, a dining room that seats 12, and maybe even a transporter that can beam passengers back to Monaco if they need a break.

Speaking of transport, one auction lot proposed for donation to the NWWF was a trip into Earth orbit aboard Virgin Galactic. The event's attorneys, of whom there are many, appeared before the committee, trembling, ashen-faced and dry-throated, driven to their knees in fear of unprecedented exposure in a liability lawsuit, and talked them out of it. About the only thing not up for auction were high political office and ownership of emerging nations in obscure parts of the world.

Back to the MS Katharine. Charter it for around $240,000 a week, or bid $400,000 at the auction, and start packing for Monaco with six friends. After all, they've been eating meals prepared by legendary chefs, drinking wines that mostly never leave the vintner's personal cellar, and were feeling expansive, so the idea of paying retail is quickly abandoned. This is for the kids. The air is alive with paddles.

"C'mon George," the tent resonates with good natured

taunts. "It's only four hundred grand. You ain't gonna take
it with you!"

Hungry? They raise their paddles and buy themselves a
week in an 18th Century apartment in the Le Marais district
of Paris, certain that the place has been handsomely and
sumptuously renovated, at least since the fall of the Vichy
government. Included are lunches and dinners at Michelin
Three-Star restaurants, and personal tours of world-famous
vineyards.

There were also vacations that included transportation
in private jets, walk-on roles in network situation comedies,
lunch with Judge Judy, and it went up from there, but that's
the ballpark they play in. In a good year, they raise $14 million
in a single day. In a bad year, only $12 million.

Ah, well. I despair of ever having $8,500 to spend
on something like that. My car isn't worth that much.
Volunteering was obviously the only way in for the likes of
us, which is why I told Larry to put our names on the list.

We poured wine, kept track of the lots, and helped load
the ten-thousand-dollar bottles into the Bentleys and BMW
Z-8s when it was all over. We donated our time to a charity,
saw Kyle McLachlan close-up, poured for Judge Judy, and
reverently handled bottles we'd never get to taste (the thrill
is much like erotic denial). We even saw Rusty Staub. It
was worth it.

CHAPTER 26

The Lady Who
Wrote the Bible

*he wine life has put us together with
fascinating people whom we'd never have met any
other way. One special treat...lunch with Karen
MacNeil, the author of one of the most influential
and informative wine books ever written. And she's
nice, too.*

October, 2005

Miles and Tony aren't the only people who have led us
to pleasant and important relationships with winemakers
and other wine lifers. Larry, though he doesn't live anywhere
near Napa, has, sometimes unwittingly, facilitated other
friendships that have become dear to us. Shortly after the
Winter Wine Festival revelation, he invited us to the annual
private tasting his company holds for trade professionals,
and we met Diana Schweiger Isdahl. Debi was wearing a
pair of slacks adorned with cute little embroidered wine
glasses (the wine life having influenced her wardrobe, as
well), and Diana, who was pouring her family's wine,
thought they were just the cutest thing. The friendship

grew from there, and we made it a point to visit her at the winery and family farm. She happened to mention that her next door neighbor up on Spring Mountain was Karen MacNeil. My senses came alive. Karen, among her many other oenophilic accomplishments, is the author of *The Wine Bible*, a book I treasure and have referred to previously. Anyone who writes a book with a title like that damn well better know what she's talking about. I've read it three times, and she does.

"Really? I would absolutely love to meet her."

"Okay," said Diana, sweetheart that she is, "I'll invite her over for lunch." And so she did.

At lunch, I asked Karen about a statement she made that wine is the only beverage in the world that draws us in intellectually, that it is unusually compelling because it involves the mind. It matters. The previously-quoted Matt Kramer has said the same thing.

Even earlier in the obsession I had read tons of similar statements from other writers, and they explained the fascination that crept up on us when we were first initiated. Unlike Coca-Cola or lime Kool-Aid, say, the world of wine will grab susceptible souls (like me) by the cravat (if they happen to wear one, which I don't) and bundle them merrily off to New Places. As soon as we began suffering from the passion, the moment we went beyond the Chianti bottle in the basket, we discovered wine we never heard of from places on the globe we never thought about even once, let alone twice, and it became progressively more difficult not to ask, while savoring them, "why is this wine the way it is?" Why does it taste this way? Is it because of the kind of grape, where it's from, who makes it? All of the above, of course, but once I was hopelessly into the research, I discovered yet another new dimension, and other reasons why wine things are as they are.

If I were a descendant of Dr. Welch, or a member of the Riedel or Laguiole families, I wouldn't have a problem making unlimited visits to the places where they grow wine. (It's a quirk of the wine life world view that the process is referred to as "wine growing," and not just growing grapes to make wine from. Probably a nod to the philosophy that wine is made in the vineyard, and the winemaker's job is to get it from the vine into the bottle without screwing it up). Alas, unlimited travel is not available to us. Fine wine grapes are never, never grown in ugly places, and that means going to those places, which are expensive because they're not ugly, and renting lodging in them, what with the obligatory meals in tiny restaurants in tiny villages accompanied by not-so-tiny bottles. All this can rupture a credit line, generating angry form letters from our friendly family bankers and credit managers. So, if we can't spend months cruising the byways of Bordeaux or Burgundy, we have to crack an Atlas to find out something about the village or region or appellation that's listed on the label. When the bottle says "Chimeres," what does that mean? What's the place like, what are the grapes, how are they grown, do they have a Starbuck's, all that sort of thing. As was underscored earlier, some people—maybe even most—are interested only in what's in the bottle and subsequently what's in the glass. For them, the sensations of the wine are reward enough, and that's just fine, but others are burdened (or cursed) with an inquiring mind, which is always a bit more obsessive and all-consuming.

This particular brand of curiosity springs not from noble

impulse, intellectual questing, or any desire for educational self-improvement, however peripheral. For our part, it arises from an aversion to paying a lot of money for wine. Years before, we understood that it was strictly a question of economic necessity (survival, too) to be able to look at a wine label that says it's from the Libournais or Bolgheri or the Bekaa Valley in Lebanon and have at least some crazy, ridiculous idea what the wine might taste like, and whether it's worth the obscene, usurious price the store is charging for it. Numberless are the times we've paid $40 for a bottle of something that looked good on the shelf, seduced by masterful marketing or the cute little critter on the label, only to gag on it when we brought it home.

If we're going to enjoy wine, and spring for the upper-end bottle on occasion, why not get the most out of it? If wine brings to us what we bring to it, let's bring as much as we can.

Among my earlier readings was a book by Andrea Immer Robinson, a Master of Wine, called *Great Wine Made Simple*, which took the approach that learning about wine springs from what she calls a "wine map." Know where it's from, and you know more or less what it'll be like. It's one way to spot the bargains, and it works. At least knowing the geography (warm weather means more lush fruit, cold weather means more acidity and white fruit, like pears and apples) goes a long way toward figuring out whether the wine on the neighborhood shelf will be to our taste.

Guy Whitesman, my attorney and primary care spiritual advisor, receives a monthly newsletter from a big discount wine store about two hours up the road, and becomes, monthly, very exercised about all the wonderful bottles and bargains he finds. One time, he conned me into splitting a case of red from the Languedoc. I broke a cardinal rule in buying it, because I hadn't tasted it first, but it was well-reviewed, garnered about 90 out of 100 points from the critics, and didn't cost too much, which was the best part. It turned out to be clean and tasty, and at the price we paid, we wanted more. Guy was ready to move on to the next new find, but I wanted to know if there were any similar Languedocian bargains out there, which drove me to my trusty wine atlas, asking some Serious Questions. Where the hell is the Languedoc, anyway? Why is it there? Are they happy? What's the weather like? Do they have any good Mexican restaurants?

As it turns out, the Languedoc is in the south of France (I actually guessed France right away), running roughly parallel to the Mediterranean coast, a bit inland. To its enduring shame, the area is woefully shy of enchilada establishments, but the inhabitants compensate by doing nothing all day but growing sensational grapes and make wonderful wine which they insist on selling at comically low prices. They all live in tiny villages with names like Nissan-les-Enserune, which means "Your Japanese car has leaked brake fluid on my new Reeboks," and Aspiran, which means either "heavy breathing" or "headache relief," depending on the local dialect.

Beyond these few keen insights, there's even more to learn about the Languedoc. It's the most abundant wine producing region in France, surpassing even Bordeaux, and the people have had a lot of practice squishing grapes and letting the juice go bad in barrels. Many of the villages, no matter what their names mean, were well known as sites of wine commerce in Roman times. Problem is, I couldn't find out a thing about the wine without reading about the past, and as soon as I started reading about the past, I got hit in the face with history.

New revelation, even after eight or nine years of wallowing around with diminished discretionary income and a head full of information that nobody, but nobody, wants to hear: sometimes wine is the way it is not just because of the grapes, or the ground, or the guy or gal who made it, but because of a tide of happenstance that swept across the place centuries ago.

The Languedoc is a perfect example, thanks to the Albigensian Crusade, which was so named because it was centered around the town of Albi, the birthplace of Toulouse-Lautrec, though he was not home at the time.

Somewhere in the clammy, distant mists of my college education in the Liberal Arts (which are the arts of being entirely unemployable after graduation), I studied (or was at least exposed to) world literature, history, an elective course in the New Testament, the names of innumerable people, places, and events, memorization of the prolog to the Canterbury Tales in Middle English, and practically every soliloquy Shakespeare ever wrote, all of which are now only a distant twitching memory. Actually, I remember most of the names pretty well, but have not even a whispered hint of who they were, what they did, or who they did it to. (This is also true of things that happened to me yesterday). For example, England once had a king named Ethelred the Unready (or Aethelred the Aunready, depending on which book you read). On that point my recollection is crystalline. But I can't remember what took him so by surprise.

The Albigensian Crusade used to be one of those nebulous memories—used to be—but thanks to my twisted interest, is misty no more. And, while the Crusade was mostly about the religious politics of the age, it had a direct effect on what was in the case of wine Guy forced me to buy, and explains – partially, at least – why the wines of the Languedoc are so good.

CHAPTER 27

Halloween in Venice

One year, after the Wine Experience, instead of going home we went to Italy, dragging along our friends Ralph and Trish. Strangely enough, we found ourselves in Venice on Halloween. This was the night we learned how to open Champagne bottles with a sword, which is a story in itself.

November, 2005

Ralph and Trish are dear friends, and like most of our dear friends, we met them around 1999 during a tasting at a local wine shop when we first began our descent. After a year or two of sniffing, swirling, and sipping together, and generally agreeing on what we liked to drink and what we didn't, and after Ralph had moved half of his collection into my wine room because he didn't have space for it, we talked them into coming to the Wine Experience with us. They had traveled widely, visiting places on the planet that Debi and I pillow-talked about, but we discovered in one of our many sampling sessions that they'd never been to Italy. Clearly, something needed to be done, and it was a simple matter to arrange a trip to Tuscany and beyond

right after the wine weekend. Since we would already be in
New York, we rationalized, there's no better place to find
convenient transportation to the world at large. Tens of
thousands of flyer miles later, we found ourselves in Venice.
On Halloween.

I had read about a certain wine bar that had attracted
the attention of a writer from American Express, who
praised the abundant selection of wines by the glass. That's
all I needed to hear, and insisted on dragging the group
through the interminable narrowness of the city to its door.
But when we showed up, it was only five in the afternoon
and the restaurant was still closed. "Shmuck," said Ralph.
"Nobody in Europe is going to serve us food and drink
before seven-thirty."

"Or later," added Debi.

It's not all that difficult to kill time in Venice. All we had
to do was walk. We found a café on a small piazza that
didn't have a bit of a problem offering us a selection of
wines and varietals from the Veneto, the winegrowing areas
west and north of the fabled city. Relaxing in the ancient
square as night fell, we were well into the second bottle of
Corvina when, to our total astonishment, brigades of trick
or treaters appeared, little boys, dozens of them, dressed
the way Americans think pirates should look, little girls
with sheets over their heads, peering out through raggedly-
cut eyeholes, all carrying adorable plastic jack-o-lanterns
with open tops to collect whatever kind of candy puzzled
Venetian residents would throw their way. I was betting it
wouldn't be M&Ms or Reese's peanut butter cups. Probably
more like a few slices of prosciutto. If there were a Richter
scale for cultural rupture, tricking and treating on the streets

of Venice would have registered at least an eight point five, along with the Jamaican gelato stand we'd discovered earlier in the day.

After the Halloween hallucination, we tried the restaurant again, sparing ourselves the expense of ordering a third bottle.

The owner, Mauro, was kind enough to seat us even though we didn't have a reservation, but Debi had more than one reservation about walking into the place. Mauro, personally characterized by an abundance of nose emphatically underlined with an equally-extravagant brown mustache, was dressed for All Hallows Eve in orange jeans, a checked shirt, bow tie, and pointy witch's hat, which, in a break from longstanding tradition, was bright orange. His choice of footwear consisted of Converse All-Stars. One orange, one green. He probably has another pair just like it, and he was very cheerful.

Maybe halfway through our meal, Mauro hurried past, depositing a bottle of Champagne on our table.

"We didn't order this," Debi observed.

"Why is the neck of the bottle covered with ice?" Good question, Trish. We couldn't answer. And personal as this is, I must disclose that by the time that bottle of bubbly appeared we had put the fourth bottle of Veneto's finest in the record books, and we were reading the wine list to each other again, struggling to order another bottle, in slurred syllables, with one eye closed.

But before we could make the mistake of ordering number five, Mauro, witch's hat and all, accompanied by his headwaiter, positioned himself in the middle of the dining room. The maitre d' reverently placed a medallion around

Mauro's neck, a glittering round embossed silver object the size of a salad plate, which dangled weightily from a braided red velvet ribbon, kissed him on both cheeks, and handed him a sabre. He took two steps to our table, picked up the Champagne bottle, cleanly whacked the top off with one smooth practiced stroke, put the bottle back on our table, told us it was on the house, bowed to acknowledge the enthusiastic applause, and bustled off to work the room.

We were stunned, and stared at each other until Ralph, who was by this time down to his t-shirt, said, "Look at this."

Behind him on the wall was an elaborately framed certificate, in French, in Mauro's name, from some organization like the Commanderie or Societe of People Who Open Champagne Bottles With Sabres Internationale. It looked like one of those medieval hand-illuminated manuscripts, all red, gold, and colorful, stating that Mauro was a Grand Wizard or something in the venerable organization, and certifiably skilled in doing what we'd just seen him do, even though we didn't believe it when it happened. Although I didn't know it at the time, a few years later I'd have the chance to attempt the feat myself, with humiliating results.

CHAPTER 28

How Not to Read
a Wine Label

*ine bottles offer less consumer
information than any other type of food or beverage,
because they don't have to. It took a while for us
to learn some helpful—if somewhat skewed—
techniques for deciphering the mystery and actually
figuring out what the hell is in the bottle.*

December, 2005

By the time we returned from Venice, I had learned
enough about wine to have received a wide variety of
smacks on the head from Annie and numerous friends,
current and former. It was a dilemma: I was so enchanted
and so carried away that I couldn't stop talking about
the subject, and could scarcely refrain from inflicting the
benefit of my newfound knowledge upon those around
me. People were staying away from me as though I had
developed supplemental heads and large black swellings in
my armpits and groin. And yet, I was as fascinated about
the subject as ever and couldn't shut up, so I decided to
put my obnoxiousness to good use and teach classes. My

uncle George went nuts over coin collecting and wound up opening a coin shop, and Debi's mother raises irises in her backyard that are so beautiful people give her first prize ribbons and pay her for them, so it's possible to put a passion to work, and monetize it. I made a deal with the owner of a boutique wine shop in town, and started teaching two classes a month. For the sake of credibility, I joined the Society of Wine Educators.

One of the major reasons to learn about wine is because it's one of the few nice things about life. While it's pleasant enough to listen to Louis Armstrong or Sam Cooke or somebody sing "What a Wonderful World," most people observe—and experience—the fact that pain is built in to our existence, but pleasure takes some doing on the part of the individual. Generally, we have to make our own fun. Since we need to eat several times a day, it might as well be pleasurable, which takes us to elaborate recipes that require three days to prepare, or to achingly expensive restaurants, at least once a year for a special occasion. But as soon as guests are seated and the waiter has graced their laps with napkins, the Wine List arrives, and a Kierkegaardian fear and trembling descends upon everyone at the table. So my goal in teaching the classes was to give people the information they needed to look at a restaurant wine list or pick up a bottle of something they've never heard of in a store and have some vague chance of guessing what's in the bottle, and what kind of taste experience they can expect. As Andrea Immer Robinson notes, if we know what the grape is and where it's from, we may actually have some wild outside chance of guessing what it'll taste like.

Another goal was the impulse to share, to show other people something that had enchanted me, in the hope they would become similarly spellbound, and enjoy it. Sometimes it works, and sometimes it doesn't, like the friend who did everything he could to haul me out to his garage and teach me about cars. My fire, despite his most evangelistic efforts, remained unlit.

I also tell aspiring wine lifers that of all consumer food products in the world, no package discloses less information than the label on a bottle of wine. I can grab a box of corn flakes in the supermarket and enjoy a complete nutritional analysis of each component chemical, in milligrams, to several decimal places, a rundown of all the vitamins they put in, where it was packaged, on what date, and whether or not it was raining that day. I can even find out about the FD&C red and yellow dyes number 16 and 23 they use. I bought a package of candy once, read the label, and the manufacturer was candid enough (or under enough legal duress) to disclose that his confection was coated with carnauba wax and shellac. The choice was mine…did I want to eat sweetened car polish and floor sealant, or not. At least they gave me the option.

Sadly, such is not the case with wine, though the situation is beginning to improve. Basically, as we slowly sank downward into the wine life, we found out that many wine bottles have two labels—one on the front and one on the back. The front one discloses the Andrea information: the grape, the ground, and who made the wine, even if it's a varietal we've never heard of, like Lagrein, from a place we've never heard of, like Bolzano. The front label also tells us the alcohol content, more or less. We pay particular attention to the front label if the wine is from Germany, because German wine labels (and Alsatian ones, to a lesser extent) unleash upon the prospective buyer a polysyllabic torrent of incomprehensible information that even includes the winery's national registration number, which doesn't do a thing to help you distinguish between a kabinett and a qualitatswein mit pradikat, whatever those are.

Actually, there are often two back labels, but the smaller plain one always tells you not to drink the wine if you're planning to drive an earthmover while you're pregnant. I comply with those cautions to the letter.

No, it's those other back labels that need some consideration, and even then it may not do any good. (The wine life is nothing if not challenging). Back labels come in two flavors, which I decided to call the hype label and the help label.

The hype label tells us nothing, while cleverly insulting our intelligence at the very same time. The copy on these labels is something of an accomplishment in the world of consumer marketing—a cynical ploy by the winemaker to get us to put a couple of bottles in our buggy and let some lethargic teenager at a cash register scan them for us. Hype labels usually say something like "This finely crafted Merlot is a testament to our family's centuries-long and incredibly distinguished winemaking tradition. We weep with joy as we meticulously craft it by hand in our heritage vineyards from hundred-year-old vines, laboring with love and sincere dedication to offer you melodious aromas and classic fruit profile that will enhance your enjoyment of any cuisine, and possibly bring tears to your eyes." After spending over 35 years in advertising and marketing, I've developed a keen sense of shameless self promotion, having indulged in it myself, and it doesn't get much more shameless or self-promotional than the back label of a wine bottle.

The other type of back label, the help variety, is usually better but sometimes not. At the very least it should tell the buyer what kind of grapes they stuffed in the bottle, because many wines are made of blends, bear fabulously creative proprietary names like "Conundrum," "Alexis," or "Dedication," and give absolutely no indication of the grapes they're made of. Why, we wonder, should this be?

It's easy enough to pick up a bottle of California Chardonnay or Cabernet Sauvignon and know what's inside, because helpful winemakers put the name of the grape right on the front label for all to see. But what if the front label says "Insignia," or "Pythagoras," or "Isosceles?" Should I pay over $60 for a bottle of wine named after an ancient Greek mathematician when the people who make it won't tell me what's inside? That's when a spin of the bottle and a look at the back label is very much called for. It may lead to honest useful information, but then again, maybe not. One wine I recently sampled listed on the back label nine different grape varieties that were part of the blend. It tasted like everything and nothing at the same time.

Some winemakers want the prospective customer to know what kind of grape juice they're trying to sell, and they'll specify the blend with brutal precision, offering something like, "This voluptuous red wine (hype) is a careful blend of our finest Cabernet Sauvignon, Merlot, and Cabernet Franc (help)." Or, on an especially good day, they'll reveal that it's 42.5% Cabernet Sauvignon, 31.8% Merlot, 19.7% Cabernet Franc, 2.4% Petit Verdot, and 3.6% Malbec. (If this does not add up to 100, it's not my fault.) There is, of course, such a thing as too much information, like the fireman's red suspenders, but at least, if we know what these individual varietals taste like and maybe what qualities they contribute to the blend, we'll have a remote stab at figuring out what's going to hit us when we actually drink it.

Back labels are smaller than front ones, so winemakers generally don't gush forth with information, like what the average temperature was during the growing season, or whether or not it rained at harvest time. At least we hope they don't.

But making of wine does have lots of parts. There's the which grapes should we use part, the where should we grow them part, and that whole thing about will this be a good year, or do we have to sell another one of the children. Then there's anxiety about the kind of yeast that's getting thrown into the vat and what we're going to feed it. (Yes, there's such a thing as yeast food.) These are but a few of the winemaker's worries. But they'll never put that information on a back label, and it wouldn't mean squat to most people if they did.

However, and this brings us (finally) to the topic at hand, which is that they may disclose how the wine was "elevated," or brought up. Surprise: there's a word for it in French. It's *elevage*, or upbringing, as though the winemaking process were akin to raising children, educating them, and marrying them off. Simply put, elevage is winespeak for how they made the wine and aged it. After we muddle through the parts about the cold soaking, the pumping over, the cap punching and whether or not they subjected the poor juice to malolactic fermentation, alchemy, transubstantiation, and other arcane procedures, they almost always disclose what kind of barrels were used in the fermentation and/or aging process. And this is where some background knowledge may actually pay off, which is why people take wine classes.

And the bit about the barrels came to be kind of important to us. Another pique to my curiosity.

Aside from the breakdown on the barrels, there are some few bits of information that wine labels are required by law to tell us, at least in the United States, but even the legally mandated disclosures are unhelpful at best. One of the things most people like to know is alcohol content, and it's right there on the label. Problem is, the law gives the labeler a half percent margin of leeway in either direction, so when the label tells me there is 14% alcohol, it could be anywhere between 13.5 and 14.5. Makes a difference, because some wine styles can support high alcohol content without taking the skin off the roof of your mouth, and others can't. And besides, knowing the alcohol volume can help us plan for any possible onset of consumption-related diminished capacity.

Sidebar: Cousin Annie once told us what a good time she had spending a week in Sicily, so we went. Sitting in a restaurant in Taormina, we ordered a bottle of Nero d'Avola, a wine that's right in my personal ballpark, tastewise. Big, dark, concentrated. Service was a bit leisurely, and we were in no particular hurry, so we finished the bottle and got halfway through a second, and when the food finally arrived we thought everything was funny to the point of uproariousness. I fumbled for the label. Fourteen and a half percent. Just hilarious.

CHAPTER 29

Rolling Out the Barrel

*had said earlier that there are two plants
essential to the making of wine: the grapevine
and the cork oak. That's not quite true. There are
actually three plants, the third being another type of
oak tree from which wine barrels are made. Oak, or
the absence thereof, is critical to winemaking.*

January, 2006

Since many of the help labels were careful to specify if
the wine was elevaged in this or that kind of oak, I wanted
to know what the heck difference it would make. After all,
I'm the one paying for the stuff. And drinking it. Besides, I
owed it to the people who faithfully and devotedly showed
up for my classes twice a month, eager to sip and sample,
and discover what it was that made me so crazy. Since we
usually poured five or six wines at every session, I judged
the success of the class by how long it took for me to lose
control of the group. About an hour in, they'd become very
genial and chatty with each other, and I often had to remind
them I was still there.

That being said, it's hard to overstate the role that one

species of the humble oak tree, and the barrels that are
produced therefrom, plays in the production and enjoyment
of wine. Once in the wine life, it becomes part of the "guess
what you just paid thirty-six bucks for?" game.

No other tree on the planet, I believe, has played such
a key role in the history and perpetuation of human
civilization. At least not since the one in the Garden of
Eden, and maybe the ones the Romans used about two
thousand years ago for their particularly cruel and repulsive
method of chastising Hebrews and others who incurred
their displeasure. Forget the fact that the unique qualities of
oak made it the perfect material for the construction of
the sailing ships that plied the oceans of the ancient world,
and that the Nina, Pinta, and Santa Maria were very likely
made of it; I haven't checked. But I do remember, though I
wasn't around at the time, that the invention of the steam
engine and the subsequent demise of wooden ships made
more oak available for the construction of wine barrels,
so thank you, James Watt, DeWitt Clinton, and the other
mothers of invention.

Funny thing, barrels. For dozens of centuries, they were
the containers of choice for just about everything humans
made and stored, or dragged from place to place. Why they
never used boxes, which were easier to make and more
convenient to stack, has never been satisfactorily explained.
But barrels? Oh, yeah. Even today, we can pack a properly
made barrel with goods that weigh hundreds of pounds
and one person can maneuver it by rolling it horizontally
or by tipping it up on edge, and people who know how
can even bounce them. They can be made impermeable
and watertight, and they actually do stack pretty well.
Regardless, at some point in our elevage as a species, the

divine synergy between wine and wood was discovered,
and the world has never been the same. I'd put this giant
leap for mankind right up there with moments of glory like
the discovery of fire, the wheel, and the career of Tiny Tim.

Now, it's true that barrels had been used for ages to
store wine as well as other liquids and solids. But the
barrels were relatively neutral and didn't impart any flavor
unless they were dirty, which they mostly always were,
the discovery of bacteria still being a surprise waiting
to happen. Along the way, and we don't know where, it
was discovered, centuries after people stopped mixing
wine with seawater, that wine placed in barrels of new or
relatively new oak acquired flavors that almost everyone
found to be quite yummy and intriguing.

There are three plants that are indispensable to the
world of wine, and the oak tree is two of them. The third,
of course, is the grape vine itself. The subject of the cork
oak has already been discussed earlier, in exhausting detail
at that, and I don't have the heart to do the same thing with
its sister tree the *quercus alba*, so let's return to the back
label, and it's about time, too. The one winemaking morsel
the label might impart is the kind of oak the wine was
aged in, and God willing, for how long, which is almost as
important as the kind of grape.

There's new oak, old oak, French oak, American oak,
and some from other countries like Hungary and Slovenia.
The mind staggers. Some writers compare the winemaker's
choice of barrels, and the flavors they impart to the wine,
like the seasonings a gourmet chef will put in food. And
indeed, the choice of the type of oak, new, old, French,
American, small barrels, larger barrels, is every bit as
complicated, and every bit a matter of personal taste,

as any other part of the process. I have personally driven myself nuts trying to figure it out. It has been written that what happens to wine aged in oak is almost as complex as what happens to grape juice when yeast hits it. But paradoxically enough, this complex process requires only two things: time, and the selection of the right kind of barrel.

The making of barrels is an art, and people have been doing it for a long time. Come to think of it, just about everything related to wine growing and wine consumption involves hundreds or thousands of years of tradition and history, which is another reason that wine engages the mind. It, like no other food or beverage, is a part of the human condition. We're talking generations of families making corkscrews like the Laguioles, glasses like the Riedels, and yes, wine barrels.

Take the Taransaud family in France, for instance. The first Monsieur Taransaud to become a cooper joined the trade in 1672, had a knack for it, and successive generations have followed in his footsteps until the family business was sold exactly 300 years later. Like the Welch family and the Reidels, the descendants of M. Taransaud don't need to ask how much things cost. Other barrel-making concerns in France can lay claim to similar histories.

When new wine is placed in barrels, there leaches out of the wood certain types of vegetable sugars and other elements that have transformative effects on the chemicals in the wine, imbuing it with sensations of vanilla, toffee, and other goodnesses. And, since the staves are shaped and hooped over fire, the insides of the barrels acquire a bit of toasting, caramelizing the sugars in the wood, and that brings even more flavors into play. Doesn't work with beer or Kool-Aid.

The details of every aspect of wine production are crazy-making, the composition of the barrel and aging of wine therein being no exception. Oak is capable of being shaped so the staves fit perfectly, preventing leakage, while the wood is porous enough to transmit a bit of air, helping the wine develop and age. Of course, as air passes in and out through the wood, slight evaporation occurs, and the level of wine in the barrel gradually diminishes during the lengthy aging process. The amount of wine that disappears from the barrel over time is called the Angel's Share, and I think that's just romantic as hell.

CHAPTER 30

The Aspen Dimension

*romp through the Aspen Wine & Food
Festival...just one more way we spent money we
didn't have to feed our addiction.*

June, 2006

By the summer of 2006, we had become uncomfortably
aware that our grape geekiness was way too extensive,
expensive, interruptive, and often interpersonally hostile.
We'd been to the Wine Experience six times, sat through a
number of decent conducted tastings and dinners in various
cities, volunteered for a few years at the Naples Winter
Wine Festival, watching as attendees whipped out their
American Express cards to pay for the auction lots they'd
purchased. Even the highly prized black cards, the ones
made of titanium, shuddered under the strain.

I'd joined the Society of Wine Educators and taught
classes to a small but dedicated group of aspiring grape
geeks at a local wine boutique, and the size of our modest
collection had stabilized, primarily because we'd flat run out
of money. Aside from that, we were okay.

Then along came Larry (again), who said this:

"We just absolutely gotta go to the Aspen Food & Wine Festival in Colorado."

Larry, ever the Pied Piper of wine, had already introduced us to the sister festival, held every February in Miami's South Beach, and had regularly finagled passes for us to most of the private trade events. We didn't take his urge seriously, because we'd always admired Aspen from afar. Wineweekendwise, South Beach was a two-hour drive across the state on a road through the Everglades called Alligator Alley. The trip is no problem, and besides, we get to see lots of alligators in the canals. The Wine Experience was mostly in New York, an easy and inexpensive hop from where we live. But Colorado was a continent away. Undaunted, Larry sweetened the deal.

"Our friends Allen and Kristine have a house in Leadville. We can stay there for a day or two and drive over." Leadville, Colorado? Didn't sound like much of a paradise to me, but I was wrong. Mostly.

Why Allen decided to build a second home (mostly with his own two hands) in a place like Leadville was a mystery at the time, and remains so. He picked a spot on a mountain about three miles outside of this old mining town (which, given the name, does not cause excessive astonishment), and if three or four grizzled and sunburned trail hands from the mid-1800s galloped down the main street today, they wouldn't have much trouble recognizing the place. But the area was a pleasant surprise, being imbued to this day with a certain antique Wild West charm and blessed lack of humidity that makes the four-bedroom hilltop aerie Allen and Kristine built very comfortable, up around 15,000 feet.

The place has history, too. Doc Holliday wound up in this

very town a few years after that unfortunate contretemps at the O.K. Corral in Arizona. While a Leadville resident, he managed to get himself into another gunfight in a saloon on the main street, shot his tormentor in the arm, and skated on that one, too. Doc was a Leadvillian until he died, delirious from tuberculosis, in a hotel a bit down the road.

The town is also moderately famous for being the place where the Guggenheim family turned a small fortune into one that gave them the means to build a spectacular art museum on Central Park, and a few others of similar architectural daring around the world. In the mid 19th Century, German immigrant Meyer Guggenheim, tired of his unremitting success in importing Swiss needlepoint to Philadelphia, did what Horace Greeley (supposedly) told every young man to do (even though Meyer was 60 at the time), bought some iron mines out west, traveled to the spot, and quickly decided that smelting metal ore was more tidy and more profitable than digging it out of the ground. Now, along with the Welchs and Riedels, his descendants don't have to ask how much things cost.

We were about 85% convinced about making the trek, but still hesitant, when Larry put the cherry on top and clinched the decision. Since he's in the trade, he'd have access to most of the distributor and winemaker private parties and hospitality houses. So would we.

Leadville it was, and then a drive, a few days later, over the Continental Divide and into Aspen. I've never been much interested in winter sports, or in mountains themselves, but we liked Aspen very much in June, because the weather was a crisp, cool relief from South Florida, and especially because I knew that Hunter Thompson was somewhere around, and maybe I'd run into him. We got George

Hamilton instead. Debi didn't mind.

Aspen made me reflect on the Wine Experiences that we'd been attending for several years and I realized that the WE is extremely urban in its flavor, staging, and execution. It's always held in a major hotel in a major city, with ballrooms, elevators, concierges, and sushi bars in the lobby. Aspen was different in every way imaginable. Outdoors, rather than in. Relaxed, rather than formal. The outdoorsiness made it kind of like being back in college, but we weren't drinking Mateus any more.

The collegiate vibe came from the setup. In Aspen, tastings and cooking demonstrations were held not in fancy hotel ballrooms, but in cute little tents and pavilions located in the public parks, and also in hotels around the town square, so after one session that forced us to taste ten wines from a fabled vintage in the Rhône, we just ambled across the plaza or up the street to the next seminar, like going from World History class to English Lit, but with a little more time between sessions, and with everybody in a considerably better mood.

The Aspen folks didn't include the word "food" in the name of the show just for fun. The culinary aspect was another pleasing dimension, and we enjoyed the celebrity chef seminars and demonstrations, which were much different than the show that Emeril, Wolfgang, Charlie and Mario put on at the Wine Experience.

The grand tastings were held in a huge tent that covered most of the central square, giving the town a sort of wine circus atmosphere. Around and about, wine lovers from all over the world strolled from the Little Nell to the St. Regis, sitting through one tasting session after another. And when they were over and we regained the street, there were the mountains all around, blissfully (for me) bare of snow and deeply green. I thought it was a wonderful place to learn about wine.

As may be true of many festivals and major sports events, the most engaging social enrichments took place away from the classes and seminars listed in the program guide. There were private tasting seminars, which added between $125 and $200 each to the overall event tab. But learning about wine in tastings limited to about fifteen people, sitting directly across the table from internationally-known winemakers from California, France, and Australia, discussing wines that I had only dreamed about, was the reason we'd made the trip.

I did, however, miss out on one enrichment on the second evening after Debi and I, exhausted from the effort of raising so many glasses to our lips, collapsed into bed, leaving Larry, Charlene, Kristine, and Allen to make their own fun. They wasted no time.

At our hotel, there was a hospitality party going on for some winery or distributor or other, and the four of them slipped themselves in, certain that their lack of an invitation was nothing more than an unfortunate oversight on the part of the hosts. They wound up sampling widely—and well—and were gracious enough to hand out the provided goodie bags at around three in the morning as everyone departed.

Another enrichment, and perhaps the best, was provided at no charge (thanks, Larry) in the three story house rented by a California company that made sparkling wine; one of the most historic homes in the village, built in the 1800s, a block off the main square, reserved for the week by the winery, which moved out every shred of furniture in order to offer hospitality and bubbly respite for distributors, salesman, wine writers, members of the trade such as Larry and their hanger-on friends like us, staffing the kitchen with chefs from the Culinary Institute of America whipping up macaroni and cheese with black truffles because it goes great with sparkling whites made in the méthode Champenoise.

One of the activities offered at the house was personal instruction in how to open a Champagne bottle with a sabre. Shades of Mauro back in Venice. I jumped at the opportunity.

Back in the screed on corkscrews, I mentioned that there are two ways to get a cork out of a wine bottle and that one of them required a weapon and some manual dexterity. Never having been to a feast celebrating a battle victory of the Cossack army, I'd been denied the opportunity to slice the top off a wine bottle, and I didn't think to ask Mauro to give me a crack at it, but if anyone had ever handed me a bottle and a sword, I would have at least made the attempt.

There's a trick to it. The neck of the bottle must be frozen, to make the glass as brittle as possible. That's why the bottle was so cold when Mauro put it on our table. There is a seam that runs up the bottle from the base to the neck, and it has to be facing upward, toward he who wields the sword. With one effortless blow, the edge of the sabre (which, by the way, is more ceremonial than lethal, has a dull blade, and usually bears the name of a Champagne producer somewhere thereupon) slides up the seam, catches the lower ridge of raised glass that holds the wire cage in place, and the neck of the bottle snaps apart cleanly right at the weak spot. Theoretically. If it doesn't break perfectly, the bottle gets poured out, because a few glass fragments can really ruin a nice glass of wine.

In Aspen, at the bubbly house, they let me try it. Three times, sacrificing several bottles of their not-inexpensive product to my unpracticed efforts. I will not discuss the outcome, but I will confess that my application to the Commanderie of Sabre Wielding Champagne Openers was flatly denied.

CHAPTER 31

"Sometimes, I Even Put It in the Food"

R̶eflections on wine and food pairing, cooking with wine, and how these realizations changed the way we cook, eat, and drink. The wine life has also taken us to cheese, but that's a whole other story.

November, 2006

The advent of the holidays, coming not long after the Aspen adventure, was a time for entertaining, visiting, sampling, and cooking. This led me to think back on the ways that wine and its intimate relationship with food had affected us over the past ten (had it been ten?) years.

There's a (very) small joke about the evolution of the human species since the dawn of time. In the first stage of development, we ask "how can we eat?" In the second stage, we question, "why do we eat?" And in the third, we ask "Where should we have lunch?"

The wine life made us ask all this and more many times over, so, in a way, it has taken us on a little journey through the Ascent of Man.

In most of the old world cultures, especially France, Spain, and Italy, wine is thought of more as food than drink. We didn't appreciate that when we first contracted the disease, because we were so caught up in the flavors, the aromas, and especially the sharing with like-minded people, most of whom, I was gratified to discover, had more bottles in their homes than we did, and were of a generous nature. Later, though, we came to appreciate the various Mediterranean cultures for teaching us that wine really is food, as much a part of a meal as soup, salad, and dessert. From there, it was a tiny step to finding ourselves face to face with the intimate relationship between the two (not the French and Spanish; the wine and the food).

For quite some time, we had been going out to dinner and choosing the wine first, then finding some menu items to go with it. And later on, we caught ourselves watching television and movies more closely, because any time a wine bottle appeared on the screen, we'd strain to see what it was. (Flash forward: In the movie "Ratatouille," which came out in 2007, the evil chef offers the hero a bottle of 1961 Chateau Latour, and all the wine geeks in the theatre (all two of us) almost slid off our seats. It was apparent that whoever had written the script knew at least a little something about legendary vintages.)

On the subject of food and wine pairing, food chemistry, bridge flavors, and all that, volumes have been written. I'm not deluded or Julia Childish enough to venture into that arena, but as we got sucked into wine appreciation we found ourselves thinking and acting differently about dining out and dining in.

Walk into any wine store or gift shop that sells wine tchochkes, and there will be a dish towel, place mat, coaster, or wall plaque with the following popular saying: "I love to cook with wine. Sometimes I even put it in the food." We have one, God help us, and we have others with different cute mottoes on them. When wine came into our lives, we cooked with it, we cooked alongside it, and we found our way into scary expensive restaurants.

It all started at home. Many of us well recall Graham Kerr and his television show, The Galloping Gourmet, back in the late Sixties. (It's one of the few things I do remember from the late Sixties). Kerr (who insisted that his name was pronounced "care") had the most successful cooking show on television at the time, and probably helped establish the genre in its present form. He was popular for his decadent recipes, loaded with butter and cream, his humor, and his trademark glass of red wine that he hit on, often quite liberally, throughout the show.

That's us. Whether we're making a recipe that commands us to throw an entire bottle of Zinfandel over four pounds of chicken, or just boiling up some pasta, we're previewing the wine we selected to go with the dish, hoping there'll be some left by the time dinner's ready.

All of which led us to devote a good deal of mental effort to what goes with what, which most people—quite sanely —don't worry about all that much, at least not until they have their oenological epiphany. Even when we had only a few bottles in the house, we were sliding down the slippery slope, trying to decide whether to open the Chianti or the Nero d'Avola with the red sauce.

It was an exponential enlargement of gustatory consciousness, and it happened not only because of the little we knew about wine at the time, but also because

our tastes had changed. Maybe sharpened is a better word.
Or intensified.

As the obsession tightened its grip, we started drinking
(slightly) better wines, which means they were more complex,
which means they had more layers of aromas and flavors
to figure out. Soon, we heard ourselves saying "well, there's
some cedar on the nose, but the first thing that hits me on
the palate is the dark plum, with a little bit of eucalyptus
kicking in on the finish." We truly deserved to be severely
beaten about the head and shoulders. Some of our friends
began to hate us, while others called us during office hours
from a wine store, wanting to know if 1997 was a good year
in Burgundy. (It wasn't.)

Point is, learning to taste wine is learning to taste, period.
We pulled apart the flavors of everything we ate. One day I
caught myself swirling and sniffing a glass of water, which got
me a smack on the head from Debi. She threatened to tell
Annie about it, but didn't. When we invited friends over for
dinner, we spent as much time figuring out the wine as we
did cooking the food. Wine is food.

Cooking with wine, as apart from cooking while drinking
wine, is a whole different thing. Though this may not be
universally true, it seems to me that recipes based around
wine are more complex than a French horn, running to
fourteen pages, demanding 300 ingredients, and taking
hours to prepare. This is not necessarily a bad thing, it
must be said, because part of the joy of creating anything
worthwhile and beautiful lies in the pleasure of taking pains.
A movement known as Slow Food, which originated in
Milan, Italy, has spread through the world, promoting the
pleasures of preparing good, sensibly grown food and sitting
at table, sharing with friends. Not such a bad idea.

So there are few things I enjoy more than whipping out my tattered and sticky copy of Sid Goldstein's *The Wine Lover's Cookbook*, prying apart the pages, spending four hours making a shopping list of ingredients, blowing a stupid amount of money at the gourmet market, and devoting the next three and a half days to the preparation one of his fabulous entrees that makes our glass of Syrah sing like all three tenors.

But this is not a custom appropriate to every evening... just when we find an excuse to invite some friends, cook for them, and continually fill their glasses. Getting seduced by the wine life, even a little, made us treat this aspect of our social activities a bit differently. I printed up menus to put at each place setting, spending hours figuring out Microsoft Publisher, trying different type faces, inserting little wine related doodles from the clip art file. I described the courses in fanciful terms, often in my best pidgin French, six or seven of them, listing the wine that would accompany each. I know other people who actually do this, and we're all pretty much doomed. Like anyone who suffers from a debilitating condition, it's nice to know I'm not alone. I've been searching for therapists, support groups, anything, but none of them will take me in.

Didn't matter. Most of our friends were wine lifers anyway. We sipped while we cooked, kicking up Mom's spaghetti sauce recipe with a cup or two of Sangiovese, and had long since given up hanging out with people who lacked our own extreme affection for the grape. Shame on us again.

It pains me periodically to think back on how much the wine life has changed us, but still. There's a technique in sales training called the Ben Franklin close. Divide a sheet of paper into two columns, then write all the benefits of the buying decision on the left, and all the negatives on the right. See which list is longer, and go with that choice. The wine life changed so much for us, but the positives far outweigh what's in the right-hand column. If we go to dinner with friends we knew before the evening with Larry and Charlene, and if they don't appreciate or understand why we're putting a really special bottle on the table, we can't seem to stay friends for too long. Sad, but true.

But there's good news. We've met tons of new people who are at least as hopeless as we are. At parties, when we stand in small clusters with new acquaintances, one elbow bent, casting about for a common topic after we're well past the weather and the kids, we hope that wine will inevitably emerge from beneath the surface like Godzilla coming ashore in downtown Tokyo. If it does, and if our acquaintances respond warmly, we have plenty to discuss for the rest of the evening. If the topic hits the floor with a sickening thud, there's a good chance we'll politely excuse ourselves and go to the bar, hoping our hosts have put out a decent bottle or two.

Sidebar: a friend we met through Larry owned a restaurant in the next town, and held a Super Bowl party every year that quickly became the subject of myths, legends, and the occasional television network news report. He had a show cellar in his house holding around 6,000 bottles, and on Super Bowl Sunday he pretty much opened it to his invited guests and hoped they wouldn't hose him too badly. While the 1959 Chateau Margaux was off limits, as were the 3-liter bottles of every cult wine we never heard of, most of what he offered as refreshment was astonishingly generous.

Since we're on the subject of wine parties, this may be

a good time to talk about cheese. When we invite wine friends (which are the only kind we have left any more) for dinner at the house, the pre-prandial munchies are pretty much obligatory. In the old days it would be pretzels, chips, and dip. Not any more. Now, it's pate, cute little crackers, and handmade cheeses from a small family farm in Wisconsin that started making them the day before Washington crossed the Delaware.

The wine life took us inevitably to cheese, which is just as complicated and considerably more aromatic. It's a place where Velveeta doesn't cut it, where those individually-wrapped Kraft singles my mother used to grill on bread become woefully lacking. Like good wine, good cheese costs money. *There's* a surprise.

We took the wine trip, learning about many of the different kinds and what foods they go with. It became belatedly apparent that we'd also have to make the cheese voyage, discovering Reblochon, Humboldt Fog, handcrafted artisanal products, the difference between cheeses made from sheep's milk, goat's milk and cow's milk. Monty Python's cheese shop skit became more dear to us than our previous favorite, the dirty vicar. We even went to cheese tastings, just like wine tastings, and then we met Carole.

Wine takes us places, in this case to a local woman (I believe she's Belgian) who makes her living as what I can only describe as a cheese sommelier. The only other one I ever met was at Artisanal restaurant in New York, at which every dish (except maybe for the martinis) is based around cheese of some sort. Carole holds classes and samplings, gourmet markets hire her to put together their cheese selections, and so do local restaurants. She's the area's only cheese celebrity. This much sought after woman is more than an encyclopedia of cheese, she is the Library at Alexandria.

Let's get back to the restaurants, where we encounter food, wine and, on many occasions, even cheese. Many of the better places offer a cheese course, very European, just before dessert.

Here's another part of the wine life where it really helps to be well-resourced. As the passion grew, as food and wine became more part of one another, we found ourselves choosing restaurants on the basis of the wine list instead of the food list. That divides the grape geeks into two classes…those who decide on the wine first, as I've already mentioned, and then what to eat with it, and those who tell them what putzes they are for doing that.

It's a constant wine lifer complaint: many restaurants that are reasonably good or very good at food pay ridiculously little attention to the wine side of the business. Either the list will be too limited or (more commonly) they'll sell us a decent bottle and give us those birdfart Libbey glasses to drink out of.

Which brings me (and many, many other wine lifers) to a peeve that's more than just a pet—it's an adopted child. Wine prices in restaurants. Among wine lifers, this is a constant conversation, and a constant gripe. This is where too much knowledge is a dangerous and upsetting thing.

Once we were up to over 100 bottles we had our arms pretty well around the topic of what wines cost how much, and where. And, driven out of sheer economic necessity, we'd rooted out some bargains—the $10 wines that were well regarded, and very much to our taste.

So it's hard not to get our knickers in a twist when we read a wine list and see a bottle of very nice wine that costs

$10 in the supermarket being sold for $40 and up. I'm not all that good about figuring things out, but this should be a classic no-brainer for restaurant owners. And there should be a special circle of Hell for people who charge quadruple the retail price for a bottle of vin ordinaire.

I mean, really. Wine is the one inventory item in restaurants that is all good news. It doesn't go bad all that much, takes up little space, is relatively easy to store properly, and actually increases in value (sometimes) the longer it remains unsold. Plus which, a wine display, even a small glassed-in cellar, adds mightily to the décor and cachet of the establishment. Since twenty per cent of restaurant customers generate eighty per cent of the wine revenue, the more reasonable the prices are, the more the wine lifers will buy. Am I the only one who understands this? Excuse me while I strike my forehead with the palm of my hand.

Sidebar: there is a genre of restaurant—my favorite kind—that's attached to a gourmet market or similar establishment. We can go into the market, buy a bottle at retail, take it to the restaurant and they'll serve it to us for five bucks. We eat there all the time.

We should have paid attention to the signs. Wine lifers spend considerable discretionary income on dining out. If we had discretionary income, we would, too. Like everyone else, we go over the top on special occasions, but in our family there are only two birthdays and one anniversary in a year. So we find other reasons (excuses) to dine finely, or we make them up. For example, it has become a tradition for us to arrive at the annual Wine Experience a day early, so our group can share a dinner the night before the event starts. Sometimes this works, and sometimes it gets way out of hand. Friends invite other friends, who invite others, and while most of them bring a bottle or two of something good, the attendees at our dinners have grown so numerous that half of them are lost to us in the atmospheric haze of distance, all the way down at the other end of the table, over the horizon and out of sight. Last time we did it, we had thirty people, and didn't know half of them.

In the "find other reasons" category, there is the dinner that's enjoyed in the domain of some world famous celebrity chef like Alain Ducasse, Wolfgang Puck, or Thomas Keller, such as the repasts I just mentioned, the ones we save up for all year and share with our Wine Experience buddies. Being on vacation is also a reason, so maybe there's a place in the countryside way outside of Brussels sporting a Michelin star or two or three, and we drive a hundred miles knowing we'll have to leave them the car to pay for the meal, but we're willing to take the train back to the city. Or that time we were in Paris, and through some kind of miraculous interruption in the natural order of the universe we were gifted by unseen powers with a reservation at the Jules Verne in the Eiffel Tower, where Debi's menu didn't have prices on it so she ordered the $75 bowl of soup, and we were lucky to get out of there for $250 a person. For lunch. We probably won't do that again, but at least we can cross it off the bucket list.

On the "make something up" list are dinners we've planned, seduced by or accompanied by wine lifer friends, when we declare our own Special Occasion, which may be a real one, such as Valentine's Day, or completely fictional, like an odd-numbered Thursday. First, we find a restaurant that will let us bring our own wine and won't charge us a $50 per bottle corkage fee, and then we work out the menu with the chef and manager. This is not a recommended course of action, because the food usually winds up costing more than a BMW.

The evil genius behind all this is Jack Dilman, introduced to us by (guess who) Larry and Charlene back in maybe 2002. It's not just the 3,000 bottle cellar behind his kitchen that makes him a great guy, nor is it the fact that his fabulous wife Lana is an internationally-trained gourmet chef and being invited to their house for dinner is like going to Nobu Matsuhisa's house on New Year's Eve. No, it's that Jim has a talent for coming up with deliciously corrupt ideas about dinner and wine and the like.

"Let's do a Chateau Latour vertical," he pipes up one night. "Five couples. Ten bottles, five vintages. Jerry, you find the wines." It took us six months to put it together, haunting the Internet auction sites for the wines, and after I spent an unconscionable amount of our mutual money on them, he tells us he's arranged dinner at the Ritz-Carlton.

There is a physical sensation known as a "klong." It is a sudden rush of fecal matter to the heart. The feeling I got at the Ritz when they brought the check. I braced for the call from the credit card company, but it took them several days to catch up with me.

The wine ran us about $3,000, so that's $300 a person, the dinner was another $150 a head, and the two bottles of white we bought with the appetizers upped it another $50 a person. Okay, it was a once in a lifetime splurge, and we'll never do it again until Jack comes up with another degenerate wine inspiration and, fools that we are, we climb on board.

CHAPTER 32

It's a Guy Thing.
You Wouldn't Understand.

No doubt about it. Wine is a guy thing, and a harsh mistress. This chapter offers a slightly twisted discussion of why this is.

January, 2007

"Will somebody please explain to me," Deb asked soon after New Year's Eve, "why wine is such a guy thing?"

After sitting through some of the big time tastings, and taking those first not-at-all reluctant steps into the wine life, and attending our seventh Wine Experience, I had to reflect on that one. When we go to a tasting or wine event we see plenty of women, and mostly, they know their stuff. Female winemakers are famous, like Pam Starr, Heidi Barrett, and Helen Turley, whose wines can sell for as much as a mid-sized car. As I've mentioned many times in previous pages, Debi's sensitivity to the nuances of what's in her glass impresses me constantly. And yet.

In contrast to Tony's wife Patty, who bolts in the opposite direction when she hears the pop of a cork, Debi is interested and analytical, and will sample pretty much any kind of wine I open, unless it's one of my nine-dollar-a-bottle "finds" from an allegedly up-and-coming wine region like East Kishinev or Lower Burundi. But perceptive as her palate is, she doesn't tickle in the direction of reading books about it, haunting the wine sites and chat rooms on the web, and stopping in every single wine store she sees on the off chance she'll find a rare treasure in the clearance bin. Her appreciation tends much more to the sensational than the cerebral, and she points out subtleties of flavor and aroma that I sadly miss while I'm reading the back label about the blend and the harvest and how the juice rested for 27 months in French oak barrels, 60% of which were new.

We know several wine-loving couples (the rest of our friends having deserted us, or us them), and in each case it's the husband who buys the wine, stocks it, makes lists, puts his inventory on an Excel spread sheet, writes out the tags for the bottles. These activities seem not to call to women, and I haven't found many exceptions.

Debi has been to wine tastings without me, and has come home with her own discoveries, which she searches out and buys, but that's where it ends, except for the drinking part. I'm the one who has to keep track of them, find out when they're drinkable, inventory them, put them away, and remember where they are in the cave.

I've given up trying to figure out that dynamic, but I'm really sure of one thing: when it comes to complete obsession with hunting down a bottle, taking it home and killing it, the boys are way out in front.

How to explain this particular anomaly of gender? I conducted my own intensive personal research into the phenomenon, which consisted of informal interviews with those male friends who share my interest/obsession (the only friends I have left), usually over a glass of vin du jour. They all suffer from the same hunter-killer hard-wiring, though some of them, like Jack Dilman, are wired a little harder than others. He's been known to buy so many cases of wine at one time that they get delivered to his house on pallets with a fork lift.

The one thing wine-obsessed men all seem to have in common is that they don't want their wives to know how much they buy. There's some sort of cultish mysticism to male wine acquisition, a scurrying in the dark, folded arms clutching a bag that clinks mysteriously, or a small cardboard box that's heavier than its size would indicate. It's the hard hormonal buzz that comes from discovering, on the wine store shelf, stuck way in the back behind the new stock, one bottle, and only one, of a favorite wine that I drank the last of a few years ago and could never find anywhere else ever again. Like the hunter-gatherer I am, my clutching hand whips out, I grab it, take it to the cashier. And find out it's half price.

Debi says that luck happens when hard work meets opportunity. In the case of men and wine, the hard work comes in the reading, the acquiring of information, the hunting, the going about daily affairs with antennae aquiver for that lucky bottle in that unlikely place. For my brothers and me, the opportunity comes from looking at every wine display we can find, in every store, supermarket, discounter, closeout bin, no matter where. And sometimes, it's all opportunity and no work at all. I know a man who acquired a complete collection—about a thousand bottles—of really fine wines, great producers, excellent vintages, sensational selection, from an incipient retiree who owned a mom and pop supermarket in some Midwestern city. The former grocer sold the inventory cheap, because all those bottles had been in the basement for so long (under coincidentally excellent storage conditions). He'd never put any of it out on the shelves, and given the inner-city location of his store, wouldn't have sold it if he had. Besides, all of it was so *old*. I have so much faith in the personal integrity of this accidental opportunist I am confident he offered a fair price even though he had been, for a brief period, a guest of the state.

In wine buying for men, the thrill of the hunt meets the art of the deal, but it's even more intense and visceral than that. It's like having a mistress. I have to smuggle the stuff, for God's sake, into my own house. And if I couldn't do that, if Debi weren't gone enough, I'd consider renting an apartment for it somewhere across town. Ron my dentist friend is firmly in this category, with 2,000 bottles hidden in three wine storage facilities in widely-separated parts of the county. Does he go visit them? What does he tell his wife when he slips out to sneak home with a treasured bottle of 1966 Romanée-Conti La Tache? How does he explain the cork dust on his hands? The faint drip of red on the front of his shirt? How will he keep his wife from reading this book?

It's ridiculous. A guy will spend $225 on a bottle of wine (a lot more than we spend on a case) and sneak it home, but a woman will get the same surreptitious pleasure out of finding a designer dress on a back rack marked down to $25, hustling it out of the store, and then buying a $200 pair of shoes to wear with it.

I think it's probably just tradition. The world of wine is more conservative than any established religion. The making of wine dates from the time when men hunted and gathered, and women cooked and bred. Today, there are plenty of women involved in the making and selling (and drinking) of wine. Most of them have better taste buds than the men, and several of them are truly famous. But when women plunk down $600 plus for a case, they don't keep it a secret. Too bad, because they never experience the dubious thrill of sneaking it into the house.

CHAPTER 33

Maybe It's Not a Guy Thing, After All

In the new world of wine, women are not only catching up, they're starting to take the lead.

July, 2012

It's easy to think of the wine world as bound by tradition, since the practice of winemaking started before the discovery of fire, and because there are places in the world where people still crush grapes with their bare feet. But today things are changing quickly, and in spite of all the musing I've done about wine being almost solely the province of people of the masculine persuasion, women are making their mark. The influence of female winemakers and drinkers is being felt in the way wines are made, served, marketed, and consumed. Which brings me to Isabelle Forêt.

Isabelle is one of France's premier wine critics and journalists, and occupies a unique position in the wine world because she's female. Not only that, her books and blogs treat wine appreciation and consumption purely from a woman's point of view. She believes that wine evaluation has been hijacked by "macho snobs" whose arrogant pronouncements created what she calls "intellectual tyranny." Strong words, but not entirely off the mark.

Since forever, waiters in restaurants would invariably hand the wine list to the man at the table. Isabelle didn't like that. And, in the major wine journals and magazines, the vast (and I do mean vast) majority of the critics are men. Other than Isabelle, I'd be hard pressed to name more than one or two other serious female wine writers.

And, based on my own experience, I do believe that men have exercised, if not intellectual tyranny, at least some control over the historical and philosophical dimensions of this ancient beverage. As I said, the appeal for women is generally hedonistic.

When I was a sophomore in college, I took a course called "Marriage and the Family." On the first day of class, the professor, a kindly-looking, smallish woman in her sixties, entered the lecture hall as the bell rang, and the first thing she said was "Boys and girls are…different."

After the hooting and nudging and exclamations of "duhhhhh" died down, she amplified on that statement, and much of what she said back then applies today to how and why men and women approach and appreciate wine so differently.

In her excellent book *Women of Wine: The Rise of Women in the Global Wine Industry*, Ann B. Matasar profiles women who have had a major impact on the business. She deals with winemakers like Helen Turley and Heidi Barrett, and women on the business and marketing end, including Alexandra Marnier Lapostolle and several of the daughters of well-known winemakers (Gina Gallo comes to mind, as does Gaia Gaja, both of whose families are household names in the wine world) who have grown up in the family business and taken over both winemaking and marketing responsibilities. Today, women own several of the greatest, most historic chateaux in France. Going even further back, there's the tale of the Widow Cliquot, whose husband died in 1805 when she was 27. She took over her husband's winery in Champagne and was among the first successful businesswomen in the history of the country. So it's clear that feminine sensibilities have slowly crept into the way wine is made, and how it tastes when it comes out of the barrel. The operative word here is "slowly."

For Isabelle Forêt, wines made by and for men have mostly been "coarse swill," destroying the taste of the meal. Today, the collective consciousness skews toward the idea that wine is at least as feminine as it is masculine. And indeed, wines are often described in those terms by the (mostly male) wine critics who write for the major magazines. A wine can be "masculine" or "seductive," "silky" or "muscular." This whole sexist thing has been around for a long time.

I've already noted that for my wife Debi the appeal of wine lies in the sensual and hedonistic. Her sense of smell is unparalleled, and her palate, exquisitely attuned, often picks up layers of flavor and complexity in wine that escape me utterly. The only time she cares about how the wines are labeled and stored in the cellar is when she can't find the bottle she's looking for.

Boys and girls are different. There's no arguing with the cosmic divergence of our respective body chemistries and their influence on our behavior (as any married man can confirm) and chemistry alone is probably enough to control the way our taste buds and olfactories respond to the wines we expose them to. Isabelle maintains that women have a more "refined" sense of taste than men, and are better at perceiving the subtleties and complexities of beverages like wine. I believe her, because Debi is living proof, and while I'm sure I could find some science to cite right about now, I'd rather spare us the boredom.

It's probably easier to be snobbish about wine than about any other luxury item. I went to a wine dinner once at a local restaurant, and it happened that the Ferrari Club was having happy hour in the bar. The parking lot was full of gorgeous, artistically sculpted Italian iron, each one worth a significant fraction of a million dollars. But the owners I talked to were very down to earth about their cars and their passion for them, exotic as they might have been. Not so with many wine lovers, and they know who they are.

The whole point is that wine should be pleasurable, accessible, and easy to enjoy for everyone. At least that's what Isabelle maintains. Sure, the guys like to play wine trivia once in a while (Quick! Name the ten crus of Beaujolais!) but for women it's all about what's in the glass…and on the plate…and the company at the table.

Okay, so how do women really influence the experience of wine? Well, first of all, it's estimated that women buy 60% of the wine that's sold in the world. What we don't know is what kind they're buying, and how they decide to pull this bottle off the shelf instead of that. Before I really started digging into the matter (having no life otherwise), my guess would have been this: since women do the food shopping, the wines they purchase are of the supermarket variety: wines in the under-$20 range, meant for everyday drinking. There are, in fact, more kinds of wine on sale in the average supermarket (over 300) than any other product category. Imagine if we had to choose from 300 different breakfast cereals or varieties of tomato sauce. The men, on the other hand, do the research, read the wine journals, and seek out the really good stuff.

Wrong again, grasshopper. The wine industry, being very interested in selling wine to women, and eager to reap the dollars involved, has commissioned extensive research into just this issue. The gathered data are subjected to slicing and dicing in every direction, and probably run through the beta-binomial theorem just for good measure. The results run exactly opposite to my pitiful guesswork. In general, women buy wine more often and spend more on it than men do. Plus, some surveys suggest that almost 57% of wine drinkers are women, and 43% are men. Who'd've thunk it?

There's one effect of the female wine consumer that is pretty clear: many wines are being made in a softer style, with less tannin and more fruit. Of course, this may also be due to the fact that most people who buy wine don't lay it down in a cellar to age for ten years. We want to buy it today and drink it on Saturday, so it has to be approachable right now. However, one influence of the female wine drinker may be the increasing popularity of rosé wines, which, as I write this, are enjoying a new en vogue status.

Another recent phenomenon is the ease with which women can band together to share their interest in wine. Thank you, World Wide Web. There are sites called "Women on Wine," "Women With Wine," "Women and Wine," "Women for Wine," "Women Who Just Like Wine," and just about any other permutation you can think of. The purpose of these web endeavors is to allow women to learn about the topic, share information, and join together for appreciation sessions. They seem to hold a lot of events where the central purpose is to drink wine. Gets my vote.

But how are men reacting to women's increasing interest in—and knowledge of—the wine world? Right off the bat, it's nice when two people find they have something in common. In this era of rampant singledom, match dot com, eharmony, and in general getting hooked up on the Internet, anything that starts a conversation and gets you quickly closer to the person you just met would certainly be welcome. Debi and I know several couples (more than three or four) who met through dating sites and went on to create successful marriages, so the Internet hookup thing apparently works better than hanging around in bars or trolling for sailors on the docks. What if, at the first face to face meeting for coffee in a very public place, they had discovered a mutual interest in wine? I'd consider that a big boost to the progress of the relationship. Isabelle says that wine can release a woman's passions and sensitivity. Men need to get the hint.

CHAPTER 34

Birthday Surprise, French Style

*I*sabelle takes us on a roll through the wine country of the Loire Valley.

October, 2007

On Sunday morning after the Wine Experience, Debi asked, "You know what today is?"

I knew, but pretended to my usual bewildered state. "Huh?"

"It's Sunday."

"So?"

"Today's the day you tell me about my birthday surprise."

It was, as I well knew, Sunday, October 28th, 2007, four days after Debi had one of those milestone birthdays. I know better than to disclose which one, but it ended in a zero. We had arrived in New York the previous Wednesday for our 8th annual trip to The Purpling of the Teeth. Debi elbowed me constantly the whole time, expecting her big birthday gift on the actual day, which was pretty reasonable, and wanting to know what it was, which was not reasonable at all. I had my own personal motivations for holding things back.

Actually, I was planning to spring it on her at the airport on the way home, but decided to cave in and avoid the incessant questioning I was sure would ensue for the rest of the day. So I gave her a birthday card, and her passport was inside.

"Where are we going?"

"Paris."

"Really!?? When?"

"In a couple of hours."

She jumped up and down and wet my face with kisses.

My original intention was to get us in a cab that Sunday afternoon, drive us innocently out to JFK, and astonish her by winding up at Air France instead of Jet Blue, but Debi pried the truth out of me, as she always does.

Cousin Cynthia was an accomplice in this plot, keeping a straight face in spite of the tricky situation. She was especially helpful because I didn't know that the surprise had been partially blown a few weeks earlier, despite all my efforts to make Debi's birthday what the government likes to call a Black Op. Some unknowing soul at the airline had phoned the house to tell us that one of our flight times had changed, and Debi had taken the call. She told Cynthia she thought something was up and that it involved Paris, but Cynthia hadn't spent all those years in law school for nothing. She nuanced her response like the trained attorney she is, and with such consummate evasiveness that Debi didn't catch on. Cynthia also was silent to me about Debi's inkling, but I attribute that to the mystical bond that exists among all women in all places.

Debi is something of a jumper to conclusions, and sort of assumed that if there really was a secret trip in the offing we would first be going home from New York, then continuing on from there. I reminded her, gently, of what they say about people who assume. Due to her assumptions, she wasn't sure about the parameters of the overall trip. She also didn't know that the final destination of the journey was not Paris at all, but far beyond.

"We're leaving...now?"

"Couple of hours. Later on this afternoon."

"But what about the dog? What about my job? What am I going to wear? What about..."

All taken care of. For the previous five months, I had spent hours in clandestine conversation with Debi's managers at work, with our trusted house-sitter, and with Cynthia. Knowing that France is on roughly the same latitude as Labrador, I was sure the weather in late October would be uncomfortable, so I asked Cynthia to tell Debi that there was a cold snap in New York, and to bring warm clothes. Good thing, too.

Nobody loves Paris when it drizzles, and I don't care what the song says. It was cold and drippy when we got there after a typical journey. Two hours late out of JFK, watching several passengers die of old age waiting for their bags at Charles de Gaulle, hoping our names wouldn't appear on the dreaded Lost Luggage Screen, which had happened to us during other trips, when they gave us the bad news along with a hearty handshake and little zipper pouch containing a t-shirt, toothbrush, and miniscule stick of deodorant. Then there was the always-insane crush of traffic from the airport into town.

It was old home week in Paris, also part of the plan. Cousin Cynthia's son Brian, whom we had initiated into the Wine Experience experience a few years earlier, was raised with his parents' palate for wine, and he showed up promptly at 6:30 the evening of our arrival, commuting in from his teaching job in Lille. I made a lame excuse to Debi and dragged Brian onto the Metro. Our ex-pat friend Ed, with whom we'd shared that fateful bottle of grappa in Florence a few years earlier, was waiting for us at the Gare de Lyon, because he had arranged our rental car, which Debi also didn't know about. Ed would be our assistant tour guide for the trip, and was charged with doing most of the driving, because I'm not nearly deranged enough to drive in Paris, no matter what my friends think.

After getting it all straightened out with Ed, and pestering Brian with questions about the Lille life and what his job was like, we dragged ourselves all the way back across town, picked up Debi, and Metroed back the other way, to Bofinger, our favorite brasserie. Charming little quirk about Bofinger. They didn't take our names while we waited for a table, but instead gave us a card with the name of a classical composer on it. When they called out "Rossini," for example, Brian, intellectual that he is, hummed a few bars of William Tell. The couple that held the Mozart card heard us whistle the opening notes of the Jupiter Symphony as they walked past us. Our card said Salieri, which stumped us both completely.

Another typical Parisian dinner experience, waiting an hour for a table, but it was worth it – if you can call eating a huge mound of Alsatian sausage and sauerkraut at 11PM

while suffering from atemporal circadian disrhythmia a fun
thing to do.

Next morning, I sprung the rest of the surprise.

"We need to pack."

"Pack? We just got here! Are they throwing us out of the
hotel? Is our credit card screwed up again?"

"No and no. But this is not a Paris trip. We're going...
elsewhere."

I had two reasons for picking the Loire valley for the
wine surprise. First, it was close enough to Paris that we
could drive down there conveniently, spend a few days, and
drive back. Bordeaux would have been a better choice, but
we didn't have that much time. Second, I wanted some of
Debi's birthday trip to be spent in the chateaux that litter
the countryside in that region of France, and third (okay,
three reasons), we had both, over the years, become hugely
charmed by the Sauvignon Blancs that come from Pouilly
and Sancerre.

Ed picked us up at the hotel with Isabelle Forêt riding
shotgun. She was another part of the surprise, our guide to
the Loire, thanks to Ed, who has more French connections
than Popeye Doyle. After living in Paris for over 25 years,
Ed knows all the Important People. Not normal important
people like politicians, or the mayor or the chief gendarme,
but really Important People. The woman who literally
wrote the book about all the best restaurants in the city
that tourists like us have never heard of and will never find
on our own, the guy who let us in through the back door
of the D'Orsay when the line stretched all the way to the
Trocadero, and Isabelle, whose credentials and wine chops
have already been disclosed.

Sidebar: when we were early into our wine lives, we visited Ed in Paris, and he found us a woman whose husband worked in the Champagne industry. She bundled us off in her car at eight in the morning, drove us northeast, through World War I battlefields whose names I recognized, past low hillsides flooded with unending seas of brilliant yellow mustard flowers, to the ancient city of Reims. The chalk caves beneath the major wineries were astonishing, but it has been our experience that the best winery visits are the ones scheduled for half an hour and wind up taking three.

In a tiny village south of Epernay, low stone houses lined the only two streets, some more historic than others. On vacant land between the buildings, in back yards, and in every space on the street that wasn't cobblestoned, Chardonnay vines marched off in every direction. M. Fournier and his daughter Gabrielle had turned one of their homes into a winery, in the basement of which they managed to make about 500 cases of excellent Champagne a year. I've seen many basement recreation rooms, bars, and foosball facilities, but the Fourniers had decked theirs out with huge cement fermentation vats, a crusher, destemmer, and a bottling line. On the ground floor, in what may once have been the living room, was a tasting area and hundreds of bottles displayed on racks and shelves.

As Gabrielle poured and we sipped from a few different bottles, I became distinctly uneasy, because one of the wines gave off a distinct flavor of…mushrooms. I was far along enough to know that wine can taste like a lot of bizarre things, but mushrooms? I'd never encountered that in any sparkling white wine. Did I dare to remark on it? Wouldn't it be an insult to the winemaker?

Finally, I whispered to our guide, "Champignon?" Gabrielle heard me, and stopped in mid-pour, her face alight with pleasure.

"Champignon! Oui! C'est ça!" She complimented me on the acuity of my palate, because she *wanted* the wine to taste like mushrooms. Who knew?

Isabelle believes (and can pretty much prove) that men and women taste things differently due to physiological distinctions that go far beyond the obvious (and delightful) divergence in the nature of their reproductive equipment. Her contention is that female taste buds are built as differently as everything else, and that women are especially sharp when it comes to identifying, understanding, and appreciating certain types of flavors. Her book, and the annual wine guides she publishes, are all based on that premise.

Ed and I had worked for months, frantically emailing plots and plans about the trip. Which chateaux to visit, who Isabelle knew and where she wanted to take us, scheduling how many days in this place, and how many days in that. Since Isabelle knows almost everyone in the French wine trade, she made the recommendations and finalized details, leading us down back roads that no wine tourist would even remotely consider.

The only thing good about driving in Paris is driving out of Paris. I found that out in 1995, when we were shooting a television show at the Chateau de Thoiry, about 40 miles from the city. (The Chateau, owned by the Baron de la Panousse, is a game farm, with all sorts of animals living in a kind of outdoor zoo. Ostriches (mean ones) roam freely, there are giraffes and hippos, zebras. Weird. No Parisian school child gets out of sixth grade without making a field trip to this attraction.) Leaving town in the morning was a motorist's delight, but coming home, even at 10:30 at night, was agony of the purest kind. We missed more than a few dinner reservations, and if there's one thing that Parisians take seriously, it's restaurant reservations. They even have brokers who arrange them on behalf of clients, and people who don't show up can never eat dinner in that town again. There's probably a blacklist of delinquent diners.

The Loire River rises in the massif centrale of France, runs north, then bends gradually westward, babbling across the country until it empties into the Atlantic at Nantes. Frankly, it's not all that much to look at. Mostly shallow and sluggish, with low mud banks along the edges, long, brown and narrow, winding out to the middle of the slow-moving stream. A desultory river, lazy and disappointed.

At the easternmost end, right where the river bends from its northerly course, there are two towns, Pouilly and Sancerre, right across the river from each other, and that was the first stop on the pilgrimage. The reason: we desperately wanted to visit the wild man of the Loire, Didier Dagueneau, about whom more in a moment.

When we finally reached Sancerre, we were so thirsty that we almost didn't have time to admire the view. But when we got up to the village, we changed our minds. Deliciously medieval, the town is built, as are all towns from that combative era, on the very defensible top of a hill. I admit that we haven't covered France the way we've explored Italy, but I'm convinced that there are few villages more visually delightful and downright charming than Sancerre. Despite its obvious lack of cathedrals and similar obligatory structures, the streets are lined with warm, inviting buildings that date back to the 1600s, made of stone in every shade of brown. The population is small, so there aren't many people wandering about, or many cars driving down the main drag. I don't remember noticing a traffic light, or even any stop signs. But there are intriguing side streets, a delightful village square, an impossibly old stone tower, and a couple of restaurants that make the trip even more worthwhile. It is a town for wandering.

First stop: the winery of Pascal Jolivet, a favorite of mine for quite some time. He makes an archetypal Sauvignon Blanc in the under-$20 range that invigorates with its minerality and clean fruit flavors. We had met him several times at the Wine Experience, including the one we had just attended two days earlier, and I wish I had his head of hair.

After a tasting in the cellar of Pascal's place, we staggered to lunch in a restaurant on the square, and about halfway through the meal our day veered in a whole new direction. The reason: the explosive arrival of Alphonse Mellot, who, if he isn't the mayor of Sancerre, should be.

Alphonse simply overflows with good will, geniality, and bienvenu. Sandy haired, bespectacled, open-faced and smiling, he bustled into the restaurant trailed by a befuddled wine writer from Australia who could barely keep up, grappled Isabelle firmly to himself, kissed her wetly on both cheeks and absolutely insisted that we join him at his winery immediately after lunch. Good thing, since we were planning to do that anyway.

The Mellot family has been making wine in the area since the year 1513, though Alphonse doesn't look nearly that old. He is, in fact, maybe 50. His winery is smack in the middle of the village and his caves descend hundreds of feet into the hill below the streets. Most of his barrel storage areas are at least 400 years old, with connecting tunnels between them so low that we had to Quasimodo our way around. The main winery is at street level, and its stainless steel computerized modernity is a shocking disconnect with all the 17th Century cobblestone picturesqueness right outside the door. If not for the fork lift rumbling down the street loaded with cases of wine, the scene could have been a snapshot back in time.

As soon as we arrived, pleasantly satisfied with our lunch, he started opening bottles, tapping barrels, and loosening the valves on the tanks. Long story short, we were willingly trapped in his winery for over five hours, glasses never empty, stumbling through the deep underground from cave to cave, bent over because of the low ceilings, swirling, sniffing, and spitting into the drains in the floor. (There wasn't enough spitting).

When we arrived after lunch, Alphonse was in the midst of hosting a visiting American couple accompanied by two young men in their mid-20s who told us they aspired to be winemakers. But their visit (how shall I say this), did not fulfill their ultimate expectations, because Alphonse hadn't seen Isabelle in quite some time, and shortly after we got there he devoted all his attention to her, and to us, and to keeping our glasses filled, and to discussing and commenting on his wines in a bizarre mixture of English and French. The four unfortunates trailed along behind, hating us for usurping their face time with Alphonse, victims of unfortunate neglect and an uncharacteristic lapse in hospitality which was entirely not our fault.

The last stop on the tour was Alphonse's office, the

other visitors having long since departed, disappointed, unfulfilled, and more than a little pissed off. The office shelves were not bearing up well under the weight of his personal wine collection, many of which he absolutely insisted on opening for us, disregarding our less-than-convincing protests.

By the time we tore into his stash, it was getting dark and cold, which is typical of northern France around the first of November. At that point we had no choice but to invite Alphonse to dinner.

He suggested a place in the neighboring village of Menetou-Salon, but first offered to guide us to our first night's lodging, and asked us to follow him there. It wasn't easy, because his driving was a solid reflection of his exuberant personality, and we lost him immediately in the dark, narrow country lanes, glimpsing his taillights far ahead only once or twice.

We arrived at the chateau well behind schedule, since Alphonse had coerced us into sampling so widely for so many hours. It's well known that the Loire valley is home to many of France's most spectacular chateaux, built by 17th and 18th-Century nobles who just couldn't wait to get out of Paris in the summer. The Chateau d'Ivoy is one of these.

One fact needs to be clear. There are chateaux in the Loire, and there are Chateaux. Many, like those abandoned villages in Tuscany, became tempting targets for large hotel chains who converted them into luxurious hostelries that extract 400 euros a night, and there's nothing wrong with that, because the places are breathtaking, and they concierge the hell out of their discriminating guests. We were looking for an experience that would be a bit more personal, more intimate, and less costly. We found it.

The Chateau d'Ivoy is owned by Jean-Gerárd and Marie-France Gouëffon-de-Vaivre, whose names have far too many diacritical marks and hyphens for me to contend with, so we just called them Marie and Gerard. The main building sports characteristic round towers on the corners and must cover a couple hundred thousand square feet. It was once the home of the treasurer to Mary Queen of Scots, and from the looks of the place, he kept most of her money for himself. But the couple, who are overwhelmingly gracious, run it more like a bed and breakfast than a luxury hotel. A B&B stuffed with priceless antiques, embroidered pillows depicting various species of hunting dogs, canopied beds, Hermes toiletries in the bath, outdoorsy artwork on the walls, and jaw-dropping objets d'art, but the experience was more like staying with friends than putting up in a hotel. No front desk, no bellhop, no valet parking. We were guests in someone's home. Someone's really, really big historic home.

After we checked in, Marie and Gerard showed us around the place and asked if we liked dogs. Well, we do, but were completely unprepared when they opened a back door and admitted a lumbering Irish Wolfhound, which, I now understand, is the biggest dog they make. We lost the capacity for speech. A moderately sized child could ride this animal, which weighed every bit of 220 pounds and stood hip high to Debi. This is the kind of dog that, when he licks you, you stay licked for a long time. Big damn dog.

Suitcases stowed, we were off once again, attempting to follow Alphonse as he careened, Mr. Toad-like, along narrow tree-lined country lanes in utter darkness (do they have to plant those trees so close to the road?) at a maniacal pace, roaring into the tiny village of Menetou-Salon and coming to a shuddering, squealing halt in front of a low, nondescript cottage. This small town has its own distinction as a winemaking area, and we've seen its name on several labels, but its products have never achieved the renown of Sancerre or Pouilly. It was sort of creepy, actually, because when we arrived it was around nine, and we gathered, Ed, Isabelle, Debi, Alphonse, and I, in eerily empty unlit streets. All the inhabitants were most emphatically in for the night, every window closed and tightly shuttered against the cold. Not a glimmer of light escaped anywhere. All was gloomy and lonely and vacant. Alphonse assured us that people lived there, but the place looked as though the zombies had marched through and cleaned it out.

The restaurant was very country, and I don't mean Cracker Barrel. We sat at long trestle tables with other diners, confronted during the course of several hours with plate after plate, bowl upon steaming bowl, a family-style deluge of rabbit, duck, chicken, fish, fresh grilled tomatoes, pasta, and several barrels of the local wine. We'd been drinking whites all day so a few bottles of Cabernet Franc were a welcome change.

After a tour of the kitchen (if you could call it that) where Grandmere did all the cooking on an ancient wood-fired stove (did I mention that this was a country restaurant?) thing got a bit out of hand, wine-wise. We finally bid au revoir to Alphonse and the new friends we'd made during dinner at about one in the morning, a good 12 hours after we'd first met.

Next morning, rough around the edges, we were up early (again), enjoying an extensive breakfast on silver service with Gerárd and Marie-France, then pulling our meager belongings together for another day of touring and tasting. Our first stop: a much anticipated meeting with one of our winemaking idols, and pretty much the main reason we'd come to the Loire in the first place.

CHAPTER 35

The Wild Man
of the Loire

*ne of the main reasons for the trip to the
Loire was to meet Didier Dagueneau, known as the
Wild Man of the Loire. Single-handedly, he changed
the way wine is made in a part of the world that
takes tradition very seriously indeed. He wasn't there.*

November, 2007

The Loire being the spiritual and biological home
of the Sauvignon Blanc grape, and the Loirese having
made this wine since well before Caesar trisected Gaul,
the atmosphere wasn't exactly welcoming when Didier
Dagueneau showed up in the town of Pouilly years before
and decided to show everybody How It's Done. If there is
a stronger word than outspoken, he was that. Critical of
tradition, too, which kept his neighbors from clasping him to
their collective bosom, but despite the inertia of the area,
most people agree that even though the prices he charged
were astronomical, Dagueneau pretty much redefined what
Sauvignon Blanc from that particular area is supposed to
be. Maybe revolutionized is a better term, since the offices

of his winery were decorated with pictures and posters of
Che Guevara and others of his political persuasion.

Big, burly and bearded, hair out to there, red flannel
shirted, accompanied everywhere by dogs only slightly
smaller than himself, anyone who saw Dagueneau would
label him a wild man at first sight, just on appearance alone
and before knowing anything about his wine. He looked
like he'd be more at home in Humboldt County than in
the outer reaches of Pouilly. He had no formal training as a
winemaker, having spent most of his life riding motorcycles
at high speeds and winning world championships in
dogsled racing. Most of his offerings sell in the $75-$120
range, which is painfully high for a Sauvignon Blanc, since
many quite quaffable and highly rated examples of the
varietal from New Zealand cost well under $15, and
excellent Pouillys and Sancerres are widely available for
under $25. But this is a case of getting what you pay for,
because his healthy disrespect (or maybe disdain) for the
way grandpere used to do it, his limiting of the yield he
took from his vineyards, and his pioneering application of
biodynamic agricultural principles led him to make wines
of transcendent elegance and purity. Critics worldwide
consistently rated his wines at 95 points and upward for
their style and finesse. So when it came to setting prices
for his products, he parted ways with the populist and
socialistic philosophies espoused by his Cuban revolutionary
hero, and headed straight for the profit motive. He felt that
his pricing strategy, called "charging what the market will
bear," was justified.

We had discovered Dagueneau's wines at the Florida
Wine Fest in Sarasota, the same one that allowed me to
converse in hesitant French with Paul Pontallier from

Chateau Margaux. The Sarasota tasting was another epiphany, though somewhat more modest than the one Larry had inflicted on us. Sampling several Dagueneau wines during the seminar, Debi and I looked at each other with eyes wide and knew that something important and expensive was being revealed to us.

****

"Oh, no! Not you people."

The first words we heard when we walked into the cool recesses of Dagueneau's winery on Thursday, November 1 came from—hard to believe—the four people we had encountered (or who had encountered us) the day before at Alphonse Mellot's.

They looked at us as though we were scrofulous lepers with body parts peeling away before their eyes. The way they said "you people" confirmed my impression that, after their experience of the day before, they hoped never to see us again, but they did, and we saw them.

Isabelle enjoyed the same relationship with the people at this winery as she did with Alphonse, so the older couple immediately harrumphed off the premises, deciding to wait in the car, while the two young aspiring winemakers toughed it out for about half an hour, hanging on the fringe of our group, angry and disappointed yet again, listening uncomprehendingly as Isabelle told us everything in the world about the wines, in French. Then they, too, gave up and pushed on to their next tasting. I felt badly, because I wouldn't want to come all the way to France, drag myself down to the outer reaches of the Loire Valley, and get cut out of the fun by four strangers with an inside track. But it honestly wasn't our fault.

When we arrived at Dagueneau's winery, which was tucked back on a private side street that he had named Rue Che Guevara, we were told that he'd been called away on some sort of vineyard emergency. We all suffer disappointments in our lives, but this one was particularly crushing. We were, however, hosted by one of his sons, who demanded that we taste every wine in every barrel and tank, which took about five hours, but no Didier, and we left without meeting him. On September 17, 2008, at 52 years old, he crashed while flying an ultralight aircraft, and was killed. His picture is still on my office wall.

Speaking of walls, even though Didier was not there to meet us, his personality permeated the entire winery, and not just because the iconic images of Fidel's best friend Ernesto were so much a part of the décor. The inside of the main tank room was lined with white plastic wallboard, upon which Dagueneau had written, with felt markers, quotations from Che and Chairman Mao, as well as a complete assortment of irreverencies, such as "The future belongs to fools, drunks, and thieves." We felt right at home.

As many wine geeks discover early in their travels, most tasting rooms just run their visitors in one door and out the other, hoping that someone will buy something on the way through. But we also found out that those who know even a little about wine, who ask informed questions, who demonstrate an appreciation for the effort, the culture, and the experience, are, in every case, warmly welcomed, whether in Sancerre or Sonoma. It didn't damage our cause to be accompanied by one of the country's premiere wine writers and critics, because that excited them more than somewhat, and impelled them to open the bottles, barrels, and tanks. Thanks to Isabelle, we had very deep bilingual discussions and very deep tastings. My French couldn't keep up with most of what Isabelle said (a friend of mine was married to a French woman who told me I spoke the language like a Spanish cow), but as our glasses were being continually topped off, it started to make sense. Didier's son, like Alphonse, opened every barrel of every vintage of every cuvée they make. We were late for our lunch reservation.

That Thursday afternoon Isabelle had arranged another tasting at de Ladoucette. Once again, there are chateaux, and there are Chateaux. Well, Baron Patrick de Ladoucette lives in a Chateau and a half. The place, a massive, sprawling white structure with lead-colored roof and a cluster of soaring circular towers, sits off the road and down at a lower elevation, looking like Cinderella's castle at Disney World, complete with turrets, crenulations, and, if I remember correctly, a flying buttress or two.

Many of the major vineyards in the Sancerre and Pouilly areas have been owned by the Comte Lafonde and the Ladoucettes ever since their purchase in 1787 from the illegitimate daughter of Louis XV. Bad timing, because France had a bit of a political dustup in 1789 which caused the family to fall on hard times. Unlike most of their noble friends, they were allowed to keep their heads, and once things had calmed down a bit, built the properties back up over the ensuing centuries. To this day, they make some of the finest examples of the appellation. However, from a stylistic standpoint, they and the Dagueneaus might as well be on separate continents, if not separate planets. Ironically, the two wineries are separated by only about 200 meters of vineyards.

At Dagueneau, there were oak barrels at every point of

the compass, and we must have sampled the contents of them all. The oak was one of Didier's heresies, because at de Ladoucette, there wasn't a barrel to be seen anywhere. It was a completely oak-free environment, the family being devout believers in the virtues and traditions of neutral containers for fermentation. The winemaking facility absolutely glittered with the refulgent brilliance of stainless steel.

Then it was on to the Chateau de Gizeux in Bourgueil, our home for the night, which Ed said was about 100 miles away, but he was criminally mistaken. It was more like 200 miles. We drove and drove and it got darker and darker, on the autoroute, off the autoroute, through villages, through the fast food and chain restaurant section of Tours, back out the other side, forever. We arrived in the deadest part of the night, but the owner, Geraud de Laffon, whose name, thankfully, requires no accent marks, acute, circumflex, or otherwise, still welcomed us with the same geniality that we'd encountered from Gerárd and Marie the night before.

The Ch. de Gizeux is the largest chateau in the Loire, which is saying quite a lot, but most of it is uninhabitable. These days, the upkeep on a house with 109 rooms (plus hallways, galleries and grand salons) is a bit beyond the means of most people, even those who are hereditary members of the French nobility. In fact, Geraud spent most of his working career as a sales representative for Zodiac, the company that makes those little rubber boats used by Navy SEALS and the descendants of Jacques Cousteau. When his father wanted him to take over the chateau, he didn't exactly jump at the chance. The oldest part of the building dates from 1338, and it's a bit much for one couple to handle.

To give us an idea of its size, Geraud told us that the roof covers 5.5 acres. There are riding stables, endless hallways, chambers and salons decorated by Italian artists imported to do the work in the early 17th century. Geraud is working hard to get grants from historical societies to help with the expense of cleaning and restoring the artwork.

Even though we had arrived late, dinner was ready, prepared by a chef from the village, and served in one of the many salons. Crystal chandeliers, dim light and a tang of smoke from the fireplace, high ceilings, glass upon glass of the valley's traditional wines, and Geraud's extensive line of ancestors, who regarded us, stern-visaged, from the ancient paintings on the walls.

An old world delight, and over much too soon. The next day, Debi's birthday having been celebrated in elaborate style, we had to go home.

CHAPTER 36

How I Caused a Constitutional Crisis

ertain states allow wine to be shipped directly to consumers, others do not. It's a Supreme Court kind of thing, and very controversial.

March , 2006

Okay, it wasn't just me. There are many others of my ilk.

Back when we started getting crazy and buying wine from the auction sites, we weren't much concerned about whether we'd actually receive the product or not. As I mentioned, the visits by the FedEx and UPS people who strained the capacity of their handcarts and their lumbar muscles wheeling cases into our office were both regular and reassuring. We bought, they shipped. But early in 2008 that started to change. For the worse.

Actually, the pressure had been building, on and off, for many years, but it seemed to come to a boil right around this time.

Not even the cork vs. screw cap controversy is as inflammatory as the battle that's constantly being waged across the country about direct shipping of wine to consumers. Like everything else connected with the wine life, it is an issue both complicated and comical, but it all comes down to the fact that some states will allow wineries and wine stores to ship directly to a buyer's home, and others will make the buyers rot in rat-infested jails for it. In about half the states, direct shipping is a felony, right up there with possession of crack and kiddie porn.

Why the difference? Partly because of what it says in the Constitution, and partly because some state liquor lobbies are more powerful (and greedier) than others.

The 10th Amendment specifies that "the powers not delegated to the United States by the Constitution, nor prohibited by it to the states, are reserved to the states respectively, or to the people." That includes the regulation of the sale of alcohol, which, because there's so much tax money involved, the states jealously guard for themselves.

But then there's the question of the Commerce Clause, found in the same august document, which says that states may not "erect barriers" to the free flow of goods across state lines.

And then, just to put a little lagniappe on the issue, there's the 21st Amendment, passed in 1933, which put an end to America's disastrous Great Experiment with prohibition, for which wine drinkers are especially grateful. To really screw things up, the amendment states, in part, that "the transportation or importation into any state, territory, or possession of the United States for delivery or use therein of intoxicating liquors, in violation of the laws thereof, is hereby prohibited." Clearly, this was intended to put an end to the grip that organized crime had on the liquor trade, but there have been…unintended consequences.

The states and their liquor lobbies point to this provision in court so forcefully that they almost dislocate their elbows, just the way gun enthusiasts point to that "keep and bear arms" phrase, and that's what makes gun and wine control such judicial tar babies.

(In most serious wine-producing countries, the making of wine, and the selling of it, is controlled by a central government authority, such as the INAO in France. In the United States, it's controlled by the Bureau of Alcohol, Tobacco, and Firearms (and, I think, Explosives), which demonstrates fairly clearly, I think, the position that wine occupies in our culture, in contrast to other countries.)

Sidebar: I once called the ATF to find out what kind of wine I should drink with my Smith & Wesson .38. The agent said, "Depends on what you're smoking." (I know…old joke.)

It's hardly surprising that wine enthusiasts, wineries, and other concerns that try to sell wine on the web would come down solidly on the side of the Commerce Clause. The liquor wholesalers and state governments who count on the tax money see this movement as a bad moon rising, and a serious danger to the very fabric of our society.

Flash forward: In mid-2010, the House of Representatives began to consider yet another bill that would control wine shipping on a Federal, rather than a state, level, and the arguments, like those that have gone before, get pretty silly. Especially since the bill is supported, solidly backed, and mostly written by the National Beer Wholesalers Association. I'm still trying to figure that one out.

The wholesalers who control the "three tier" system of liquor distribution (wholesaler, retailer, consumer), constantly spread dire predictions that direct shipment will allow persons under legal age to buy alcoholic beverages without ever going into a store. They have a point, but only if we try to picture some 16-year-old hacker in Wyoming stealing his father's platinum Amex card so he can order a case of Beaucastel Chateauneuf du Pape Hommage a Jacques Perrin for his own personal use. Besides, every reputable shipping company has a provision for "adult signature required" delivery. But that's their story and they're sticking to it. Frankly, I'm surprised they can state this argument without a giggle, wink, and elbow nudge.

At bottom, the real issues are, as always, money and power. It is in a government's basic nature to try to control as many aspects of human activity as possible. That's what governments do, and why people go into politics. Since states control alcohol sales within their borders, it's a natural conclusion that direct sales to consumers would fall under that purview. Some states control liquor sales more strictly than others, and there are others that don't care one way or another if UPS hauls cases of Cabernet to the doorways of their taxpaying registered voters. Some states allow access to alcohol only through state-owned stores, or, like Florida, are home to a liquor lobby that has enjoyed a virtual stranglehold on alcoholic beverage legislation for a very long time. Virginia is similarly clutched about the throat. There, one man was arrested and charged for selling a single bottle of wine to a friend.

And there's the sales tax issue. States cry and moan that they'll lose tons of revenue since purchases made on the Internet generally avoid state sales taxes. The consequences, say the states, are nothing short of apocalyptic. If I receive a case of wine at my home or office, government services will cease, schools close, garbage will pile up in the rat-infested streets, civil servants will go unpaid, and hordes of the undead will rise from the earth, ravaging our cities and eating our brains. Here, they have a point, if only a minor one. If I buy $400 worth of wine from Winebid, and they ship it right to my office, the state loses around $24 in sales tax. Now, I've spent a lot more than $400 on Internet wine purchases, and admit that I've absentmindedly neglected, on one or two occasions, to render unto Caesar what he's supposed to get. What if everybody did that?

But everybody doesn't do that, because of the nature of the product being sold, and the nature of the addict who's buying. Nobody goes on the Internet to buy a common wine that can be found at the supermarket or the local fine wine shop. For the vast majority of wine sales, the three-tier system works just fine, because it's set up to handle a large volume of supply and demand.

But when we prowl the web, we're in search of the rarities like the wines that will never be available in our state, or that have long since been snapped up by insiders. (Sad, but true…many wine store owners, receiving a shipment of a limited-allocation wine that's in high demand, either sell it privately to their best customers, or keep it for themselves.) So the state isn't losing any significant amount of money, because if the wine isn't available, the sale will never be made in the first place. One can but shake one's head in wonder and pity.

Despite the simple clarity and obviously impeccable logic of the arguments in favor of direct shipment, this continues to be a hotly contested issue in state courts all across the land. Anyone, even children, can go on the web and buy prescription drugs, unlicensed music from unknown bands, even automatic weapons. But in 26 states a private person can't buy a bottle of wine. The trade press insists that the tide is turning in favor of the consumer, so we'll see, and most important, the direct shipping dilemma is solved, or at least neatly sidestepped. My favorite winery in California might not be able to ship to me, because if they do, they risk being charged with a felony, losing their license to make wine, and spending time in the slammer with the father-rapers and mother-stabbers. But my brand new wine-loving best buddy in Ohio is blithely qualm-free on this matter. I bought his wine at auction on Wine Commune, and he sent it to me person-to-person, plainly wrapped. It's a private transaction, and generally well below the radar of the state's wine police.

The American Vintners Association, bless them, believes, I hope not too fondly, that rational thinking and civilized discourse will ultimately conquer the political contribution coffers of the wholesalers. And, in fact, Supreme Court decisions have been handed down that have favored those who wish to ship freely. But my prediction is that the issue won't be resolved completely or clearly for quite a while yet.

CHAPTER 37

The 39 (or so) Steps

There have been occasions during the long slide into the wine obsession when even the most hardened and mentally corrupted addict pauses, looks around, and tries to figure out "what the hell?" We define the stages of the addiction into which we had descended. A cautionary tale.

January, 2009

As I noted previously, there have been occasions during the long slide into the wine obsession when even the most hardened and mentally corrupted addicts pause, look around, and try to figure out how they got where they got. One of those moments occurred that time when our friend referred a local writer to us to do an article about our back bedroom slash home office slash wine room. Another was one afternoon during our trip to Italy with Ralph and Trish, a few days after the Halloween Champagne decapitation, sitting on a hotel balcony along the shore of Lake Como, slowly realizing that if it hadn't been for our meeting at a wine tasting, none of us would have been there enjoying the stunning scenery and equally stunning wines.

Early 2009 was a third time, and I'm not really sure what caused the stopping and looking around, except for the belief that the unexamined life is not worth living. Deb and I had been written up in the papers, I had become the Wine Director of the Southwest Florida Wine and Food Festival, the regional lifestyle magazine devoted an entire page to my less-than-stunning visage and brief wine life story, I was teaching classes, holding staff training wine workshops at fine dining restaurants, and seriously considering going for a certification as a real sommelier. We were far down the road from Boone's Farm.

One thing became clear, and I was very excited about it, because things don't become clear to me very often. I was hit with the inkling that as we fell down the rabbit hole into the wine life, we went through stages, steps if you will, which are, according to ongoing research conducted among a large sample of wino friends, moderately well defined. It's like the stages of a disease, or grief, only better.

Psychologists who study huge human experiences such as death and grief enumerate the emotional stages people normally go through when they lose a loved one. Denial, disbelief, bargaining, like that. Since visual acuity is more profound when directed at the past, I now see that we, too, went through some stages as the passion for wine consumed us.

Curiously, many issues related to alcoholic beverages seem to come in a certain number of steps. When alcohol is consumed, it's the only way to keep track. Twelve-step programs have, no doubt, done a lot of good for a lot of people, but the wine thing has steps, too. How many? They go on forever, depending on the intensity of the passion and the dimensions of the trust fund. There are people in the world with twelve bottles in a rack on top of the refrigerator, others with a hundred bottles in the bottom of various closets, and still others with 35,000 bottles in a commercial storage facility that costs them 25 grand a year, or in a custom-built wine cellar under an Alp.

The word "progress" can mean many things. Sometimes it's good, like the progress we've made as a civilization, giving up witch burning, slavery, and the gold standard. It can also be evil and inimical, like the progress of a debilitating disease. Looking back on the "progress" of our obsession, I find myself asking, more than once a day, what kind of progress is it? What the hell happened to us? Where have we journeyed since that first Mondavian kiss on both cheeks? I came of age during an era when long strange trips were a regular occurrence, but I never expected to go on this one.

It's just that the culture of wine is so deeply rooted in the development of civilization in this hemisphere, which makes the curiosity about it, the attraction to study, both daunting and exhilarating. Daunting because nobody can learn it all, daunting because I know, just like the gunfighter in 1800s Leadville, there are always people who have a broader grasp of it than I do, who are quicker on the draw, and who have much bigger cellars.

We all cope as best we can with limitations in personal funding, but the indisputable fact is that we get from fine wine what we bring to it. I admit that we've spent several hundred dollars on a bottle of wine more than once, and by gum, we want the most out it, in terms of hedonistic pleasure, cultural dimension, the satisfaction of having visited where it's made, even an afternoon with the winemaker, when a half hour visit turns into a getting-to-know-you that's five hours long, sitting at a small table on the edge of the vineyard, the air cooling off, even in summer, preparing to open bottle number two, then three.

So our wine lives arose from a mixture of curiosity, limited income, opportunity, and luck. Since the attempt to impose order upon chaos is a natural human desire (albeit a mostly futile one), it occurred to me that our "progress" had stages to it, steps, even, not noticeable at the time, one flowing into the other, but distinguishable now, brought into focus with the perfection of hindsight.

The situation in which we ultimately found ourselves was a culmination of the "progress" we've made, the good kind and the bad. I know people (we all do) who are wrapped up with bike riding or radio controlled model boats or traveling to experience every major roller coaster in the country. They all, at one point or another, met their own personal Larry and Charlene…people who opened up the top of their heads and poured in a delight they hadn't known about.

In our case, the discovered delight was the life beyond beer, the experience that transcended the anonymous Italian swill in the carafe at the restaurant with the red-checkered plastic tablecloths, bottles of elegant liquid that absolutely embarrassed the sweet pink fizzy Portuguese stuff we drank from brown stone bottles back in The Day. It was difficult, but we came to terms with the fact that once, long ago, we liked Mateus and Lancer's, and we begged for forgiveness. Today, people serve it at Sixties parties for laughs. We took, with a good deal of encouragement, a first impulsive, irreversible step. We drank what Larry poured and thought, "I wouldn't mind having a few bottles of this to come home to after a hard day." The road we traveled could have been made of yellow brick.

We looked back on the bringing home of the wine racks, the signing up for the lists, and the big plunge of blowing our allowance on our first annual wine blast in New York. We remembered the few upscale wine dinners, tastings, and samplings that expanded our perspective about where good wine comes from. The dinners also brought us into some peripheral contact with a group of people who are farther down the wine path than we'll ever hope to be, mainly because they have insane amounts of money. The "progress" we made came into focus.

I now understand that phase, more or less, as Stage One, when it dawned on us that buying an entire case of wine was a much bigger commitment than buying a case of beer, for several reasons. First, it's more expensive (even a case of the ten-dollar bargain bottles sets us back a hundred-twenty bucks plus tax, and for that money we could buy almost two buckets of popcorn at the movies). Second, before our epiphany, Deb, me, and a small number of weekend house guests could demolish a pony keg between quitting time on Friday and tee time on Sunday, and never think about it more than once, if at all.

But if we were to go through 12 bottles of wine in the same period, we'd start to question ourselves intensively, and we'd have incurably purple teeth. Back then, in Stage One, we hadn't discovered all the fancy stoppering systems I mentioned earlier, or the nitrogen that's sprayed in the bottle to keep the air away from the wine, or the refrigerated cases that can adorn a countertop, holding four bottles at the perfect serving temperature with cute little spigots on the front. We never used any of that, because screwcaps notwithstanding, pulling a cork is a ceremony, a commitment. Some unfinished bottles hold up well for a few days with those little sucky stoppers in them, and others die overnight. We didn't know, and we didn't want to take the chance, so if we opened it, we finished it.

About six months later, in Stage Two, we were looking at 55-60 bottles. We did not consult the experts about this, but we're told that some of them believe the feverish clawing of the obsession can be arrested at this point, and the obsessor gradually guided back into a normal life through therapy, dedication, hard work, and the occasional strategically-applied electric shock. Other experts, equally eminent, maintain otherwise. Stage Two got us into a couple of wine clubs, and in possession of our first wine rack, in the second bedroom, groaning in anguish under its new burden of bottles. At the 99-bottle mark, we also found ourselves more comfortable in stores that sold wine than in those that didn't.

In Stage Three we took the first big step. Larry's wine racks were disposed of, given, if I recall, to an up-and-coming wine buddy to whom I'd passed along the bug. There were the 500 bottles we never thought we'd have, in an ex-bedroom transformed into a wine study home office with its own write-up in the local lifestyle magazine. The do-it-yourself wine refrigerator hummed happily in the closet, and I absorbed every wine tchotchke catalog that showed up in the mailbox. Those little dinky-butt wine racks we got at Crate & Barrel? History. Cases stacked in closets and under beds? Now in their own special room. We didn't know it at the time, but we were staring straight into our (dark) future.

By Stage Four, there were, sitting on the floor of the new wine room, at least two or three cases of impossibly obscure wines that I knew nothing about. Somehow, they worked their way into the inventory, so I was reasonably sure I must have bought them. Teroldego. Lemburger. Frontignan. Piculit Neri. And something called Abbaye de Belloc, which is supposedly made by Benedictine monks who live in speech-free seclusion high up in the Pyrenees.

As mentioned earlier, there will always be people who have more wine than we do. A lot more. Rock stars, celebrity chefs, cybermillionaires, movie producers, guys who pitch perfect games, brain transplant surgeons. They've been playing with wine for so long that they've kind of leaned back into it and put their feet up. It's like they've climbed the mountain, attained the summit, and are coasting comfortably back down the other side. When you ask them how many bottles they have, they say, "At which house?" But it doesn't make any difference, because they probably have every bottle there is. So do their friends. These are people who made $360 million selling the computer parts company they started in their garage with a $700 loan from their uncle. Many of them buy vineyards in Napa.

My eighth-grade friend Curtis had an older brother who used to say he wanted to marry a nymphomaniac who owned a liquor store. Ron the dentist has over 2,000 bottles primarily because he married the liquor store part. (Information on his connubial pursuits is sadly lacking). His father-in-law managed a wine store, and Ron started collecting right out of college, back in the late Sixties. He's way past Stage Four, and coasting comfortably. Wouldn't dream of building a wine room, never reads *Wine Spectator*, disdains our yearly trips to the Wine Experience, and stores only about 100 bottles in square bins he installed in his hall closet. No refrigeration, no custom redwood racking, no cute little tags hanging on the necks of each bottle. He's had them in there so long he knows every one personally. No fancy wine storage unit, either, just a standard slightly surplus refrigerator in the laundry room next to the cat box where he keeps his 20-year-old grand cru white Burgundies. He is Mister Life After California Cabernet. No tchotchkes for him.

Another inevitability that we didn't clearly foresee is that our tastes would change over time, and they've come full circle, in a way. In college, I was nonchalant, suave, and blasé as I ordered that fifth of Lancer's on a special dinner date, but that was then. Back in Stages One and Two we looked for good bottles of ten dollar wine, drank them, and were satisfied. Then we got a bit more refined, because our attendance at the wine club tastings gave us a hint that there were wines of more refinement, elegance, and hedonistic fulfillment. I kept a spread sheet inventory of the bottles we bought, so I could calculate the total value of the collection, and the average price per bottle. Over the years, the collection expanded, and the average per-bottle price increased in alarming multiples. Once we were given a Northern Italian single-vineyard Barolo that was so scarce the winemaker himself couldn't afford to buy any.

There's hard material evidence that our tastes change over time, and I have it right here. Whether they get more sophisticated or more pretentious is still a matter for discussion. Ron built those nice square little wine bottle bins in his hall closet when he moved in to his house, around 1980. They worked fine, because the California Cabernet and Bordeaux he was drinking at the time came in bottles with nice straight sides, so he could stack them lying horizontally with Teutonic precision. But he became a victim of his own improvement in palatal discrimination. He disdains the up-front, in-your-face Cabernets, those made in a concentrated style that whack the drinker so hard they're called "fruit bombs." After more than 40 years of buying, collecting, and drinking, he favors what he says are the more subtle, more complex sensations and aromas of the fine Pinot Noirs from Burgundy, of which he has a stunning collection. But Burgundies come in bottles with curved sides, so when Ron puts them in the bins, only the grace and good humor of the wine gods keep them in place, and then just barely. When he tries to extract a bottle (and being a dentist, he should be good at extractions), they all come sliding joyously out onto the floor. He doesn't catch as many as he used to, and loses two or three a month.

The obsession has stages that flow one into another imperceptibly and do not proceed in a clear smooth upward curve. Some collectors, with means far beyond those of mere mortals, build show cellars, like a doctor friend of mine whose billiard room has a thermal glass wall, floor to ceiling, looking in on a stunning display of hand carved wooden racks holding thousands of bottles dramatically set off by cleverly engineered lighting that comes up through the floor. Other friends have overcome the desire to display their treasures, preferring to keep their $3,400 bottles of Pétrus and Le Pin in the basement, safe from the prying and admiring eyes of visitors.

What to take away from this? On the plus side are the relationships (first of all), the travel and dining experiences, the physical flush of tasting a liquid that can bring tears to the eye. Also a plus is learning that the best wine friends are those who own more bottles than we do. Wine lovers are not miserly, and they love to share. We let them.

Mostly, it's the friends, winemakers who have been unfailingly cordial, warm, and welcoming, and fellow grape geeks who we've met at weekend events. If not for wine, we never would have connected with cousins Douglas and Cynthia, and the other family members to whom they've led us. Once, at a wine tasting on a cruise ship, I met a young man who obviously understood what he was drinking, and we've been email buddies ever since.

But we are obligated to write the friend issue on the minus side, too, because we may well have lost as many as we've gained. Our tastes, our interests, simply diverged. We retreated from them because they didn't share what became so important to us. Sweet sorrow.

CHAPTER 38

"What's the Best Wine You Ever Had?"

I've mentioned more than once that our passion for the wine life has been impossible to conceal. And I've also observed that ultimately, the only friends we have left are either similarly afflicted or have stuck around in spite of our condition, either out of morbid curiosity or because they were waiting for me to open another bottle. I was at times, I admit, boring and insensitive. The whacks on the head I'd received from Cousin Annie (she delivered some of them personally, some over the phone, and others on Skype) generally wore off over time. We described to everyone in agonizing detail all the tastings we'd been to, told them about the trips to Napa and Tuscany and Champagne, and ushered them past the wine cases stacked on the floor in various rooms of the house. Honestly, I believe they benefited from our enthusiasm, since they graciously offered to help us consume some of our better bottles. And, *mirabile dictu*, a few of them came to believe that I might actually know what I was talking about so incessantly. They began to call me from the wine aisle at the supermarket, asking for recommendations.

Invariably, believing foolishly that I might know something about the subject, they will ask about the best wine I ever drank. The more puckish wine lifers I know will invariably say the best wine I ever drank was the last wine I drank, but I'm not usually that much of a smartass.

Some wine lovers will rhapsodize about the Château d'Yquem 1945 that caused them to moisten themselves in public, and others will reminisce fondly of that once-in-a-lifetime chance they had to swill some perfectly matured Haut Brion or Romanée Conti La Tache. (There are wine lovers among the international business and banking elite who gather in places like Hong Kong a few times a year and do wine tastings where they each chip in something like $25,000 per person, but that's not what this is about).

We all, initially, tasted something that changed our lives. And for the lucky ones, it happens more than once. But even though wine spurs most of the senses, gives us what we bring to it, involves us intellectually, promotes civilized dining and conversation, and incites curiosity and scholarly obsession, there's one more wonderful thing about wine, and it's this: it's not what we drink, but where we are, and who we're with. Julia enters, upstage right.

Julia Scartazzoni is a brilliant designer of fabric, textile and home furnishings whom we love for reasons other than she lives in a quaint, picturesque, historic, restored village in Tuscany. She's blessed with Sophia Lorenesque Sixties Italian movie-star good looks, so she's a knockout. Her personal attractiveness is surpassed only by her talents as an artist, designer, decorator, all those things, so anyone among the international business and banking elite who wants to fulfill the fantasy and restore a farmhouse in Cortona or somewhere else in Tuscany as so many people seem to do, just cruises the back roads around Siena, buys a place, gives Julia the keys and a huge amount of money, goes back home, and waits. A year later, they'll move in and love everything she did. There's nothing about her that isn't exquisite and delicious.

In Tuscany, people own whole villages. Julia's is called Argenina, thought she doesn't really own it. That honor— and stress inducer—belongs to her neighbor, a woman with a daughter in the Tuscan equivalent of high school when we met. Doesn't matter. Julia lives there, in a place that consists of about six unspeakably ancient houses, a modest church (deconsecrated), and the traces of what might have been the piazza back around the time Columbus was packing for the cruise.

For some reason, there seem to be dozens of villages throughout Italy, maybe hundreds, tiny places that have, over the years, simply curled up and died. Of course, the young people who don't want to make wine or olive oil or grow figs until they die all take off to try their luck in Siena or Florence or Rome as soon as they can make it to the train station on their own. More commonly, creeping modernization overwhelms the simple infrastructure of the village, and there isn't enough water to run all the new flush toilets and washing machines. Most of these places are on hills, and the water is way, way down.

So individuals or consortiums (consortia?) or hotel chains have bought up whole towns (small ones), and restored them, selling the houses to wealthy Germans for princely sums, or simply turning the entire village into a hotel. San Felice is like that. Not far from Argenina, it's a brand-new thousand year old village, founded in the year 990, completely renovated only a millennium later, operated by an international super-luxury hotel chain that was established somewhat more recently. Guests stay in suites in the old city hall, or in what used to be a private apartment, or in a sumptuous guest room above a 15th century barn. Kind of strange, actually, the way the place looks. Almost too perfect, like the people at Disney built it, using the most contemporary techniques and technologies with the most consummate skill to create the illusion of antiquity in a place that truly doesn't need it.

Argenina is a tiny village close enough to Siena that you can see the skyline out the kitchen window, at the crest of a hill off a completely invisible gravel road, and it's so antique and picturesque and quaint it gives me toothaches. At the apex of sweeping green vineyards, Julia's terrace commands a vista of orderly rows of ancient vines that curve and flow with heartbreaking grace in every direction, sloping down and away in the misty distance. Straight across the valley there are similar hills, and at the top of each one sits another Argenina. It's considerably less sanitized and considerably more authentic than San Felice, because those who restore places like Argenina don't have to impress a highly-moneyed international clientele paying $500 a night. Julia's neighbor, after years of going through the kind of nightmares that only Italian zoning and permitting bureaucrats can inflict, not only succeeded in preserving the deep timelessness of the place, she actually enhanced it. Maybe it's the dirt road, or the little things left undone and crumbling, but living there (or staying for a week or two, as we've done) allows the primeval energies of the region to flow within and without.

The first time we went to Argenina (and Tuscany in general), we'd come to Florence to shoot that television show about a jewelry designer. Janice, the show's producer, had worked with Julia on a previous program about the most beautiful inns in Italy. Seems that Julia knows the subject better than most because she and her ex-husband the Baron owned a country hotel at one time, just outside Radda in Chianti. It had been a 14th century monastery which they restored, operated for a while, and sold.

The day before the grappa episode, Janice drove us two hours south from Florence, pulling over once in a while for a photo op, or when we saw an interesting wine bar or vineyard, passing through Poggibonsi, a place which is everything the modern age can do to devastate an old world city, a dreadful, repulsive, squatty, smoky gray sprawl of gas stations, truck stops, confusing traffic circles, and the skewed Italian interpretation of convenience stores. When we got to Argenina, in shock that Janice could actually find the undetectable gravel path off the side road, the town was in the midst of its own little renaissance. A huge flatbed truck with some kind of yellow engine mounted on it squatted in the middle of the village's one muddy street, trembling and bellowing like a hippopotamus in heat, boring into the earth and belching sickly brown slurry down the hillside. The buildings were bare stone inside, tradesman's trucks clogged the area, plumbing fixtures, ancient and modern, were strewn about the grounds, and Julia greeted us in a pair of L.L. Bean's finest hip boots. She looked terrific.

The visit lasted only a few hours, because restoring and rebuilding a 1,000-year-old Tuscan village makes an inconvenient mess. The place was crawling with dampened men spattered with mud the color of a school bus, soggy figures with drooping mustaches and saggy pants and waders, shouting and cursing polysyllabically at the laboring well drilling equipment that shuddered and trembled on the bed of their truck, and every inch of ground was covered

with the thick viscous goo that the machine sucked up
from the innards of the hillside. When we went back a year
later, the restoration was not only completed, it was
perfect. Julia's little slice of this ancient redoubt (Argenina
was mentioned in government documents as early as the
year 900) was a two story house of irregular beige stone
with an open terrace on the second floor, facing her studio
from the far side of the weathered stone courtyard. Under
the house was our apartment and the showroom where
she displayed her hand-painted draperies, bedspreads, and
other inspirations. She'd decorated the area with wagon
wheels, old barn doors, and objects with a richness of
character that comes only in old Tuscan farmhouses, and if
a couple of centurions had ridden by just then in a chariot,
it wouldn't have surprised me a bit.

Julia had a real wine cellar, too. Not one of these California
redwood custom designed "wine cellaring systems" with pin
racks and diamond bins, but an honest-to-God wine *cave*,
deep under the house, carved from the solid rock God
knows how many centuries ago by people who may have
painted animal fetishes on the walls with their own blood,
or at least fed a few Christians to the lions. The room was
low-ceilinged, dim and delicious. It smelled of the ages, and
the air was thick with time, innumerable bottles stacked in
cobwebby crannies hewed into every vertical surface.

We stayed a week, spending at least some of our time
above ground. The bushes that clung to the pitted stone
walls were bursting with roses all the way to the roof,
the grapes were ripe enough that we could reach out the
window to pick them, and Julia had not only prepared our
complete week's travels for us, she'd color-coded everything.

"See? Tomorrow you follow the blue, Monday the

yellow, Tuesday you relax, and Wednesday you follow the green." She handed us photocopied maps from the guide books, highlighted with colored markers the routes we were to take to the hill towns during the day, and to the restaurants in the evenings. Since Julia is pretty much a one-woman Tuscan Board of Tourism, we didn't argue with her choices…until we tried to figure out her maps. One day we wound up at a farm, all the way up a remote hillside, surrounded by the cutest long-haired baby goats. If I didn't speak a small amount of nasty Italian, we'd still be there.

There are country restaurants all over America, I guess, but I don't think we've ever been to one. I can't recall driving 100 miles to some village in the middle of Alabama farmland countryside just to have lunch at an incredible restaurant owned by a celebrated gourmet chef. (There are, I have been informed, places like this in remote areas of Virginia and Maine). In Europe, for reasons that have always puzzled me (as so many things do) the more Michelin stars chefs have, the more they feel it necessary to put their dining establishment in a village that has maybe five permanent inhabitants, and is at least a hundred kilometers from any center of civilization, out where God forgot His shoes. Maybe it's the cheap rent.

One year, we went to Switzerland to visit a friend who worked for a huge drug company doing pain-killer research on lobsters. (Don't ask). Anyway, we took a little day trip, starting from Basel first thing in the morning and driving maybe a hundred miles total. We had breakfast in Switzerland, lunch in Germany, and dinner in France, each meal in a charmingly remote old house or barn or stable that had been transformed into an internationally-renowned destination restaurant. Same thing in Tuscany. Around Argenina, there are tons of restaurants that serve dinners after which suicide is essential because any future life event would be pointless by comparison. Many of these places own a couple of Michelin stars, and if they don't, they should.

We'd driven down from Florence, spent our first Argenina afternoon unpacking, and getting to work on the bottles of the local Chianti Julia had put in our room. Of course, we'd never heard of any of them, but as I think back, our lives were changed again that day. Our common taste in wine was imprinted, patterned by the extensive sampling of that local production, and inside of us a bell tinkled and a voice exclaimed, "This is the way wine's supposed to make you feel." It was the first glimmer of something we'd learn later on in the Loire. We were drinking the Real Thing, made from grapes grown on eighty-year-old vines right outside the door, and crafted in small batches by a family that's been doing it much the same way for a thousand years. This wasn't the stuff we got at home, shipped thousands of miles, cooking in the hold of a ship for a month, brutalized by the very system that put it on our table. Or did it taste that way because we were simply in that place? It's probably a good thing we weren't in Bordeaux, having our tastes imprinted by the local production in the same manner, and much more expensively.

Drinking it where it's made offers an incomparable emotional component. On Debi's birthday trip, we'd had lunch just outside of Bourgueil, at a restaurant called the Moulin Bleu, because, not coincidentally, it had a blue windmill in the middle of the parking lot. But better yet, the restaurant nestled amidst the vineyards of Yannick Amirault.

I'd read about Yannick because big, extracted, powerful

wines have always appealed to me (despite the derision of grape geek friends who prefer a quaff more subtle and refined). When we'd turned off the main road, I saw his name on the fence, and thought "Hmmmm."

Of course, Ed, Isabelle, Debi, and I were obligated to taste our way through several of Yannick's bottles during lunch, and, while the flavors and complexities elevated me, it tasted ten times better because I could look out the window at the vineyard and know that the wine in my glass came from right over there. Like Matt Kramer says, travel to a wine's geographic and cultural source certainly does kick the flavor in the butt.

Following the green marker lines on Julia's map, our first dinner destination was the Bottega de 30, a few miles down the road. We'd read about the place, had been looking forward to the meal for months. It was going to be a real highlight-of-the-trip experience. The restaurant, we found out, was in a village that boasted 53 permanent residents, none of whom looked to be under a hundred and six, and all of whom were sitting on low benches against the brown stone walls when we pulled into town. Another unexpected stumble into the past: at golden sunset, the bent-over shapes of great-grandmothers, draped in black from head to toe, shuffling along, casting long shadows on harsh stone streets that breathed gently with the ages.

Convinced that we were on the verge of the world's most complete Tuscan Gourmet Dining Experience, we walked down about six steps into the restaurant, and it was gorgeous. Decorated with dark evocative woods, unspeakably old artifacts, beamed ceiling, terra-cotta tile floor, it was the very Platonic Ideal of a Tuscan Gourmet Dining Room. It was also very empty. Our reservations were for eight o'clock; it was about seven-thirty, and there wasn't a single human person in sight.

On our right, a few steps below us, a door opened, and a young man stepped out. He was about 25, wearing an immaculate white chef's coat and toque.

"*Mi scusi,*" I said, beginning to unreel a sentence I'd practiced for three of the previous four hours, "*Habbiamo una prenotazione per otto hore.*"

"You guys Americans? Where ya from?" A pause, and a stare.

"Uh...Southwest Florida."

"Hey, good to meetcha. I'm from Jersey City."

So much for the authentic experience. Actually, Jimmy (that was his name, Jimmy) had won a culinary scholarship that liberated him from the gastronomic wasteland of northern New Jersey and privileged him to apprentice at the Bottega completely without pay for six months. He'd never been outside the States before, was insanely joyous at the opportunity, and could have flown to Florence unaided by the customary machinery, until he discovered that he'd be living in a village of fifty-three people, all of whom were dead or close enough to it not to matter. Miles from the nearest real town. Light years away from any woman under a hundred and six. Without a car. He worked late every evening, and crazed away the days.

In Tuscany, the wine lust courses through internal organs, and the journey becomes one long pilgrimage. Bottega de 30 was only the first stop, because the second restaurant Julia recommended was at the top of a hill (aren't they all?), up a one-lane rutted dirt road, in a village that had only two permanent human residents and about four hundred cats.

Sorry to say, but the voyage of which I speak took place when our addiction was in its infancy, and we didn't know enough to set up or seek out tours or tastings at the millions of vineyards in the area. The black rooster is the official symbol and trademark of the Chianti Classico region. But we didn't know the significance of all those black rooster signs that we saw along the twisting roads. So we contented ourselves with a day in the holy city of Montalcino, suffering up the steps to the fortress behind an overweight yet genial Belgian couple we'd met at lunch, and spending a shameful portion of the afternoon in the tasting room, trying to decide whether to buy the Rosso (about which we knew nothing) or take a deep breath and spring for some good vintage Brunellos (about which we knew even less).

"Let me taste that last one again," said Deb. The wine pouring guy was starting to give us mysterious Italian looks. "Did we like this one" (sip) "or that one" (sip sip). By the time we settled on twelve bottles and came to terms with the fact that we'd have to personally shlep them all the way back to the States, the Belgian couple had become incapable of speech, the wine guy had made six or seven unenthusiastic trips down and up the prehistoric stone stairway, hauling bottles from the cellar, deep night had fallen, and so had we.

Julia is only one good thing about Argenina. Another is that her ancient home is right down the road from where they were later to film "Stealing Beauty," and just outside Siena, which the Italian government has officially designated a Very Old Place. Those Siennese people have definitely won a victory over modernization, especially in the critical area of plumbing. The place is a Gothic rather than a Renaissance city like Florence, and if much has changed since the 1300's aside from electricity and motor scooters I'm damned if I can tell. Somebody once said that Italy is just one big museum, and Siena proves it.

But as any wine lifer will tell you, the most attractive and important historic monument in Siena is not the city hall, with its architecture reminiscent of the Palazzo Vecchio in Florence, nor the world famous piazza with its seashell shape. It's the imposing red brick fortress, the Fortezza Medicea, which today houses an official government agency with a name that translates to "Council for Bringing Every Good Wine in Italy to One Place at One Time So You Can Taste All of Them, All Day Long."

The regions of Italy are steeped in long tradition, and when we've swirled and sipped in Friuli or the Veneto or wherever, we've been offered mainly the wines made in the local area, because they match the food. But the Enoteca Italiana in Siena is possibly the one and only place where the intrepid wine lifer can sample wines from every single producing region in Italy. It takes quite a bit of time, a dedication that borders on the monumental, and a constitution equal to the task. Fortunately, the tasting bar serves food, and Advil.

As much as we might love to pursue new wines in other countries, we inevitably discover, sooner or later, that no matter how wonderful they are, and how inexpensive, we will wizen and crumble to dust before we find them at our friendly neighborhood wine merchant, and if we do discover one, it'll cost more than our house. Even if we encounter it at a price that doesn't make us quake like the proverbial aspen, we can take it home and drink it, but it won't be the

same. We won't be in Siena, relaxing in the tasting room
of a Medici fortress, behind 12-foot-thick walls, looking out
over a centuries-old cobblestone courtyard where Cosimo
and Lorenzo may have walked. Which brings me (neatly)
back to the original question: what's the best bottle of wine
we ever had?

Outside Julia's atelier, right at the top of the hill, there is
a stone patio bounded by a low wall separating the building
from the grapevines that slope away just below. One night,
Debi and I sat out there at sunset, chilling a bit along with
the air, looking over a scene that probably hasn't changed
much since Nero played his last recital, and shared a bottle
of local Sangiovese that a man down the road made in his
garage. No label, no foil, no cork, no nothing. It was the
best wine we ever had. It cost two dollars.

CPSIA information can be obtained at www.ICGtesting.com
Printed in the USA
LVOW05s1808281213

367243LV00001B/3/P

9 780981 822259